THE VETERAN'S SURVIVAL GUIDE

Also by John D. Roche

The Veteran's PTSD Handbook:
How to File and Collect on Claims for Post-Traumatic Stress Disorder

THE VETERAN'S SURVIVAL GUIDE

HOW TO FILE AND COLLECT ON VA CLAIMS
SECOND EDITION

JOHN D. ROCHE

POTOMAC BOOKS, INC.
WASHINGTON, D.C.

Library of Congress Cataloging-in-Publication Data

Roche, John D., Maj.
  The veteran's survival guide : how to file and collect on VA claims / John D.
Roche. — 2nd ed.
    p. ; cm.
  Includes bibliographical references and index.
  ISBN 978-1-59797-051-8 (alk. paper)
  1. Military pensions—Law and legislation—United States—Popular works. 2.
Disabled veterans—Medical care—Law and legislation—United States—Popular
works. I. Title.
  [DNLM: 1. United States. Dept. of Veterans Affairs. 2. Veterans Disability
Claims—legislation & jurisprudence—United States. 3. Veterans—legislation &
jurisprudence—United States. W 32.5 AA1 R673v 2006]
  KF7276.R63 2006
  331.25'29135500973—dc22

                              2006008905

Potomac Books, Inc.
22841 Quicksilver Drive
Dulles, Virginia 20166

10 9 8 7 6 5 4

CONTENTS

PREFACE

Billy Kidwell's letter to the editor of *Veterans Post*, dated June 2005, expresses the anger and frustration that is common among veterans who have unsuccessfully dealt with the VA.[1] Publications like this are a great forum for all the GI Joe Veterans to express their thoughts on what they see is wrong with the system. Here are Mr. Kidwell's thoughts:

Dear Editor,

The Veterans Court Continues to Cover Up Wrong-doing By VA General Counsel

Evidence keeps mounting proving that the Court of Appeals for Veterans are extreme right wing zealots, who believe that Veterans should have no Veterans Court, and do not deserve benefits.

An investigation by Vets For Justice, has discovered that although the Veterans Court was established by Congress and "supposed" to be for Veterans, that the Court is nothing more then a sham, a hoax, intended to deceive Veterans, by making them believe they have a real Court, a fair, and impartial, Court to go to when the VA arbitrarily denies their VA Claim.

In reality, the Veterans Court is "fixed," and stacked, with extreme right wing zealots, most of whom were appointed by the Bush Family, all of whom are bias against Veterans and believe Veterans Benefits is really welfare.

The numbers show that a Veteran has a better chance of hitting the lottery then of receiving a fair trail in Court of Appeals for Veterans.

The Veteran has prevailed in 13 cases out of 14,000!

Hanging Judge Roy Bean was far more lenient and impartial, then the Judges on the Veterans Appeals are!

We have found that there is a pattern that veterans who proceed Pro Se before the Veterans Court when they are unable
to obtain an attorney, are taken advantage of by both the Veterans Court, and the General Counsel of the VA.

Billy Kidwell
Via Internet

I think you will agree that Mr. Billy Kidwell is correct in naming the invisible underlying theme of veterans' frustration as the
political agenda of those who are at the very top of the food chain.
For the powers that be, the real issue is bottom-line cost. What can
we do to reduce overhead and still look like we are behind our
troops and veterans without creating a major backlash?

The real source of veterans' problems is not the Court of Appeals for Veterans Claims, the Board of Veterans Appeals, or the
VA's General Counsel Office. Mr. Kidwell touched on one very
important issue, which is probably most responsible for the remands
and denials made by the system. The veteran is under the impres-
sion that all that is required of him is to file a claim form and the
VA will do the rest.

Big surprise! Approximately six weeks later the veteran receives his first letter from the VA. He is confused. It is asking for
hard evidence that the injury or disease did in fact occur. Talking
out loud to himself he asks "what evidence . . . it's all in my military records." The telephone counselor told him over the phone
not to worry, the VA would get his records.

Surprise number two! He receives a second letter three months
later. This time the letter is brief, stating "claim denied." "Your
claim failed to meet the standards necessary for the VA to trigger
the VA's Duty to Assist." The telephone counselor never explained
that the United States Court of Appeals for Veterans Claims ruled
previously that unless the claimant submits sufficient evidence, the
VA was not obliged help him.

For the veteran, the only option is to appeal the denial of benefits. He is bound to lose the appeal because of his initial failure to provide evidence that would convince an average person to conclude it was possible that the injury or illness was service-incurred.

This is a well-orchestrated technique to deny claims by the hundreds of thousands and focus the blame on the veteran. VA facts sheets titled "VA Disability Claims Processing" for the fiscal years 2003 and 2004 state that during this period 1.53 million veterans were notified of the final decision concerning their claim. One million two-hundred twelve thousand veterans received "Dear John" letters. This is a real victory for the White House. These 1,212,000 veterans will receive no compensation benefits, require no mandatory healthcare or vocational rehabilitation training. The White House can now divert the billions of dollars for projects that are in agreement with their political agenda. On June 23, 2005, Secretary of Veterans Affairs R. James Nicholson made known to one and all around the beltway that, due to mistakes in computing the veterans' health care budget, the bureau had underestimated by over a billion dollars for fiscal year 2006 the cost just to provide the current level of basic services.[2] It is hard to understand how they could make such an error when military and veterans' organizations repeatedly and publicly protested that their estimate to operate all the required health services was insufficient.

Tighten up your seat belts, for veterans are in for a rough ride in the near future. The VA is rewriting title 38 of the *Code of Federal Regulations* (CFR). The plan is to completely delete Part 3, "Adjudication," and reorganize it as Part 5. The dangers that advocates and veterans alike must be alert for are subtle changes in words like "will" to "may" or "shall" to "shall at Secretary's discretion" and the omission of subparagraphs used to explain the law more clearly.

Here is an example where the VA introduced wording in a revision (38 CFR §3.304(f) "Direct service connection; wartime and

peacetime") in 1993, which left unchecked the discretionary judgment of senior claims examiners when deciding the merits of a
claim based on PTSD, POW, and personal assault. This revision,
as it was touted, read as follows: "if evidence establishes that the
veteran engaged in combat," direct service connection will be approved. Who would have suspected that one little word like "if"
could generate so many denied claims or generate complex requirements for securing proof that a veteran in fact engaged in combat
with the enemy? In one case I worked on the VA wanted proof as
to the date, place, and details of vet's traumatizing experiences.
Military records in the VA's possession confirmed he engaged in
combat with the enemy because he was awarded the Purple Heart,
Combat Infantry Badge, and the Bronze Star. The question that
should be asked is, why would they ask for such detailed evidence
when the veteran had these combat awards?

One reasonable explanation is that merit pay raises hinge on
how many claims an individual examiner is able to clear month
after month. Every Monday morning each of the fifty-seven
Regional Offices (RO) has to report to the "powers that be" in
Washington how many claims it cleared. If an RO performs poorly
under this set of guidelines, the RO's director most likely will be
replaced and the reduction in the annual performance bonus will
hit one and all in their pocketbook. How many claims examiners
do you think will prolong the development process until the veteran has provided every possible bit of evidence? The most common practice is to deny the claim and let the claimant struggle with
it during an appeal.

INTRODUCTION

It has been six months since the VA signed the certified return receipt attached to Richard Jameson's application for 100 percent rating for Total Disability Due to Individual Unemployability (TDIU). His wife noticed his symptoms seemed to be multiplying daily. He no longer had contact with anyone but her. The only income the family had was his Social Security Disability check of $900 per month and a VA Comp Check for $1,147. Maria, his wife, would work double shifts at times at O'Sullivan's Irish Pub to bring in enough money to keep their heads above water.

Chronic Post Traumatic Stress Disorder (PTSD) never unchained him from the terrifying events that were his alone to endure every day for the rest of his life. In Vietnam he could no longer enjoy the companionship of close friends within his squad. He was their leader and he would do everything to protect them; but he did not want to know them because they might be dead in five minutes.

Five of his closest friends died horrible deaths. He would think about them every night as he tried to sleep in the wet, mucky swamp, reliving their tragedies before sleep came. Every night he would feel guilty because he was still there and his friends were not. Some nights he found solace wondering if he would die during the night from a poisonous snakebite.

His last week in Vietnam was the longest he ever endured. Each morning he said to no one in particular "only six days to go and a wake-up." Then it was five, four, three, two, and the wake up. "This is my day. I just might make it."

That little voice inside him was saying, "Who are you kidding? A million things could go wrong; how about you tripping a bamboo death trap? Here's one that has a good chance of getting you, being ambushed on the way to the 'LZ.'" He made it to the landing zone (LZ) and the sound of the approaching chopper was almost too good to believe. But that little voice inside was saying, "Remember your old buddy Harry on his way back to division for rotation processing when out of nowhere a VC pops his head up and fires a stinger missile. Seconds later a giant ball of flame erupts in the sky above and Harry's trip back home is cancelled forever."

Home at last and he tried to fit in, but somehow it just did not seem to happen. For a while after his return, he felt things would work out. Shortly after leaving the service, he married his high school sweetheart. With a job delivering courier packages he was his own boss. He was dealing with postservice transition until a small group of other drivers started to heckle him. When one called him a baby killer, he exploded. With no thoughts about what he was doing, he beat the man so badly he required hospitalization for the injuries. He was fired and arrested, and served three years in prison.

In prison, he was given extensive testing by the prison psychiatrist. His diagnosis was chronic PTSD with very low social coping skills. He tried to find steady work after leaving prison without success. He was fired from every job he tried for insubordination, fighting with coworkers, or absenteeism.

He applied for Social Security Disability Benefits and VA Compensation Benefits. Both benefits were granted. That was some help but without his wife's extra income there was no way they could make it day to day.

It was nearly eight months before the VA letter arrived announcing the decision concerning his claim for Permanently and Totally Disabled status. The letter came right to the point: claim denied. With shock and disbelief, Richard called the VA's 800 number, hoping to plead his case. He was politely told, "If you don't agree with our decision you can appeal it." With anger in his voice, he asked, "What the hell does that mean? How do I do that?" The service center counselor tells him, "Send us a letter stating you don't agree with our decision. In return we will send you a statement of the case which will explain why we denied your claim."

Unless Richard understands the appeal process, he is looking at three to five years before this one issue is resolved—that is, if he can successfully argue why his claim is superior to that of VA. More than likely, he will end up losing his claim. He has no idea what to do. At this stage hiring an attorney is against the law unless the attorney will accept a payment in full of no more than ten dollars.

A veteran in this situation could go to a service organization for help, but in most cases, that is an extremely limited choice, meaning little comes of doing it. The last thing the VA wants is a force of qualified advocates attacking its decisions. So the vast majority of service officers are not trained to be advocates. In many cases, they are nothing more than an extension of the VA network for outreach services. In all these veterans' external outreach organizations, some very outstanding advocates go head-to-head with the VA and successfully champion their clients' claims.

In the thirteen years I was an active service officer representing veterans, I ignored the code of performance that prohibits judging the merits of a veteran's claim. We were told this was the VA's job, not ours. However, I believed it was my duty to determine the merits of a claim, and if the evidence did not support the claim, I would have a frank talk with the vet. Working together, we would build a well-grounded claim. It was my business to know the laws, regulations, and internal manuals so I could put together a winning claim for my client. No way was I going to be a clerk for the VA and submit a claim I knew would not trigger their "duty to assist."

A joint initiative of the Department of Defense and the Department of Veterans Affairs in 2002 expedited the initial processing of claims so individuals leaving the service would receive compensation benefits thirty days after separation. DOD examiners, VA Medical Center personnel or VA contract medical examiners using the VA protocol would evaluate the alleged injury or illness.

After a moment's thought the question arises, how accurate and thorough are these examinations? Do physicians conduct all exams or do physician assistants or nurse practitioners perform them? If doctors, are they specialists or generalists? A tragic event occurred recently at the James Halley VA Hospital in Tampa, Florida, when a gravely wounded combat veteran from Iraq died after being released by the VA because the staff was not trained or familiar with the techniques his condition required.

Anyone who is separating from the service and has an injury or illness that may be service related should always remember that he or she is an expense for which the powers that be do not like being liable. Never forget they are not giving you anything. They owe you what you paid for in blood, physical pain, deformity, and psychological trauma.

Here are ten rules I recommend to anyone doing business with the VA.

Rule # 1 There is no claim if it can not be proved.

You bear the burden of providing sufficient evidence that your injury or illness is more likely than not to have occurred in the service. Otherwise the VA will deny your claim.

Rule # 2 Don't file for compensation benefits unless you have all the evidence.

This is especially true if you are filing while on active duty. Instead file an "informal claim" for the benefits. This action protects your date of entitlement up to one year and allows you to do the job right. It prevents the VA from prematurely denying benefits because you have not submitted sufficient evidence for them to rate the claim.

Rule # 3 What do you do if your claim is denied? *Appeal it.*

The VA isn't right just because it said no. Claims for complex issues, such as PTSD, undiagnosed illnesses, and heart disease, often are denied because the individuals responsible for rating the claims have no experience in law, medicine, or occupational limitation imposed by injuries or illnesses. Another reason for so many errors is that the adjudication groups are pressured to clear as many claims as possible or it affects their annual performance pay bonus. If the claim is denied, they get credit for completing a claim action.

Rule # 4 Know the rules the VA must follow.

It's easy to access their statutes, regulations, manuals, legal opinions, and pertinent case law. If they in any way stray from the golden rule then drop the hammer on them.

Rule # 5 Take your medical records to a non-VA specialist along with the appropriate VA diagnostic code.

It is more likely than not that VA medical evaluations will be performed by a physician's assistant, nurse, nurse practitioner, or a retired general practitioner. The findings of these marginally qualified medical staff members are another reason why many claims are denied. If this happens to you, start yelling "flawed examination" by filing a "Notice of Disagreement" (appeal) immediately. Take someone with you when being examined. Later they can offer a sworn statement as to what kind of questions you were asked, how long the exam lasted, what the medical findings were, if the examiner followed the proper protocol, and if the Compensation and Pension (C&P) examiner had your claim file and reviewed it prior to the exam. One last thing: C&P examiners have been known to tell you one thing and file a report that is entirely different. Remember to yell "Flawed" and file a NOD.

Rule # 6 If you are claiming a disability based on a combat injury or illness and have related awards or decorations, be sure to mention this in your claim.

The VA must accept your explanation if your service records show you have a Combat Infantry Badge, Purple Heart, Bronze Star, or Air Medal with V device along with other awards and decorations. This cuts out all the guesswork on their part. They only have to evaluate the degree of disability as indicated by the medical evidence.

Rule # 7 Become a paper PI, learn how to track key evidence to support your claim.

Here are several examples where evidence may be hiding: after-action reports, unit's history, sworn statement from those who were with you, and your sworn statement detailing the events and circumstances.

Rule # 8 Look for a qualified advocate if you need assistance.

You can measure their worth by how well they know VA regulations, manuals, and case law. You do not want to join up with a service officer who can only fill out VA forms. Ask them how many appeals they have filed and how many cases they have won. Look for the service officer who says "Hell yes! I'll go head to head with the VA."

Rule # 9 Read every letter from the VA with great care.

Immediately after filing a claim (approximately three months later) the VA will send you a notice titled Expedited Action Attachment. Don't let yourself be forced into allowing them to expedite the processing of your claim. You have one year by law from the date they received your claim to submit all the evidence before they can render a final decision. They may even send you a notice after sixty days to say that they are denying your claim for failure to provide compelling evidence. Don't ever believe them! Respond by sending them a Notice of Disagreement stating you have by law one full year to submit the necessary evidence to support your claim.

Rule # 10 Join and support service organizations. Always remember you are not a "*Customer.*"

In VA facilities throughout the country there are signs and banners stating "We support our veteran customers!!!" American Indians expressed it best by saying "The big Washington chief speaks with forked tongue." Always remember the White House, Office of Management and Budget (OMB), and the Department of Veteran Affairs see you as nothing more than an expense they wish to minimize. You have paid dearly for these benefits. Therefore, to keep what you are entitled to, band together with your fellow veterans and dig in. Hold the line when they want to cut benefits. Make them comply with the laws as provided by Congress. A report establishing how many of the White House staff, including the executives, OMB, and all the political appointees in the Department of Veterans Affairs have had actual combat experience would make interesting reading.

The only way veterans can tip the odds in their favor is to know exactly what their rights are and how to go about protecting them. To this end this revised edition of *The Veteran's Survival Guide: How to File and Collect on VA Claims* will show how to build a winning claim and what to do if you have to appeal a VA denial of benefits.

1 | A HISTORY OF SHAME

The United States veteran's benefits system traces its roots back to the seventeenth century when the Pilgrims of Plymouth passed a law protecting citizens who joined the colony army to defend it against the hostile Pequot Indians. The colony made certain that any soldier disabled in the defense of the colony would be supported by it.

When the colonies banded together and declared their independence from England, the Continental Congress of 1776 addressed the needs of its soldiers. To encourage enlistments during the Revolutionary War, the Congress passed legislation authorizing pension benefits for soldiers. This was the first move by the fledgling republic to protect all citizens who took up arms to defend the republic. However, in 1783 mutinous Pennsylvania troops surround Pennsylvania's Independence Hall to press the Congress for back pay.

Medical and hospital care for veterans in the early days of the Republic were the responsibility of the individual states and communities. Nearly thirty-five years later, in 1811, the federal government authorized the first domiciliary and medical facility for veterans. Throughout the 1800s, the nation's veteran's assistance program was expanded to include benefits and pensions not only for veterans, but also for their widows and dependents.

Following the Civil War, many states established homes for their veterans and included domiciliary. Medical and hospital treatment was provided for all injuries and diseases, whether or not of service origin. Homeless and disabled veterans of the Civil War, Indian Wars, Spanish-American War, and conflicts of the Mexican

Border period, as well as those discharged from the regular service, were all cared for at these homes.

During the late 1800s Southern Democrats in the Congress successfully introduced the first major legislation to chip away at veteran's entitlements. Angered by the South's defeat in the Civil War, they blocked receipt of concurrent benefits to Union troops who were retiring with service-related disabilities. Military retirees were now having to pay a kickback to the United States government for the privilege of being eligible for compensation and medical treatment. The informed and political elite were careful to minimize verbal support of this policy. After all, weren't such entitlements another form of double dipping by a select group of individuals who served in the armed forces? This practice has been on going for more than a hundred years. In 2004 the first step was made to correct this disguised form of taxing retiring career military members who qualified for compensation benefits pay for their care. Every veteran who retired from the service with a disability should know this change was made possible by the tenacity of Congressman Michael Bilirakis. With sword and shield he charged the dragon of deep-rooted establishment.

The Origin of the Runaround

When the United States entered World War I in 1917, Congress established a new system of veteran's benefits. Programs included disability compensation, insurance for military members, and vocational rehabilitation for the disabled. The swelling ranks of veterans in the 1920s led to a division of responsibility in the administering of benefits. Three different federal agencies would now administer them: the Veterans Bureau, the Interior Department's Bureau of Pensions, and the National Home for Disabled Volunteer Soldiers. Veterans had to fend for themselves with three separate federal agencies, each with its own laws and regulations. Confusion and contradiction within the agencies about who was in charge left many veterans wandering from agency to agency.

The Hoover Administration's Legacy

The practice of declaring missing combat troops dead when bodies were not recovered started in the early 1930s. A simple memo from the Acting Assistant Chief of Staff ordered the status of any missing GI to be changed to deceased effective the date he or she was noted as missing. The benefits of changing missing in action status to killed in action effective the date a GI was declared missing pleased the Hoover administration for several reasons. It would no longer have to set aside accrued pay due the missing service members. With an election coming up in November, Hoover could push for all the boys from World War I and the Russian Expeditionary Force to be accounted.

In 1930, Congress authorized the president to "consolidate and coordinate government activities affecting war veterans." The three former agencies that independently exercised control over veterans' benefits were reorganized into the Veterans Administration.

HOOVER AND THE WORLD WAR I WAR BONUS MARCH, 1932

One of the most shocking acts ever committed in our time by the government against veterans was in 1932. The Veterans Bonus Expeditionary March to Washington, D.C., was to be a peaceful petition to the government to pay the World War I Bonus now and not wait until 1945.

The country was in a great depression. Veterans, like so many others, lost everything: their jobs, their property, their self-respect. Some lost their loved ones to disease and starvation. In the big cities like New York, Chicago, and San Francisco veterans found temporary shelter and food from the Red Cross and Salvation Army. Elsewhere they were forced to live on the streets with little more than the clothes on their back and maybe some kind of bedroll. They panhandled for nickels and dimes hoping for enough money to buy a twenty-five cent "Blue Plate Special" lunch or dinner.

Those veterans living on the streets equated it to the "hell of trench warfare."[1] There were no German shells, bullets, or mustard gas attacks to deal with, but they had all the other horrors of living in the trenches. Nonexistent sanitation conditions, rats, flies, and lice infected these homeless veterans with all kinds of deadly diseases. Public health services could not deal with a nation of millions of homeless sick people. World War I sergeant Walter W. Walters from the Portland, Oregon, area decided he had to do something.[2]

The government could not stand by and do nothing while conscripts of the Great War were barely staying alive. They had not asked to be drafted or fight a war thousands of miles from their homes. Three hundred combat veterans from the Portland area set out to peacefully petition Congress to pay the $1,000 bonus authorized by the World War Adjustment Act of 1924.[3]

They needed the money now, not in 1945 as the act required. It wasn't long before other groups around the country joined the march on Washington. By the end of May 1932, the ranks of the Expeditionary Bonus Force swelled to 3,000 veterans, who camped out on the Capitol lawns. By July 1932, there were nearly 30,000 veterans, wives, and children camped on both sides of the Anacostia River.

Sergeant Walters organized all these people into military-style encampments. He had a chain of command that set rules of behavior at each campsite. The men paraded up and down Pennsylvania Avenue carrying American flags while singing war songs and chanting their grievance. This was a peaceful petition made by the people to the government.

On June 15, 1932, the House of Representatives passed the Patman Bonus Bill, authorizing early payment of the bonus, which was cheered by veterans. President Hoover was madder than hell and stormed out of the Oval Office while telling an aide *"You* go over to the Senate and tell them if they pass the Patman Bonus Bill I will veto it."** He was not going to let a bunch of veterans force him to spend two billion dollars. He was going to keep his balanced budget.

On June 17, 1932, thousands of veterans waited for the 9:00 PM Senate vote. The Senate knuckled under and voted to kill the bill. Although veterans and their families disbursed in a lawful manner, Senators slipped out the back way hoping to avoid a confrontation with them.

The veterans did not leave Washington but stayed in their "Hooverville" Camps on both sides of the river. They had no plans to leave. They would not give up the bonus fight. The veterans were an embarrassment to the Hoover administration for the entire world to see.

President Hoover called Secretary of War Patrick Hurley to the Oval Office, saying "I want these people out of the city. You will evict them from every vacant federal building, warehouse, shanty, and cardboard box shelter in the metropolitan area. The local police cannot do this. The police have already shot two veterans and the situation is getting worse. Use the Army to move them to the other side of the Anacostia River."

General Douglas MacArthur, chief of staff for the Army, was ordered to evict all the squatters in the city limits. This sparked tempers on both sides. Some marchers were taking physical action against the eviction order by throwing rocks at the police.

On July 28, 1932, the army forcibly moved veterans out of the city. To justify his actions he would not yield his belief that this was a Communist-orchestrated affair. General MacArthur ordered two squadrons from Major Patton's 3rd Cavalry Regiment and one battalion from the 12th Infantry Regiment to lead the attack. They were not to shoot the veterans or their families but were use their horses, swords, gas, and bayonets to roust the veterans from out of the city. Reports soon circulated that many veterans suffered wounds and injuries as they retreated to the bridge that crossed the Anacostia River. The news media reported the death of two children by tear gas.

General MacArthur was given a direct order from the president through the secretary of war: "Do not cross over the bridge into the encampment area of these veterans." The frantic president was afraid of the political backlash and repeated the order a second time.

MacArthur told his aide Major Dwight Eisenhower, "People are coming down and pretending to bring orders from the president and I am too busy to see them." MacArthur gave Maj. George Patton the order to move his two squadrons of cavalry units and one infantry battalion across the Anacostia River Bridge at 11:00 PM. With sabers drawn Patton and his troopers charged into the encampment.[4] Fires erupted in the camp as the troopers herded the people out of the camp. The horizon was one great wall of flames, as every shanty and shack was torched.

Attorney General William H. Mitchell's report to President Hoover concluded,

> This experience demonstrates that it is intolerable that organized bodies of men having a grievance or demand upon the Government should be allowed to encamp in the city and attempt to live in the community like soldiers billeted in an enemy country.[5]

His report emphasizes active Communist manipulation of Bonus Marchers at the heart of the problem. This of course added weight to MacArthur's contention he was fighting Communists. However, the VA released findings that 94 percent of the bonus marchers were former members of the armed services. The findings also showed that 67 percent of the demonstrators had served overseas and 20 percent were disabled. The creditability of the Attorney General's report was seriously challenged by these findings. The marchers were not legions of lawbreaking individuals with histories of criminal behavior. They were legions of veterans asking for help.

Roosevelt No Supporter for the Bonus Marchers, 1934

In 1934 the World War I veterans finally received their bonus when Congress prevailed over President Roosevelt's veto. The attitude of the incoming president did not change in regards to veterans. President Roosevelt proclaimed, "No one [merely] because he wore a uniform must therefore be placed in a special class of beneficiaries over and above all other citizen. The fact of wearing uniform does not mean that he can demand and receive from his government a benefit which no other citizens [sic] receives." Lack of postwar support and care of veterans by commanders in chief crosses party lines. Republican and Democratic presidents alike have looked for ways to trim, shave, and remove commitments to veterans.

The Eisenhower Gift to Those Who Served

In the 1950s, during President Eisenhower's second term, he and the Republican Party pushed to change the retirement guideline for those leaving the service after twenty or more years. The plan passed by Congress no longer permitted retired pay to be computed based on the active duty pay for the individual's rank. Future raises would be based on the cost-of-living scale used by the Social Security Administration. At the same time, a simple change in the language of the law concerning health care for retirees leaving the service was put into effect. The wording of the statute was changed from "shall provide" to "may provide" health care for retirees. This had great impact on those in retired status.

Lyndon Johnson's Years and Agent Orange

A specific blow to the welfare of those who did battle in the jungles of Vietnam was the failure of the Congress to acknowledge that Agent Orange was responsible for numerous illnesses. The Johnson and Nixon administrations successfully denied service connection for just about every known illness associated with exposure to Agent Orange for nearly twenty years.

A successful battle in Federal Court established that exposure to Agent Orange was responsible for numerous medical problems. The attorneys for the veterans successfully argued their case, winning an enormous settlement from DOW Chemical Company. The VA could no longer hide behind the justification that only Chloracme was a condition resulting when exposed to Agent Orange.

The Ronald Reagan Administration, 1981–1989

During the second term of Reagan's presidency the Court of Appeals for Veterans Claims became a reality. The power of the second largest agency in the United States government was defanged. No longer could the VA play judge, jury, and bearer of bad news. A supervisory body now existed that made the VA apply the law as Congress had intended. This court took years to reshape the BVA's review role. It was not a total success as the regional offices have difficulty grasping the concept of Preponderance of Evidence and the Doctrine of Reasonable Doubt; thus many legitimate claims are denied at the expense of the veterans and gratification of the "Bean Counters."

The George H. W. Bush Administration 1989–1993

The initial complaints of undiagnosed illness that plagued the first Gulf War veterans were met by the "Papa Bush's" administration with great skepticism. It was several years before Congress jumped in and passed legislation that added "undiagnosed illness" to the illnesses considered to be service related.

The Department of Veterans Affairs (VA) was established as a cabinet-level position on March 15, 1989. President Bush hailed the creation of the new department by saying, "There is only one place for the veterans of America, in the Cabinet Room, at the table with the President of the United States of America." The first secretary of the Department of Veterans Affairs was a former Republican congressional representative named Edward Derwinski. However, contrary to President Bush's statement regarding the recognition of the Department of Veterans Affairs, nothing of momentous benefit to veterans in general has yet escaped from the president's cabinet room.

The Clinton Years 1993–2001

Despite the "we can't do enough for you" rhetoric that has bombarded veterans since the early 1980s, benefits are constantly being downsized. The ruling parties in Congress since Ronald Reagan have measured veterans' benefits only by bottom-line costs. Gone are the sincerity and pledges from a grateful nation to those who have served and sacrificed. When politicians look at the fact that there are nearly 27 million people who served in the military and each has a potential claim for benefits they see an immediate threat to their special interest projects.

When politicians attack veterans' benefits with cuts, they might as well attack motherhood, apple pie, and the flag. To forge ahead on the same path would be a strategic blunder. By encouraging personnel downsizing, submitting budgets below actual expenses, and instituting an early retirement incentive for senior claims and rating-board members they will create logjams of sufficient magnitude to reduce the number of veterans receiving benefits.

George W. Bush's 2001 Administration May Outdo His Father's

Reorganization of the adjudication function now has claims dragging on endlessly before a decision is reached, and there is a mixed level of technical skill by the new generation of rating team members and claim examiners, resulting in a higher rate of denial of benefits. There has also been an effort to make VA compensation benefits taxable, which if voted into law, would reduce the spendable income of the disabled.

The following is a direct quote from a news release from Senator Byron L. Dorgan, dated March 1, 2004.

BUSH TO VETERANS: PAY MORE, WAIT LONGER, RECEIVE LESS HEALTH CARE

President Bush has not submitted an adequate budget for the Department of Veterans Affairs since he took office. Year after year, he has offered budgets that have sought to make veterans pay more and more out of their own pockets for health care. Not only has the Bush Administration tried—and been successful in one case—to dramatically increase copayments for prescription drugs, the Administration has also proposed various methods of generating additional revenue and artificially reducing demand for VA health care. The Administration uses the projections from these measures to pad their inadequate budget requests for veterans' services so that they can claim budget increases. Some examples of this include the counting of revenue from copayments and third-party insurers as part of the President's request, which has become standard practice for the Administration, and shifting retirement funds from another government agency. The following is a year-by-year summary of the President's budget proposals for veterans' programs.

Fiscal Year 2005: Increased Fees and Longer Waits, Even as Troops Come Home

INADEQUATE FUNDING

This year, President Bush's proposal would increase VA health care spending by $500 million, an increase that would fail to provide the VA with enough resources to maintain current services. With 60,000 veterans already on waiting lists for health care, and tens of thousands of military personnel scheduled to return from Iraq and Afghanistan as the newest generation of veterans, this under-funding will only further reduce the quality and availability of vet-erans' health care.

VA Secretary Anthony Principi admitted at the House Veter-ans' Affairs Committee's budget hearing that he asked the White House for $1.2 billion more than what VA received. As a direct result of President Bush's failure to meet Secretary Principi's re-quest, valuable specialty services like long-term care and mental health treatment will see significant cuts in capacity and staffing—at a time when the demand for these services is increasing. More-over, the President's budget slashes $50 million from critical medi-cal and prosthetic research programs at the VA.

THE REVIEW OF 72,000 PTSD CLAIMS
It was announced in October 2005 that the results of a quality re-view by the VA Inspector General that 72,000 veterans granted service connection benefits for PTSD at the 70 percent and 100 percent level will have their claims reviewed. The inspector gen-eral alleges that 25 percent of claims granted for PTSD did not qualify for benefits. If this is the case, then 18,000 veterans are going to be dropped from the rolls. What could that mean in dollar cost savings for the VA on an annual basis? Try this estimate on for size: one billion, two hundred million dollars per year. I arrived at this total by estimating that at least 60 percent of the 18,000 vets in the 100 percent and 70 percent range would be dropped by the VA to the 40 percent level. They can do this very easily simply by telling the veteran that they want the who, what, when, and where for each stressor that he or she alleges caused the PTSD. If the vet can't verify these stressors from government sources, "Sorry about

that but its bye-bye compensation benefits. The boss asked me to pass this on to you: 'It's nothing personal. It's just business.'"

HOLDING THE COURSE

"Holding the Course" as our president has said many times, has motivated members of his administration to develop ways to come up short four billion dollars for direct medical services in 2005. This revelation surfaced as a big surprise during the 2006 fiscal hearing in Congress. The politically appointed leadership works from only one playbook, written by the White House and the Office of Management and Budget (OMB).

Because the VA cannot compete for highly skilled physicians, it hires many immigrant doctors who will work for what they can pay. The VA will accept language limitations in an effort to maintain hospital-staffing requirements.

The VA has reduced the size and configuration of its rating board; doctors and lawyers are no longer members of the three-member board, and a single individual can now decide almost any type of claim considered by it. These individuals do not have a medical or legal background to call upon when deciding an issue. Very few, if any, have the ability to evaluate complex medical issues requiring specialized training and experience.

VA regional offices are noted for frequently making decisions contrary to the decisions of the court. In the past they have changed the intent of regulations and manuals without authority to do. In recent years, in order to reduce the backlog of pending claims they have employed such practices as telling veterans they have sixty days to respond with evidence. When a veteran fails to respond in sixty days, they deny the claim.

What you do not always hear about is what happens to the rank and file when employees fail to meet the assigned goals in moving pending claims. When an RO director is looking at the Monday morning stats dispatched to Washington and sees a decline in claims being cleared he immediately braces for a frontal assault from one of the gung-ho presidential appointed bureaucrats.

I would like to relay a fictional scenario that illustrates this bureaucray. Blessed with being able to become invisible at will, I decided to spend a morning with Harry Goodman, the director of the St. Oslo's Regional Office, on October 24, 2005. The hotline phone rings in Director Harry Goodman's office and his internal system is shot full of adrenalin. I hear him say, "Damn, it's Noseringer" as he picks up the telephone and grits his teeth. His caller is none other than Justin Noseringer the third, better known as "Rambo in a pinstriped suit," who is famous for going for the jugular. "What's going on down there Harry; your boys are not meeting the weekly goals for clearing backlogged cases? You know, of course, the annual bonus for your RO is riding on how well they do. Oh, yes! Sad news about Orville Smith, head of the Phoenix RO, had to replace him because his boys were unable to get the backlog under control. I always liked Orville, good man, hated to see him get the ax, Harry! Hope I don't have to call you again."

Director Harry Goodman shouts out to his secretary, Sally, "Get all the team chiefs up to the conference room ASAP and tell them I'll be looking for answers why they are letting the rank and file goof off." Thus starts another week in the second-largest agency of the government.

MR. PRESIDENT, IS THIS THE WAY TO TREAT THE WOUNDED?

The *St. Petersburg Times* ran an editorial on November 4, 2005, titled "*No Way to Thank Troops*." The editorial was based on an article published in the *Philadelphia Inquirer* on April 10, 2005 concerning a severely wounded infantryman and his alleged debt of $7,000 to the Army. The facts as outlined in the article were as follows: The soldier's left hand was so severely mangled by a land mine explosion that it had to be amputated; the army failed to reduce his combat pay when he was air evacuated out of Iraq; because he was air-lifted out of the battlefield, his equipment was left behind and the quartermaster had to charge him for unreturned equipment; the bureaucratic solution to this indebtedness to the United States of America was to outsource his debt to a collection agency close to where he settled; this poor GI now knows how grateful all the president's men in the DOD are for his sacrifices and endured hardships.

Know Your Adversary

Perhaps this first chapter was not the most acceptable way to introduce a book, but it really is on point. It all boils down to this: know your adversary. The VA will swear they are not adversarial. "Don't you read the signs we have posted in our buildings, 'Veterans are our best customers'?" The hallways in any regional office or medical center have signs everywhere expounding their dedication to those who served.

Think about this, you are on one side of the street saying "I am entitled to compensation benefits, I was injured in the service." On the other side of the street the VA is shouting back "Oh, no! You have not proved to our satisfaction that your injury is service related." This is now an adversarial contest. The definition of adversary is "somebody who opposes somebody else in a conflict, contest, or debate." [6]

During the past fifty-five years the tenure of seven Republican presidents and three Democrat presidents failed to stop the erosion in caring for those who bore the battle. The source of the problem is the White House, and the Office of Management and Budget tries to make the human costs of going to war a nickel and dime expenses.

The mighty fist of the man sitting in the Oval Office slams down on the desk, telling the secretary of the Department of Veterans Affairs to pass this on to all those appointees under him: "I don't care how they do it but the VA budget will come in below last year's level. I don't want to hear we can't do it because of injuries and death in the Middle East. If we are forced to deal with that situation then find ways to cut benefits by cutting services and treatment, stop being so generous with granting benefits, and reduce the number of employees.

"Don't give away the store to all people claiming to be suffering from PTSD." [7]

Are We Making the VA Better?

There are concerns by the Congress, service organizations, watchdog groups, and individual veterans that the VA is not doing its job. Since the first edition of this book, the Department of Veterans Affairs has launched a major media blitz trying to convince everyone they have taken steps to correct all their shortcomings and improve their day-to-day operation. This new operational strategy is known as the Claims Processing Improvement Model.

To accept this new initiative as a major breakthrough in claims processing, you have to overlook that the backlog of pending compensation claims in 2002 topped 432,000. Undersecretary for Veterans Benefits Administration, Daniel L. Cooper testifying before the Senate Veterans Affairs Committee in May 2005 advised that by implementing this new management concept the fifty-seven regional offices would be able to reduce the backlog to 253,000 by September 2003. [8]

On October 20, 2005, the upbeat message from the good Admiral Daniel L. Cooper, Undersecretary for Veterans Benefits, about moving claims along fell overboard. The backlog increased by 100,000 claims between 2004 and 2005 and now stands at 350,000 veterans waiting for help.

You Can't Always Win

The Paralyzed Veterans Association sued in Federal Court to stop the VBA from denying claims sixty days after notifying the veteran of the evidence they were seeking and won. The judicial opinion rendered stated, "no negative decision on any claim issue could take place for at least one year from the date of original notification." It took the VBA three months to find a way around this court order with the help from members of Congress friendly to the administration. However, in that short period, 100,000 claims were added to the backlog.

Undersecretary Cooper advised the Senate Committee that there were several other factors slowing efforts to clear the backlog of pending compensation claims. Firstly, the total number of new claims received in 2001 was 674,000; by 2004 the number leaped to 771,000, which leads the VBA to estimate that over 800,000 new claims will be filed in 2005. Secondly, it appears that veterans are naming more disabilities on each claim filed. Approximately ten years ago, the average was 2.5 medical issues per claim, and in 2005 it has jumped to ten medical issues per claim.

Another factor that cannot be blamed directly on the VA is the level of technical competence at the local service organizations. These service officers are told to file a claim whether or not a veteran has proof that he or she was injured or had illness in the service. The once- or twice-yearly training meetings are not sufficient to give a volunteer service officer a working background for helping his or her comrades.

A parallel goal of the Veterans Benefits Administration (VBA) was to reduce processing time from 223 days to 145 days. Some information made public is not always right on point. This was noted in the General Accounting Office (GAO) audit in 2002, which stated the number of days the VBA implied for processing compensation claims was 223 days. The audit revealed that compensation claims were taking 241 days, pension claims were running 126 days, and Dependency Indemnity Compensation claims for widows and parents were being processed in 172 days. The question that comes to mind is why choose an arbitrary number of 223 days for each of the three categories instead of simply citing an accurate count for each group.

In some ways they are really caught between a rock and a hard place. At the very top of the government food chain, the Oval Office and the OMB are telling all the administration's appointed secretary and undersecretaries they don't care what they have to do but cut the flow of money on veterans' issues down to a trickle. "We have to pay for wars, protect tax cuts currently in place, and influence international events."

There have to be some appointees who go home at night knowing 1.23 million veterans were denied benefits just to satisfy the White House's mandate to hold the line on veterans' costs. The secretary of the Department of Veterans Affairs is doing a "Texas Two Step" trying to explain why his Health Administration's 2006 budget for medical care came up nearly two billion dollars short. According to the rationale being played back, they had no idea the budget needs would not be met. Isn't that a strange one, when just about every major service organization was on record stating the medical budget was not sufficient. What about the budget for the Veterans Benefits Administration: how many billions of dollars would they come up short if they granted even half the 1.23 million claims they denied? I do not know how many billions would have to be added to the budget, but I do know the man sitting behind the big desk in the Oval Office would have a cow. I also believe that the trickle-down effect would reduce the number of appointees traveling the beltway each day for their failure to stop the flow of funds to veterans.

Chapter One Highlights

For over 300 years, it has been the law of the land that those who were wounded, injured, or diseased in the defense of this country would be provided with the care and financial assistance necessary to go on with their lives. As the ranks swell with those who served this country's interest by taking up arms to either defend it from a hostile enemy or enforce its national political agenda, the number of individuals disabled by this service has also sharply increased.

In less than a century, this country has sent its young men into harm's way more than ten times.

Members of our military have been used in tests of biochemical agents and nuclear radiation and in other experiments without their knowledge or permission. Since World War I our country has deserted thousands of American troops who were missing in action by declaring them "killed in action—body not recovered." There has been no real aggressive action on the part of this country to follow leads and account for these individuals. That isn't to say it hasn't spent millions of dollars in the quest for "answers." Our government and politicians deserve high marks in producing catchy slogans and speeches in expressing their sympathy for these people.

The bottom line is this: It is less sending members of the American military into combat than supporting those who survived the wars, police actions, and the dangers of daily military duty that is so expensive. The politicians want to cut the costs of this country's obligation to its veterans, but this must be done covertly. They do so by reorganizing the internal structure of the Department of Veterans Affairs in the name of streamline management.

The Department of Veterans Affairs, having been the focus of severe criticism by service organizations, veterans, and congressional oversight committees, has experimented with various management concepts in efforts to appear more responsive to the needs of veterans. The Claims Processing Improvement Model (CPI) is the latest attempt to increase efficiency in processing compensation and pension claims and reduce the number of errors.

The internal structure of the Adjudication Division in each of fifty-seven regional offices is divided into six functional groups composed of "x," a fixed number of teams in each group. The groups are identified as Triage, Pre-Determination, Rating, Post-Determination, Appeals, and Public Contact. Is this really that much different from the organization of the Adjudication Division in the 1970s? The groups did not have the same names, but the functions were almost the same. If you were to chart both claims processes, they would look something like this:

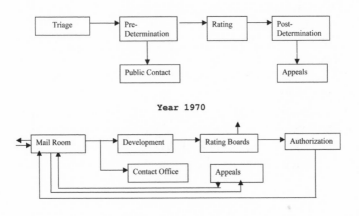

Year 2005

| Triage | → | Pre-Determination | → | Rating | → | Post-Determination |

Public Contact

Appeals

Year 1970

| Mail Room | → | Development | → | Rating Boards | → | Authorization |

Contact Office

Appeals

Triage Team

VA manual M21-1M, Part III Subpart I, Chapter 1 highlights the following duties as the sole responsibility of the Triage Teams.

*   Teams will review all incoming mail to determine if it is within their area of authority to decide the issue immediately. It is so only if the claim requires no in-depth development and does not require the review of a claim file.
*   Teams are to determine if any internal controls should be initiated for these reasons: claims establishment in share, control of Veterans Records System, modern award processing development and routing mail.

The mailroom is the first stop within the VA adjudication process. There are times when a veteran's problems start in the mailroom. It would not be an exaggeration to say that some regional officers receive more than 100,000 pieces of mail per month. Moving that much mail almost guarantees that documents and evidence are going to get separated from the primary correspondence. You can avoid this problem if all your pages and evidence are securely fastened together. The second most important precaution you can take is to print your name and VA C-Number or Social Security number at the bottom of each page. Precaution number three is *never*, *never* send documents or correspondence to the VA without first making a backup copy. Precaution number four is if you are mailing your information to the VA, send it by certified mail with a return receipt required. Many individuals have regretted not doing this, because their evidence was lost in the system. The VA's position has always been, if you cannot prove we got it then it was never sent.

You also have to take into consideration that the mailroom is not an exciting place to work. Upward mobility is extremely limited and job satisfaction is not a ten. These inherent problems can lead to a claim being denied or delayed. With thousands of pieces of paper floating around on a daily basis, it is a sure bet that some pieces of evidence will get misfiled. Don't let them be yours.

TRIAGE WORK FLOW
So what is the day-to-day routine that starts in the mailroom? In a nutshell, M21-1M mandates as follows:
Mail Incoming
- Mail must be reviewed at least once a day.
- Mail must include records for additional processing.
- No claim file will be ordered by the Triage Team to be worked by team members, meaning if they order a claim file they cannot work the claim.
- Mail that is worked will be processed/completed at once or by the next day.

Mail Internal Routing
- Each piece of mail must identify the issues pending.
- Each piece of mail must show the action taken by a Triage Team member.
- Each piece of mail will show proper routing instruction.

Is there a danger your claim could be denied at this level? Yes. A clerk could easily misfile or lose a vital piece of evidence to substantiate your claim. This action could result in the claim being denied. Remember the rule: always, always be able to prove you sent the VA a document.[1]

Pre-Determination Team

The second step in the adjudication process for an original claim, reopened claim, claim for increase in disability compensation benefits, or amended claim is to be reviewed by the Pre-Determination Team. The size and number of teams within this division will vary according to the veteran population being served by that regional office.

Complete and timely development of a claim is this team's primary responsibility. Within the framework of their accountability, they forward claims to the rating team for administrative decisions or ratings decision claims for compensation or pension. In a nutshell they do the leg work for the Rating Team. They are to determine when a claim is ready to be forwarded to the Rating Team. In theory, when a claim is declared ready to be rated, all the supporting evidence from various sources has been collected. The Pre-Determination Team is also the first stop for claims forwarded by congressional liaison sources or special interest cases.

Your claim could run into trouble here if the team member did not properly identify the government agency most likely to have supporting evidence to substantiate your claim. When your claim has been certified "Ready to Rate," it is transferred to the Rating Team.

If these people fail to collect all the supporting evidence as required by law, the Rating Team will send you a Dear John letter. If this happens you have but one choice and that is to file an appeal. This little skirmish could easily cost you three to five years in a paper war. That is if you don't quit in frustration.[2]

> Rule Number One:
> Collect your own evidence and locate comrades who might able be to give testimony favorable to your claim. Do not assume the VA will jump in with both feet and build your case for you. Only you can do that job and that is how it should be.[3]

Rating Team

By the time your claim has been certified ready to be rated, seven to eight months have passed. The backlog pending a rating decision could easily add a month or two the processing time.

With a complex medical claim there is a good chance that the first time out of the chute the claim will be denied. Post Traumatic

Stress Disorder (PTSD) is one of the claimed disabilities with an exceptionally high denial rate. The trigger that trips this bamboo booby-trap is the requirement to present hard evidence that you were exposed to an event that deeply scarred the psyche. This is especially true when you were not awarded one of the medals that allow direct service connection.

I know of one case in which the veteran, a helicopter crew chief, for nearly a year had to regularly clean his chopper of blood and body parts left behind by the wounded air-evac to the medical treatment facility at his base. He was also required to pull perimeter guard duty. On several occasions, he was fired upon.

VA doctors diagnosed him with PTSD, Social Security granted Supplemental Social Benefits because of PTSD. He has been unable to work because of it and for the last thirty-five years he has had absolutely no life.

He was there, these things did happen to him, he was diagnosed with PTSD, and he was never exposed to an event after leaving the service that could cause PTSD. The rating board has as much as told him, "We don't believe you and if you can't find the evidence, that's too bad." Claim denied![4]

Rating Teams members are chosen on the assumption they have a solid foundation of "hands-on experience" and a broad understanding of the laws, regulations, and medical knowledge essential to adjudicate a claim. With so many claims being denied, one might suspect that claims are being outsourced for adjudication to save money and effectively attack the backlog. "Only kidding Mr. Government, you wouldn't do that, would you?"

There are factors at work that disrupt efficiency and the equitable processing of claims. For openers, they only have so much time to review a claim and all its evidence. There is a daily requirement to complete "x" number of claims per day. Failure to do so invites lightening bolts from the director's office. Since raters are not trained in all aspects of medicine or law, many issues are just over their heads. And they do not have the luxury of researching

the background of a particular medical problem to see how it relates to a veteran's claim. Experience tells us that if they err, they
do it in favor of the government.

Another factor that enters into the equation is that they do not
do a "De Novo" review on a routine basis for each claim action.[5]
The only evidence considered is everything received after the last
rating decision.

Rule Number Two:
Make certain that you obtain a copy of every scrap of paper
the VA has in your claim file. This information cannot be with-
held because it is your right to know what the government has
on you. With the passage of the Freedom of Information Act
the government cannot deny the request. When requesting a
copy of your files, submit it through your local congressional
representative's office or your senator. Your request gets special handling considerations thus reducing the waiting time to
obtain the records.

Rule Number Three:
If it is at all possible for you to travel to the regional office
request that you be permitted to review your records. The purpose is to insure the VA did not leave out any internal notes,
evidence, or comments that could have a bearing on your claim.

Post-Determination Team

The Post-Determination Team addresses claims for accrued benefits, apportionments, original pension claims not requiring a rating, dependency issues, and death pension claims. Other duties
include preparing notification letters, developing and processing
non-rating products, and informing the claimant and other interested parties of the official finding of the rating decision.

This team might develop a portion of a claim that arose from
an inferred issue when the issue did not require evidence from a

third party, meaning records or evidence were in their possession. For example, a review of the claim file provided the necessary evidence to address the issue.

One common problem occurring in this group is its failure to discuss evidence favorable to your claim. Another error is it fails to list all the pertinent evidence that was used as the basis for the decision. This type of error is grounds for an appeal. Whenever you get a denial letter you should file a Notice of Disagreement (NOD).

> Rule Number Four:
> Always file a Notice of Disagreement when benefits are denied. The reason for this is that the VA is required by law to provide you with a <u>Statement of the Case</u>. This document must spell out all the pros and cons of the claim. They must clearly state what evidence was so persuasive that the only correct decision was to deny the claim. This is your chance to counter with reasons why their decision was wrong.

The Appeals Teams

A Decision Review Officer or DRO conducts reviews of NODs submitted by veterans who disagree with rating decisions. Again, the number of DROs and clerks assigned to assist them varies from RO to RO.

M21-1M, Section 3, Topic 10 states that the primary function of the DRO is the expeditious processing of appeals and remands. Within the scope of their function, they are to establish and monitor Veterans Appeal Control and Locator System records (VACOLS). Also on their list of duties are developing issues on appeal and making known any rating decision stemming from the appeal.

At times, the Appeal Team members prepare rating decisions, which includes officially making known their decision, updating the VACOLS, and preparing and releasing the notification letter.

The Appeals Team splits some responsibilities with a newly organized unit known within the Veterans Benefits Administration as
the Appeals Management Center or AMC.[6]

The best way to visualize this function is to think of it as a
spider's web. The center of the web is located in Washington, D.C.,
and from its center it has runners fanning out to each of the fifty-
seven RO. Local Regional Office AMC teams work directly with
their Washington headquarters counterpart.

By law, appeals must be moved expeditiously through the appeal process. The introduction of this newly formed function is a
back-door method to circumvent the Court ruling forbidding the
BVA to obtain evidence and adjudicate an issue not previously
considered by the RO .The story circulating the beltway is that this
new unit will improve the timeliness and accuracy of decisions. It
is still taking 700 or more days for a decision to be rendered. If a
claimant challenges the BVA's decision and takes his case to the
United States Court of Appeals for Veterans Claims, he or she adds
another two years to the process. If the Court fails to agree with the
BVA and reverses or remands the case back to them, several more
years will be added to the lifeline of this disagreement.

Public Contact Team

In the Claims Processing Improvement (CPI) reorganization plan
the Public Contact Team is the last stop for a claim being processed. This is where the VA representatives go one-on-one with
GI Joe veteran. Contact can be face to face in a contact center, by
telephone, correspondence, or e-mail. The Contact Team is expected
to exercise a two-way exchange of information with the Triage
Team, as well as with the Pre-Determination and Post-Determination teams.

The Public Contact Team must input all information from a
personal interview into BIRLS, SHARE, and MAP-D/Cover data

systems. What does all that mean? Well BIRLS, aka Beneficiary Identification Records Locator Subsystem, is a data system containing selected information from service records. Eligibility for one or more benefits available through the VA is scanned to determine if entitlement exists.

Claim information obtained by the Personnel Contact Team is recorded and stored in a data system known as SHARE. All teams have access to this data, as do selected individuals in service organizations who have the authority to review rating decisions before they are passed on to the Post-Determination Team. This information is protected by the privacy act and therefore requires a password access.

MAP-D—MODERN AWARD PROCESSING DEVELOPMENT

This application will replace CAPS as a source of timeliness data for IMS. MAP-D, according to VBA officials, contains records for all cases and will reduce the amount of manual data entry required, thus reducing the potential for data input errors. According to the Public Contact Team member I spoke with by telephone at the St. Petersburg Regional Office in Florida, the system has been in operation since 2003.

COVERS

COVERS is the acronym for Control of Veterans Record System and is primarily the responsibility of the Triage Team. From what I have been able to learn, when mail arrives it is reviewed for content and given an initial evaluation. A member of the Triage Team will review the contents of the correspondence to determine if they can deal with it or pass it on to the Pre-Development Team. If the correspondence is to be passed on, a decision is made as to which database will exercise control over the claim: CEST, COVERS, or MAP-D.

Chapter Two Highlights

The VA Benefits Administration have changed the structure of rating boards by eliminating physicians and attorneys from the boards and allowing the merits of a claim to be decided by a single individual without a medical or legal background. They're reducing the hospital medical staff and hiring foreign doctors and retired physicians from local resources. Federal statutes do not require a doctor to be licensed to practice in a VA facility. To get a job as a doctor with the VA, all that is required is a medical degree from any school in the world. Additional cost-saving measures include allowing part-time resident doctors in training from local teaching hospitals and physician's assistants to evaluate medical claims by veterans.

You think you have a claim for an injury or illness originating in the service. If you are going to do business with the VA, it is very much like doing business with a Chinese laundry service during the westward expansion of the railroads: "No ticket, no laundry." You have a great deal more to lose than a pair of overalls and shirt for failure to provide the right ticket.

The VA sorts incoming claims for compensation benefits into four distinct categories. The action the VA takes depends solely on the type of claim the veteran filed. With the exception of an informal claim, never file for benefits unless you have completely packaged the claim based on the Big Three Elements.

Remember, you can submit a winning claim, but only you can employ the necessary interest and energy to prove your injury or illness is service related. Do not let yourself be led into believing that the act of filling out a required form will bring the full resources of the VA to assist you in proving your claim is service-connected.

Where Do I Start?

The first question you must ask, "Is the evidence sufficient to convince a fair and impartial individual that the claim is plausible?" This is the key to establishing your claim. If the claim is initially denied because it was considered not to have sufficient evidence to invoke the VA's duty to assist, the only recourse is to appeal that decision. The appeal can only address the one issue of whether the evidence was adequate to satisfy the initial burden.

A great big "DENIED" at the first level will take two to four years before a decision is made on the appeal. If the claimant is successful on appeal, only then will the VA proceed with the task of determining whether the available evidence is sufficient to grant service connection for disabilities claimed. If your claim cannot past muster at all three levels, you will be denied benefits.

Problems Created by a Weakly Supported Claim

A typical claim action initiated after leaving the service can best be understood by example. Our claimant was in the United States Air Force from 1962 to 1966 and stationed in Arizona. He was a crew chief assigned to one of the fighter squadrons and performed all his duties outside on the flight line. In 1965, while home on leave, he was involved in an automobile accident that caused a cervical neck injury. He received an honorable discharge.

In January 1996 he filed an original claim for ankylosis of the cervical spine, alleging that the automobile accident in 1965 was the cause of his severe neck condition. He also filed a claim for basal cell carcinoma on the basis that he was continuously exposed to the sun for four years while working on the flight line.

A detailed statement by the claimant of the accident and a copy of the police report were not attached to the application as supporting evidence. He failed to provide any form of evidence that his skin cancer was the consequence of working on aircraft outside on the flight line for four years. The VA denied this claim as not well-grounded.[1]

The local RO's rationale for denying the claim was that the claimant did not submit medical evidence indicating his neck injury was due to the 1965 automobile accident. The claim was denied because no medical evidence was submitted to justify service-connection for skin cancer. The claimant's service records could not be found at the National Record Center, and the explanation offered was a fire most likely destroyed the records in 1973.

The appealed decision was forwarded to the Board of Veterans Appeals (BVA), who affirmed the local regional office's decision to deny benefits. The rationale given by the BVA was that since no outside medical experts' opinions had been offered, the claim was without foundation.

The claimant went back to the VA trying to reopen his claim by providing relevant dates, as well as the names and addresses of those who could give evidence to substantiate his claim. His former line chief submitted a "buddy letter" attesting that he worked outside on aircraft during his four years assigned to XYZ Air Force Base. The claimant also attached a letter from his doctor affirming that he was suffering from basal cell carcinoma that more than likely originated while he worked in the sun unprotected for four years. Once again the Regional Office denied his request on the basis that the evidence provided was not new and material as required under 38 CFR §3.156.

The decision was appealed and two years later, the BVA affirmed the regional office's denial of benefits. The claimant appealed the BVA's decision to the United States Court of Appeals for Veterans Appeals. Almost two years passed before the court ruled that the claim was well-grounded.

In deciding the case, the claimant's statement, the buddy statement, doctor's assessment, and the traffic accident report were sufficient to trigger the VA's duty to assist. The case was remanded back to the BVA with the instruction to comply with the "Duty to Assist" provision of the law. Now, more than five years later, the VA is going to determine if the claimant is entitled to service-connected benefits for residuals of an automobile accident and skin cancer.

The first time the VA denied the claim they were correct. Although he used the correct VA form, the veteran failed to provide any evidence for his claim.

Your Responsibility

Title 38 U.S. Code §5107(a) provides that:

> Except when otherwise provided by the Secretary in accordance with the provisions of this title, a person who submits a claim for benefits under a law administered by the Secretary shall have the burden of submitting evidence sufficient to justify a belief by a fair and impartial individual that the claim is well-grounded.

What this means is that if a claim is submitted based only on a belief that the current medical condition was related to your military service, without sufficient proof of this, it will be considered frivolous and denied. You cannot evoke the VA's duty to assist unless the claim is considered well-grounded.

A claim is very much in jeopardy if the claimant merely submits the required forms. There is a great deal more to claiming benefits than simply completing a form. The VA receives thousands of claims every week. How much attention do you think a claim receives? Any guess other that a quick scan would be dreaming. So if all that is attached to the claim is the original form, you have a 99.9 percent chance of receiving a Dear John letter.

> Rule Number Five: Never file for benefits when all you have is a belief your health problem is service-related and all you can submit is a claim form. Unless you can prove service incurrence, current illness related to the claimed service illness, and a causal relationship between the in-service event and the current health problem, do not shoot yourself in the foot by filing a formal claim. File an Informal Claim. You now have one year to lock down a solid claim backed by evidence.

VA's Duty to Assist

The duty to assist in terms of actually improving your chances for establishing service-connection is very limited. If for no other reason, there are hundreds of thousands of claims waiting to be processed at any given time.

Frustrated by endless complaints from constituents, Congress passed legislation known as The Veterans Claims Assistance Act of 2000 on November 9, 2000, which became public Law No. 106-475. In theory, it is a veteran's Bill of Rights that eliminates the "well grounded" requirement for a service-connected claim and requires the Veterans Administration to examine the evidence submitted by the veteran and to explain to the veteran what further evidence is needed to prove a service-connected claim.

The adjudications department at each of the fifty-seven regional offices is graded weekly on how many claims it cleared during the previous week. Job security and annual performance rewards are based on this performance standard. Think of the Triage Team as a conveyer belt. On both sides of this endless moving belt people are throwing claim forms into one pile or another. As the claims make their way to the sorting stage, where the original claim is jerked off the belt and a number 10 stock letter is assigned and dispatched. The veteran is told what is needed before the claim is rated.

The letter hits the veteran like a sucker punch to the side of the head. He is staggered by the sudden demands made for evidence, and he has no idea where to start looking. Also, they are saying, "You have only sixty days to get this in or we are going to rate the claim on what we have." The veteran thinks, "Hell, all they have is a claim form. What am I going to do? I don't know where the guys in my squad moved to after leaving the Army. I was treated for a gun shot wound in the field by a medic." The more questions the veteran asks himself the more impossible they seem to answer.

From a practical standpoint, this scenario is not necessary. Take the initiative and file an Informal Claim. You have one year to put together a claim that will pass muster. Remember, this is a real tool and it is at your fingertips. The purpose of this book is to show you how to become a "Paper PI" and track down elusive evidence.

The Veterans Claims Assistance Act of 2000 enacted by Congress and signed by the president requires that the VA

1. Provide a medical examination or medical opinion if the veteran has a current medical disability that *may be* related to military service.

2. Gather all existing service medical records and other federal agency medical records that can be obtained.

3. Make reasonable efforts to obtain nonmilitary records that the veteran identifies and authorizes the VA to obtain.

VA Regulation 38 CFR §3.159 directs the support the VA will provide during the development of a claim. Portions of 38 CFR §3.159 are quoted directly to provide you with leads as to where and what kind of evidence to look for.[2]

It is essential that you and the VA speak the same language. Here is a list of definitions published in 38 CFR §3.159a:

(1) *Competent Medical Evidence* means evidence provided by a person who is qualified through education, training, or experience to offer medical diagnoses, statements, or opinions. Competent medical evidence may also mean statements conveying sound medical principles found in medical treatises. It would also include statements contained in authoritative writings such as medical and scientific articles and research reports or analyses.

(2) *Competent lay evidence* means any evidence not requiring that the proponent have specialized education, training, or experience. Lay evidence is competent if it is provided by a person who has knowledge of facts or circumstances and conveys matters that can be observed and described by a lay person.

(3) *Substantially complete application* means an application containing the claimant's name; his or her relationship to the veteran, if applicable; sufficient service information for VA to verify the claimed service, if applicable; the benefit claimed and any medical condition(s) on which it is based; the claimant's signature.

(4) For purposes of paragraph (c)(4)(i) of this section, *event* means one or more incidents associated with places, types, and circumstances of service giving rise to disability.

(5) *Information* means non-evidentiary facts, such as the claimant's Social Security number or address; the name and military unit of a person who served with the veteran; or the name and address of a medical care provider who may have evidence pertinent to the claim.

38 CFR §3.159(b) affirms the claims examiner's *duty to notify claimants of necessary information or evidence.*

(1) When VA receives a complete or substantially complete application for benefits, it will notify the claimant of any information and medical or lay evidence that is necessary to substantiate the claim. VA will inform the claimant which information and evidence, if any, that the claimant is to provide to VA and which information and evidence, if any, that VA will attempt to obtain on behalf of the claimant. VA will also request that the claimant provide any evidence in the claimant's possession that pertains to the claim. If VA does not receive the necessary information and evidence requested from the claimant within one year of the date of the notice, VA cannot pay or provide any benefits based on that application. If the claimant has not responded to the request within 30 days, VA may decide the claim prior to the expiration of the one-year period based on all the information and evidence contained in the file, including information and evidence it has obtained on behalf of the claimant and any VA medical examinations or medical opinions. If VA does so, however, and the claimant subsequently provides the information and evidence within one year of the date of the request, VA must readjudicate the claim.

(2) If VA receives an incomplete application for benefits, it will notify the claimant of the information necessary to complete the application and will defer assistance until the claimant submits this information.

38 CFR §3.159(c) *VA's Duty to Assist claimants in obtaining evidence.* Upon receipt of a substantially complete application for benefits, VA will make reasonable efforts to help a claimant obtain evidence necessary to substantiate the claim. In addition, VA will give the assistance described in paragraphs (c)(1), (c)(2), and (c)(3)

to an individual attempting to reopen a finally decided claim. VA will not pay any fees charged by a custodian to provide records requested.

(1) *Obtaining records not in the custody of a Federal department or agency.* VA will make reasonable efforts to obtain relevant records not in the custody of a Federal department or agency, to include records from State or local governments, private medical care providers, current or former employers, and other non-Federal governmental sources. Such reasonable efforts will generally consist of an initial request for the records and, if the records are not received, at least one follow-up request. A follow-up request is not required if a response to the initial request indicates that the records sought do not exist or that a follow-up request for the records would be futile. If VA receives information showing that subsequent requests to this or another custodian could result in obtaining the records sought, then reasonable efforts will include an initial request and, if the records are not received, at least one follow-up request to the new source or an additional request to the original source.

(i) The claimant must cooperate fully with VA's reasonable efforts to obtain relevant records from non-Federal agency or department custodians. The claimant must provide enough information to identify and locate the existing records, including the person, company, agency, or other custodian holding the records; the approximate time frame covered by the records; and, in the case of medical treatment records, the condition for which treatment was provided.

(ii) If necessary, the claimant must authorize the release of existing records in a form acceptable to the person, company, agency, or other custodian holding the records.

(2) *Obtaining records in the custody of a Federal department or agency.* VA will make as many requests as are necessary to obtain relevant records from a Federal department or agency. These records include but are not limited to military records, including

service medical records; medical and other records from VA medical facilities; records from non-VA facilities providing examination or treatment at VA expense; and records from other Federal agencies, such as the Social Security Administration. VA will end its efforts to obtain records from a Federal department or agency only if VA concludes that the records sought do not exist or that further efforts to obtain those records would be futile. Cases in which VA may conclude that no further efforts are required include those in which the Federal department or agency advises VA that the requested records do not exist or the custodian does not have them.

(i) The claimant must cooperate fully with VA's reasonable efforts to obtain relevant records from Federal agency or department custodians. If requested by VA, the claimant must provide enough information to identify and locate the existing records, including the custodian or agency holding the records; the approximate time frame covered by the records; and, in the case of medical treatment records, the condition for which treatment was provided. In the case of records requested to corroborate a claimed stressful event in service, the claimant must provide information sufficient for the records custodian to conduct a search of the corroborative records.

(ii) If necessary, the claimant must authorize the release of existing records in a form acceptable to the custodian or agency holding the records.

(Authority: 38 U.S.C. 5103A(b))

(3) *Obtaining records in compensation claims.* In a claim for disability compensation, VA will make efforts to obtain the claimant's service medical records, if relevant to the claim; other relevant records pertaining to the claimant's active military, naval or air service that are held or maintained by a governmental entity; VA medical records or records of examination or treatment at non-VA facilities authorized by VA; and any other relevant records held by any Federal department or agency. The claimant must provide enough information to identify and locate the existing records including

the custodian or agency holding the records; the approximate time frame covered by the records; and, in the case of medical treatment records, the condition for which treatment was provided.

(4) *Providing medical examinations or obtaining medical opinions.*

(i) In a claim for disability compensation, VA will provide a medical examination or obtain a medical opinion based upon a review of the evidence of record if VA determines it is necessary to decide the claim. A medical examination or medical opinion is necessary if the information and evidence of record does not contain sufficient competent medical evidence to decide the claim, but:

(A) Contains competent lay or medical evidence of a current diagnosed disability or persistent or recurrent symptoms of disability;

(B) Establishes that the veteran suffered an event, injury or disease in service, or has a disease or symptoms of a disease listed in §3.309, §3.313, §3.316, and §3.317 manifesting during an applicable presumptive period provided the claimant has the required service or triggering event to qualify for that presumption; and

(C) Indicates that the claimed disability or symptoms may be associated with the established event, injury, or disease in service or with another service-connected disability.

(ii) Paragraph (4)(i)(C) could be satisfied by competent evidence showing post-service treatment for a condition, or other possible association with military service.

(iii) Paragraph (c)(4) applies to a claim to reopen a finally adjudicated claim only if new and material evidence is presented or secured.

38 CFR §3.159(d) *Circumstances where VA will refrain from or discontinue providing assistance.* VA will refrain from providing assistance in obtaining evidence for a claim if the substantially complete application for benefits indicates that there is no reasonable possibility that any assistance VA would provide to the claim-

ant would substantiate the claim. VA will discontinue providing assistance in obtaining evidence for a claim if the evidence obtained indicates that there is no reasonable possibility that further assistance would substantiate the claim. Circumstances in which VA will refrain from or discontinue providing assistance in obtaining evidence include, but are not limited to:

(1) The claimant's ineligibility for the benefit sought because of lack of qualifying service, lack of veteran status, or other lack of legal eligibility;

(2) Claims that are inherently incredible or clearly lack merit; and

(3) An application requesting a benefit to which the claimant is not entitled as a matter of law.

38 CFR §3.159(e) *Duty to notify claimant of inability to obtain records.*

(1) If VA makes reasonable efforts to obtain relevant non-Federal records but is unable to obtain them, or after continued efforts to obtain Federal records concludes that it is reasonably certain they do not exist or further efforts to obtain them would be futile, VA will provide the claimant with oral or written notice of that fact. VA will make a record of any oral notice conveyed to the claimant. For non-Federal records requests, VA may provide the notice at the same time it makes its final attempt to obtain the relevant records. In either case, the notice must contain the following information:

(i) The identity of the records VA was unable to obtain;

(ii) An explanation of the efforts VA made to obtain the records;

(iii) A description of any further action VA will take regarding the claim, including, but not limited to, notice that VA will decide the claim based on the evidence of record unless the claimant submits the records VA was unable to obtain; and

(iv) A notice that the claimant is ultimately responsible for providing the evidence.

(2) If VA becomes aware of the existence of relevant records before deciding the claim, VA will notify the claimant of the records

and request that the claimant provide a release for the records. If the claimant does not provide any necessary release of the relevant records that VA is unable to obtain, VA will request that the claimant obtain the records and provide them to VA.

38 CFR §3.159(f) For the purpose of the notice requirements in paragraphs (b) and (e) of this section, notice to the claimant means notice to the claimant or his or her fiduciary, if any, as well as to his or her representative, if any.

Duty to Assist Defined by Case Law

The U.S. Court of Appeals for Veterans Claims holds that under the Veterans Claims Assistance Act of 2000 (VCAA), the Department of Veterans Affairs cannot deny a claim until they fulfill their statutory duty and assist in the development phase of the claim. In one of the first precedent decisions (*Harvey v. Principi*, 98-1375 2001) they held that the VCAA obliges the VA to give notice to the claimants of the required information and evidence that must be submitted to substantiate a claim.

Searches of the U.S. Court of Appeals for Veterans Claims websites produces numerous nonprecedent decisions by single judges related to the "VA Duty to Assist." The findings of a single judge's opinion have value in that they will tell you the plus or negative side of an issue. This decision is only binding on the VA for that particular appeal. It doesn't mean that you cannot use the arguments in your appeal if the circumstances fit. You cannot say that in *Greenleaf v. Derwinski* the court decided that the VA had to do this or that.

Chapter Three Highlights

The best way to summarize this chapter is to first review the guidelines each regional office must use in making a decision as to the merits of the claim. Second, emphasize the claimant's responsibility.

For a claim to trigger the VA's duty to assist the claimant must show:

- For a singular condition the veteran must attach medical proof which demonstrates that he or she is currently suffering from the alleged condition and that it is possibly related to the service.
- That when the claim is reviewed, the cumulative evidence of record supports the claim and the last VA medical examination affirms the condition does in fact exist.
- That if a statement of a medical causation or relationship is made by a layperson it must be confirmed by a medical authority. For example, using a "buddy letter" contending skin cancer was caused by working out in the sun for four years is acceptable as long as a doctor's diagnosis confirms skin cancer and that such exposure could have caused the skin cancer.
- That if a medical treatise was used suggesting service connection it must be accompanied by medical evidence from a doctor that the information was relevant to the case.
- That if the claim is for multiple disabilities, the evidence for each individual disability must be able to stand alone before triggering the VA's duty to assist for that medical condition.

When a decision is reached either by the Pre-Determination or the Rating Team that the claim is denied, the notification to the claimant must clearly explain why the claim is considered an incomplete application and why further action is not being taken by the regional office. In addition, the notification must advise the claimant what evidence is necessary to trigger the VA's duty to assist. The letter of denial will also tell the claimant he has one year from the date of their notification to submit the required evidence. If the evidence submitted is sufficient to justify the Big Three Standard the effective date of any benefits awarded will be the date of the original claim.

The U.S. Court of Appeals for Veterans Claims has held that Congress specifically limited entitlement to service-connection for disease or injury to cases where such incidents had resulted in a disability; in the absence of proof of a present disability, there can be no valid claim.

4 | CLAIM ACTIONS

It is necessary to know exactly what is entailed when claiming a disability. You must know the law for the type of claim action being filed. You must know what type of claim to ask for and you must know what the VA's responsibility is when responding.

Informal Claims

When putting together a winning claim, the proper use of an informal claim is one of the best tools a veteran has to work with. **It cannot be overemphasized that when a claim is submitted it must be complete and provable.** Take time to develop evidence to support your contentions; you cannot afford to develop your claim by bits and pieces. The beauty of an Informal Claim is that the claim entitlement date is established and protected while you do the work of obtaining evidence and necessary documents.

The governing regulation 38 CFR §3.155 specifically defines an Informal Claim as any communication or action that indicates intent to apply for one or more benefits under the laws administered by the VA. Upon receipt of an informal claim, the VA must formalize the application by forwarding the appropriate form. The VA must receive the official application for an original claim, VA form 21-526, within one year from the date it was mailed to you.

There are several other regulations that call for specific action by the VA when an informal claim is filed by the claimant. Under 38 CFR §3.150 (Forms to Be Furnished) the VA is required to provide the claimant with the appropriate application. Under 38 CFR

§3.151, the specific form prescribed by the Secretary must be filed in order for benefits to be paid.

Next, the issue of how long the claimant has to file an application is spelled out in 38 CFR §3.109 (Time Limit). There is a provision, 38 CFR §3.109(b), that grants the RO the authority to extend the one-year date if the claimant can show good cause for the delay in forwarding the official application.

The filing of an Informal Claim notice should be submitted on VA form 21-4138 Statement In Support Of Claim. The reason the emphasis is on using VA form 21-4138 is that it has the same legal status as a sworn statement before a notary public. An alternate method would be to state your intentions in a personal letter to the regional office. However, sign the letter before a notary and send it to the VA via your congressional representative.

This simple procedure has one other lasting benefit—it gives you the grounds for an appeal if benefits are denied. By statute, under the Duty to Assist Rule the VA must go out and get the required records once they have been notified of their existence. If the claim is denied, the grounds for reversal would be their failure to obtain evidence known to favorable to you.

Formal Claims—Choosing the Right One

Most claim actions fall under the category of New Claims. By VA definition, a new claim generally involves a review of new evidence based on a new application. The VA will separate compensation claim requests into one of the following groups:

- ◆ Original Claims
- ◆ Amend an Original Claim
- ◆ Claim for Increased Benefits
- ◆ Total Disability Based on Individual Unemployability
- ◆ Claims Based On Medical Treatment By VA
- ◆ Claims for Adjunct Disabilities
- ◆ Reopened Claims

Department of Veterans Affairs Department of Veterans Affairs STATEMENT IN SUPPORT OF CLAIM

VACY ACT INFORMATION: The law authorizes us to request the information we are asking you to provide on this form (38 U.S.C. 501(x) and (b)). The

onse you submit is considered confidential (38 U.S.C. 5701). They may be disclosed outside the Department of Veterans Affairs (VA) only if the disclosure is orized under the Privacy Act, including the uses identified in the VA system of records, 58VA21122, Compensation, Pension, Education and Rehabilitation ords—VA, published in the Federal Register. The requested information is considered relevant and necessary to determine maximum benefits under the law. rmation submitted is subject to verification through computer matching programs with other agencies.
SPONDENT BURDEN: VA may not conduct or sponsor, and respondent is not required to respond to this collection of information unless it displays a valid
B Control Number. Public reporting burden for this collection of information is estimated to average 15 minutes per response, including the time for reviewing ructions, searching existing data sources, gathering and maintaining the data needed, and completing and reviewing the collection of information. If you have ments regarding this burden estimate or any other aspect of this collection of information, call 1-800-827-1000 for mailing information on where to send your

T NAME - MIDDLE NAME - LAST NAME OF VETERAN (Type or print)	SOCIAL SECURITY NO.	VA FILE NO.
hn D. Roche	000-00-0000	C-00-000-000 VMS -

following statement is made in connection with a claim for benefits in the case of the above-named veteran:

Please accept this notice as my informal claim for compensation benefits due to a back

njury I had while on active duty in 1967. I have been treated for this condition at the VA

Medical Centers in Lake City, Florida in 1968, Houston, Texas in 1973 and the Bronx, New

ork in 1980.

A formal application will be filed once I have collected all the evidence to support my

laim.

CONTINUE ON REVERSE

ERTIFY THAT the statements on this form are true and correct to the best of my knowledge and belief.

NATURE	DATE SIGNED September 1 2005
DRESS	TELEPHONE NUMBERS (Include Area Code)
	DAYTIME	EVENING
77 California Ct. Clearwater, FL 33770	727-484-3373	727-484-3373

The VA classifies various claims under one broad category because new claims are dependent upon new evidence, and because the decision on the claim is independent of any previous claim action. The decision to either grant or deny the claim is based on current medical evidence, service medical records, and the causal relationship between the event that occurred in the service and the current condition.

To illustrate this point, let us say our claimant is a former POW who was previously denied service connection for arthritis resulting from being beaten with a rifle butt. Because there was no evidence in the file supporting his alleged injuries, the claim was initially denied. Later, the law was changed, and if a POW was diagnosed as having arthritis disabling to a degree of 10 percent, it was be presumed to be service connected.

This time, the veteran goes back into the VA with proof he was a POW. Because of the presumptive rule, the claim will now be considered a new claim for service connection for arthritis, and his new medical evidence confirming the existence of arthritis is sufficient grounds to award compensation benefits.

Types of Claim Actions

Veterans can file many types of claim actions with the Veterans Administration. This book focuses on the four most important service-connected claim actions filed by veterans. **It is absolutely necessary** that you know exactly what is entailed for the benefit you are claiming. You must know what the law requires for each category of claim before it is submitted, as each category of claim actions require special development techniques.

Each claim must be supported by evidence that will establish it as *current illness*, *in-service incurrence*, and *causal relationship between the illness and service*. None of these links can be missing in the chain of supporting evidence. Let's call them the Big Three. Their combined power can bring any adjudicator to his or her knees. No matter what they say at the central office in Washington, the claim will be granted. But fail to support all three elements and it is a Dear John letter that reads—and I quote—"Claim Denied." Only when you have satisfied all three elements will you be successful.

Before we look closely at the Big Three, a more basic problem must be ironed out. What do we call the claim action we want to file? For example, a veteran tells the VA he wants to "reopen" his claim when in reality he wants to "amend" the original claim. The misuse of the correct terminology can at best create longer delays before the issue is resolved. For this reason, you must know the type of claim you want to file, and what the VA's responsibility is in responding to your request.

ORIGINAL CLAIM

Shaping a winning claim is an art form. It doesn't require the genius of the great masters but it does require insight into how the VA works and what you must know to successfully prevail using the Big Three elements. Properly applying each of these elements to your claim will produce a masterpiece that leaves VA no choice but to grant the benefits. Nearly all the topics discussed below are also discussed in other chapters throughout the book.

An original claim for compensation benefits is an action that has never been applied for previously. It must be filed using VA form 21-526 and must be supported with sufficient evidence to meet the standards of the Big Three.

AMENDED CLAIM

When you file an amended claim you are telling the VA you wish to amend your original claim to include additional medical problems. A good example would be filing a claim for hearing loss and claiming the acoustic trauma occurred while on active duty. For thirty years, you were a tank commander.

This type of claim would be easy to win. Your DD 214 would

be the primary source of evidence in that it confirms the total time you served in the Army and that your Military Occupational Specialty (MOS) was that of a tank commander. Before you filed your claim, you arranged for a hearing examination by a medical specialist confirming the loss of hearing. Your military health records and retirement physical show that your hearing had started to deteriorate during your service. The Army long ago acknowledged that individuals exposed to high frequency decibel sounds such as tank engines could suffer hearing loss. This was the reason they kept trying to design helmets to reduce the noise exposure and sound proof the inner compartment of the tank. This claim meets the requirement of the Big Three elements.

No Records, No Claim

If you do not have copies of your active duty outpatient or inpatient medical records, you must obtain them. Outpatient medical records and military hospital records are maintained separately at the National Personnel Record Center in St. Louis, Missouri. Outpatient records are kept with your administrative and personnel records and inpatient records are stored in the hospital records section. When requesting a search for hospital records, you will give full name, military serial number, and the military unit you were assigned to at the time of hospitalization, the name and location of the hospital, the dates you were hospitalized, and the reason for the hospitalization.

In the mid 1950s, millions of World War II and Korean War Army hospital records were turned over to the Veterans Administration as part of a special study. When the project was finished, the VA did not return the records to the National Personnel Record Center, but placed them in storage, where they were forgotten. It was not until the late 1980s that this fact was made public. If you have been advised that there are no hospital records at the National Personnel Record Center, and you were hospitalized overseas for a combat wound, injury, or disease, contact the VA and request a copy of your records.

Under the 1996 Memorandum of Understanding between the Department of Defense and the Department of Veterans Affairs, medical records of all military members retiring or separating after May 1, 1994, are transferred directly to the VA rather than to the National Personnel Records Center. The agreement calls for the military branch to forward medical records to the Department of Veterans Affairs Medical Record Center, St. Louis, Missouri, for those members not initiating a claim. If the member initiates a claim during outprocessing, their medical records will be transferred directly to the VA Regional Office closest to their future address.

How the VA Rates an Injury or Disease

When all the medical facts supporting your claim have been gathered the evidence is cross-referenced against 38 CFR Part 4, "Schedule for Rating Disabilities." This section of the CFR lists the medical problems that the Department of Veterans Affairs rates as service connected.

Note: *This section of the 38 CFR has not been updated since 1945.* There are many newly recognized disabling diseases for which there are no rating descriptions. The rating procedure used for these diseases is known as an analogous rating, which simply means finding an injury or disease that is closely related. (See the glossary in Appendix B for a complete explanation.) This is a highly subjective decision-making process by a rating-board member. When a rating under this procedure is given it should be carefully scrutinized. The last two numbers in the analog rating's four digit rating code are always 99.

Before you submit a claim for a particular medical problem obtain a copy of 38 CFR Part 4 and compare your medical condition to the rating schedule for that condition. This will tell you what the medical facts must show before the VA will grant service connection.

TESTIMONIAL EVIDENCE—A MUST

For an injury or disease to stand up as probative evidence, you must know how to prepare sworn written testimony supporting the claim. The VA is quick to disregard buddy letters as evidence. However, a properly executed deposition (see glossary) giving a detailed explanation of pertinent facts provided by you, members of your family, fellow employees, employers, or former military comrades, is all vital relevant evidence. They can disregard your sworn statements only if they have hard factual evidence to the contrary. Although they may not want to, the VA must give this type of evidence considerable weight. You must learn how to construct these statements so they relate facts, not opinions or conjecture. The deposition must demonstrate how your medical condition affects your daily routine in the work place.

The Adjudication Process

The working rules are translated from laws passed by Congress; they are not arbitrary rules which claim examiners and rating-board members create, ignore, or change at will. VA Regional Offices, contrary to former Secretary Jessie Brown's belief, violate the law all the time. If he examined the number of cases returned to the regional offices by the Board of Veterans Appeals, he certainly could not publicly state that the "Veterans Benefit Administration was not systematically ignoring the law or the court." This statement was released by Secretary Jessie Brown in 1995 and appeared in the *American Legion Magazine* in response to the criticism of the ROs ignoring the law, made by Chief Judge Nebeker of the United States Court of Appeals for Veterans Claims.

Very few veterans are aware that their claim file must be reviewed and made part of the examination by the doctor. It is the duty of the rating specialist requesting the examination to ensure that the hospital or clinic has the file prior to the examination. (See

Part XV for a complete discussion of Compensation and Pension Examinations.)

To ensure a just and fair decision on your claim, you must understand what the law requires of rating-board members during the adjudication process. Unless you are knowledgeable about what takes place during this process, it's very likely that your claim will be denied or, if granted, the award may be considerably less than what your disability justifies.

IN THE LINE OF DUTY OR BENEFITS DENIED

Determining whether your injury or disease was the result of willful misconduct is one of the first considerations a rating specialist will assess. For instance did your organization conduct a line of duty investigation surrounding the circumstances of your injury or illness? If the findings of the investigating officer determine that your medical problem or injury was in the line of duty, those findings are binding on the VA. In accordance with 38 CFR §3.1(n) the VA must accept the service department decision as binding.

The exception to the rule occurs when the VA can prove the ruling was patently inconsistent with the facts and the laws administrated by the Department of Veterans Affairs. Keep in mind that all active duty members are on duty twenty-four hours a day, seven days a week, and fifty-two weeks a year. Thus everything they did was in the line of duty, unless it involved deliberate or intentional wrongdoing with knowledge of wanton and reckless disregard of its probable consequences.

When there is a claim and there was no line of duty investigation concerning the incident, a problem is likely to arise. The circumstances surrounding your injury or disease will be left to the interpretation of a rating specialist and the decision may be based on facts not in evidence, thereby producing a denial of benefits.

There are safeguards built into the regulation that are designed to protect you from indiscriminate denial of benefits because of a mere technical violation of police regulations or ordinances. Such circumstances per se will not constitute willful misconduct. The regulation also points out that willful misconduct will not be a determinative unless it is the proximate (see glossary) cause of injury, disease, or death.

If your claim is denied on the basis of willful misconduct, the VA must give you a detailed account of how it arrived at this conclusion. If its explanation does not discuss the evidence used in determining willful misconduct and how it arrived at this decision, it is in violation of its own regulations. At this point you appeal the denial of benefits.

PRESUMPTION OF SOUNDNESS—A KEY ISSUE

The regulations governing the issue of presumption of soundness are 38 CFR §3.304(b) and 38 CFR §3.305(b). Each regulation states that a veteran will be considered to have been in sound condition when examined, accepted, and enrolled for service except as to the defects, infirmities, and disorders noted on the entrance examination. When the claimant entered the service is the difference between the two regulations. Regulation 38 CFR §3.304(b) addresses those claims filed after January 1, 1947, whereas 38 CFR §3.305(b) covers claims filed prior to January 1, 1947. There is one other important difference between the two regulations. Individuals serving on active duty prior to January 1, 1947, had to serve on active duty six or more months before the presumption of soundness policy applied to their claim.

The law provides that any defects, infirmities, or disorders noted during the entry examination will not be considered a service-related condition unless they suffered aggravation during service. Both regulations stipulate that there must be clear and unmistakable (obvious or manifest) evidence that demonstrates the injury or disease existed before entry into the service. A key point to remember is that only those medical conditions recorded on entrance examination can be considered preexisting. An isolated reference in the medical file alleging a condition existed prior to service cannot be the sole basis for denial of benefits.

The Court of Appeals for Veterans Claims has addressed the issues of denial of benefits based on preexisting medical conditions and presumption of soundness on several occasions. The case of *Parker v. Derwinski*, 1 Vet. App. 522 (1992) illustrates how the VA deviates from the regulations by applying its own interpretation to the issue before them.

Mr. Parker sought to reopen his claim for disability benefits based on an alleged vision deficiency due to a hole in his left eye. The VA position in justifying the denial of service connection was based on the absence of any indication of trauma during active duty, and an unsubstantiated statement by an army doctor referring to an injury alleged to have occurred when Parker was nineteen years old. The VA concluded that this evidence was sufficient to rebut presumption of soundness rule.

To prevail, the VA has to find that a preexisting injury or disease had been demonstrated by unmistakable evidence. The evidence did not support the VA position. It had two pieces of evidence: a statement from an Army doctor alleging Mr. Parker injured his eye playing football at age nineteen; and the fact that service medical records were silent as to an injury to the left eye. The court also pointed out that Mr. Parker's sworn statement and the statements of several doctors in evidence were ignored by the VA. The court vacated the VA decision and remanded it back to the regional office for readjudication.

This particular veteran's claim was handicapped by the fact that he waited ten years before filing his original claim for service connection. His initial claim was denied, and he filed no appeal. In 1987, after waiting another ten years, he tried to reopen his claim based on new and material evidence that was promptly denied. Again he did not appeal the denial. Each time he tried to reopen his claim he included one new letter from a friend or doctor. In 1989, after receiving another denial to reopen his claim, he filed a timely appeal. It wasn't until 1991 that his appeal made its way to the Court of Veterans Appeal.

This case is an excellent example of how a claim can be dragged out for decades. When you file your claim, its imperative that you *not* assume someone else (VA) will gather the evidence to support your contentions. *This is your job.* If you do take the easy way out and only file an application with the hope the VA will gather the evidence, you will lose.

Any time your claim is denied, you should file a notice of disagreement to appeal the decision. The rating-board members and claim specialist in every VA regional office across this country make thousands of errors each year. Don't accept a denial—do something about it. File a Notice of Disagreement to appeal the decision. Whatever you do, don't stop with just a Notice of Disagreement.

CHRONIC DISEASES

A chronic disease must manifest itself to a degree of 10 percent or more within one year of the date of separation from the service. However, there are several exceptions to this rule. If leprosy or tuberculosis develops to a 10 percent level of disability within three years, or multiple sclerosis within seven years, then service connection under this rule will be granted.

The operative word is "manifest" and is not synonymous with "diagnosis." The rule qualifies if it can be shown that during the year after separation the symptoms for the condition equate to the 10 percent rating for the disease as stated in 38 CFR Part 4, "Schedule For Rating Disabilities." No condition other then one of the forty diseases listed in 38 CFR §3.309(a) will be considered chronic under the presumptive rule. The chronic diseases are:

Anemia primary
Arteriosclerosis
Arthritis
Atrophy, progressive muscular
Brain hemorrhage

Brain thrombosis
Bronchiectasis
Calculi of kidney
Calculi of bladder
Calculi of gallbladder
Cardiovascular and renal disease including hypertension
Cirrhosis of liver coccidioidomycosis
Diabetes mellitus
Encephalitis lethargica residuals
Endocarditis (all forms of valvular heart disease)
Endocrinopathies
Epilepsies
Hansen's disease
Leukemia
Lupus erythematosus, systemic
Myasthenia gravis
Myelitis myocarditis
Nephritis
Other organic diseases, nervous system
Osteitis deformans (Paget's disease)
Osteomalacia
Palsy, bulbar
Paralysis agitans
Psychoses
Purpura idiopathic hemorrhagic
Raynaud's disease
Sarcoidosis scleroderma
Sclerosis amyotrophic lateral
Sclerosis multiple
Syringomyelia
Thromboangiitis obliterans (Buerger's disease)
Tuberculosis, active
Tumor, malignant, brain
Tumor, malignant, peripheral nerves

Tumor, malignant, spinal cord
Ulcer duodenal
Ulcer peptic

TROPICAL DISEASES

The tropics have always presented a serious medical hazard for military members. Realizing this, Congress presumes service connection for sixteen diseases and resultant disorders. It also recognizes that treatment for many of these diseases could cause adjunct diseases as a result of the therapy administered, or as a preventive measure.

However, they also wrote into the law a rebuttal rule that the VA must satisfy before presumptive service connection can be granted. The claim can be denied if the VA can show that the individual didn't serve in a locality having a high incidence of the disease, or that the disease did not occur continuously in the local population. It can also be denied if the claimant separated from the service beyond the known incubation period for the tropical disease.

One of the sixteen diseases in this presumptive group is amebiasis, a disease that is generally characterized by dysentery with diarrhea, weakness, and prostration. The disease may lie dormant for several years after exposure. When the patient does experience the first symptom, it is often diagnosed as a stomach virus and treated accordingly.

When the patient doesn't respond to the standard treatment normally given for a stomach virus, the doctor usually orders a more serious study. At this point, the findings usually show the individual as being disabled by amoebae. The patient then learns from his doctor that his chronic condition is not found to be common where he lives, and he is also advised that the disease is not known to be a common health problem at his last duty station. He is told that it is common in the tropics—such as in Southeast Asia—and is acquired by ingesting food or drink containing encysted forms.

Then the patient recalls that just before his discharge, he was on temporary duty for one week in Saigon, South Vietnam. He and his friends made a tour of the local sights and ate and drank in local restaurants. A claim is filed, and then is promptly denied by the VA on the basis of not being well grounded. The claimant's medical records do not establish treatment for the condition on active duty. His service records show he was never stationed in any tropic regions where the disease was prevalent. His records also establish he was discharged over two years ago.

This is a winnable claim, but the claimant must properly develop it before filing a formal application. In this situation, file an Informal Claim to protect the date and serve notice that a service-connected disability claim will be forthcoming.

There are three sections within 38 CFR Part 3 that govern the awarding of service connection for one of the sixteen tropical diseases presumed to be service connected if they manifest to a degree of 10 percent within a year of separating from the service. The first requirement outlined in 38 CFR §3.309(b) identifies the sixteen diseases. Next, 38 CFR §3.307(a)(1)(4) requires that the veteran have served at least ninety days after December 31, 1946, and that the disease have manifested to a degree of 10 percent or more within one year from date of separation. The third condition outlined in 38 CFR §3.308(b) requires that a veteran who separated before January 1, 1947, have served at least six months on active duty in order to be eligible for presumptive service connection and that within one year of separating from the service the disease existed to a degree of 10 percent.

There is an exception that applies to all three sections of the law: For any one of the diseases shown below, as long as the incubation period commenced during the service period, establishing presumptive service connection is possible. If you have contracted one of these diseases you must ask your physician what the incubation period is, what the disease cycle between an active state and remission is once you have been exposed, if there is a permanent cure for the disease, and if the disease is common in the location where you lived after leaving the service, or where you were stationed.

38 CFR §3.309(b) identifies the following presumptive diseases as tropical:

Amebiasis
Blackwater fever
Cholera
Dracontiasis
Dysentery
Filariasis
Leishmaniasis including Kala-azar
Loiasis
Malaria
Onchocerciasis
Oroya fever
Pinta
Plague
Schistosomiasis
Yaws
Yellow fever

Service connection will also be established for secondary medical problems originating from the original disease or for medical problems originating from the required therapy.

CHRONICITY

The VA recognizes forty diseases as chronic disorders for which service connection is granted. To determine if your medical problem is considered by the VA as a chronic disorder, consult 38 CFR §3.309(a) and Part 4.

If you were diagnosed and treated for a chronic condition on active duty or within the one-year presumptive period after leaving the service, a claim should have been filed. In order to establish service connection for a chronic disease, there must be sufficient evidence to identify the disease along with ample observation to establish chronicity. The evidence has to establish that the diagnosis was not a mere isolated finding or a diagnosis that includes the word "chronic." Having met this test, later occurrences of this condition—no matter how remote—will be considered service connected. Let's say you had a condition that was in remission when you left the service and remained that way for another ten years. You could establish service connection on the basis of chronicity without having to prove continuity of symptomatology.

However, there is an exception to the rule: If the VA can show that the current symptoms and diagnosis are attributable to intercurrent causes, then service connection will be denied. According to 38 CFR §3.303(b), "The rule does not mean that any manifestation of joint pain, any abnormality of heart action or heart sounds, any urinary findings or any cough, in service will permit service connection of arthritis, disease of the heart, nephritis, or pulmonary disease, first shown as a clear-cut entity, at some later date."

CONTINUITY OF SYMPTOMATOLOGY

A claim for service connection becomes extremely difficult to establish under the rule of continuity of symptomatology when you have been separated from the service for many years. Department of Veterans Affairs regulations state that continuity of symptomatology is required only when the condition noted during service— or during the one-year presumptive period following separation— is not, in fact, shown to be chronic, or when the diagnosis of chronicity may be legitimately questioned.

To prove continuity of symptomatology, a record of continuous medical treatment must be introduced into evidence showing that you were under continuous treatment for the disability you are claiming. The example I like to use when helping clients visualize the immense undertaking at hand involves the completion of a bridge spanning a very wide river. On one side of the river you have a completed onramp that represents your active duty medical records. On the other side of the river is the completed exit ramp that represents the current treatment record of your injury. Your job is to figure how to span the river and connect your portion of the bridge to both sides. Without the proper material and engineering plans, you cannot complete the bridge. Without sufficient medical evidence to support continuity of symptomatology, your claim will be denied.

You must accept the realization that medical evidence necessary to prove your claim may no longer be accessible or obtainable. The most common reasons for the inability to retrieve old medical records are

- Not being able to remember the doctor's name;
- Forgetting where and when they were treated for the problem;
- The doctor treating the veteran died;
- The doctor destroyed the old medical treatment records because the veteran was no longer a patient;
- The doctor sold his practice and destroyed his records;
- The doctor retired and no longer has your records.

As a claimant you must understand that when the fact of chronicity in service is not adequately supported, you must prove continuity after separation before a claim is successfully prosecuted.

COMBAT-RELATED INJURIES AND DISEASES

Official records or documents are not required to support your claim if you are a combat veteran and you file a claim for injuries or disease that was incurred or aggravated while engaged in wartime operations against hostile forces. The VA is required to accept satisfactory lay or other evidence as the basis for the claim, as long as the evidence is consistent with the circumstances, conditions, or hardships of such service.

This rule does not mean that you had to have direct physical contact with enemy forces before a claim is justified. Other actions that qualify include being assigned to a combat unit conducting tactical operations during a declared wartime or during undeclared wartime engagements such as campaigns or expeditions supporting the U.S. or the United Nations for diplomatic purposes. Operations such as those in Granada, the Persian Gulf, or Panama or temporary assignment to United Nation Forces, as in Bosnia, qualify under this rule.

Your sworn statement of the events surrounding the injury or illness is in most cases sufficient for establishing a well-grounded claim. Sworn statements from members of your unit are also acceptable evidence in establishing the basis of a well-grounded claim when there are no medical records to support your claim. This is an extremely important rule for veterans who served in a combat zone. Furnishing proof of being awarded the Purple Heart or Combat Infantry Badge can establish your presence in a combat zone. Obtaining a copy of the official unit history for the period when you were wounded or when you became ill is considered proof your claim is combat-related. Proof of being awarded various medals associated with combat operations such as the Bronze Star with "V" Device, Silver Star, Distinguish Flying Cross, and the Air Medal are excellent proofs of your presence in a combat zone.

In a very special case, *Collette v. Brown*, 95-7043 (1996), the United States Court of Federal Appeals for the Federal Circuit reversed the Court of Appeals for Veterans Claims on the issue of what a veteran must prove if they allege combat injuries are the basis of the claim. The Appeals Court held that the VA must accept the veteran's lay evidence (a statement that the injury or disease occurred in combat), unless it has proof to the contrary. The only element the veteran has to show is that he or she was engaged in combat with the enemy. The decision is absolutely binding on all VA regional offices.

Chapter Four Highlights

Now that you know you are the only one who can put together a winning claim you are ready to do battle with the VA claims bureaucracy. Not winning is not an option. Not only will you be able to play by their rules, but you will be able to beat them using their rules.

It is your job to file a claim that meets the legal and medical elements of the "Big Three." Before you forward your claim to the VA, review it carefully to be certain it addresses each of the Big Three elements.[1] They are:

Element Number 1. The claimant must be able to demonstrate a medical condition *currently exists*.

Element Number 2. The claimant must show that the condition was *incurred during service*.

Element Number 3. The claimant must be able to show a *causal relationship* between his in-service incurrence and the condition that he is presently claiming.

5 | THE BIG THREE

This perhaps is one of the most important chapters in this revised edition of *The Veteran's Survival Guide: How to File and Collect on VA Claims*. With the passage of the Veterans Claims Assistance Act of 2000, the VA is responsible for obtaining records from its own archives as well as other federal depositories before it can decide the merits of a claim.[1] This action by the VA satisfies requirement for elements two and three. In theory the veteran would be responsible for developing evidence for element one—proof of current illness or disabling condition.

The question is, will the VA get all the pertinent evidence before making a decision? The law states they will search the archives for records you point out are relevant to your claim. In chapter 2, 38 CFR §3.159 details what they will do and for how long. A few points to keep in mind:

a. If the records are not received, make at least one follow-up request to the source or an additional request to the original source. Failure after the second bite of the apple will end with a Dear John letter. What they are implying is that if the requested evidence is not forthcoming after two tries they have satisfied the intent of the statute.

b. Obtaining records in compensation claims. In a claim for disability compensation, VA will make efforts to obtain the claimant's service medical records if they are relevant to the claim. Other records pertaining to the claimant's active military, naval, or air service that are held or maintained by a governmental entity; VA medical records or records of examination or treatment at non-VA facilities authorized by VA; and any other relevant records held by any federal department or agency will be requested.

c. "If relevant to the claim" is a scary disclaimer that opens the door to all kinds of interpretation for a claim's examiners. The claimant states he thinks his medical records might have information concerning his back injury. The regulation states the claimant must provide dates, places, and circumstances to trigger the VA's duty to assist. A claim based on no more information then "I think they might have" could be interpreted to be a claim without merit, thus quickly denied.

A Dear John letter is dispatched at the speed of light. You are advised the claim was denied because no relevant evidence was received to trigger the VA's duty to assist. Your right to appeal the decision was explained along with a notice that you have one year from the date of the letter to file a Notice of Disagreement. For the VA regional office processing the claim this is a win. By denying the claim, they can be credited with closing another backlogged claim. The odds are good they made this claim go away forever because only a handful of denied claims ever end up on appeal.

Being realistic, if you have five teams processing claims at each RO, and a projected caseload input of 800,000 new claims in 2005, your claim would receive no more than one hour total processing time. That one hour would mean total combined time spent by each team group. If you further divide the hour by four team functions, then the claim would spend fifteen minutes at each stage of the process.

The pressure in ROs to meet daily goals is compounded by mandatory reporting to VBA in Washington every Monday of the number of claims cleared during the past week. Five will get you ten that the RO administrator is in the hot seat if his teams fail to meet VBA's goals. Failure is most likely rewarded with a performance review that would stop upward mobility. The trickle-down effect can reach all the way from the top to lowest clerk in Adjudication.

This does not have to be your fate when attempting to claim compensation benefits. You need to be your own team. You build your claim on these three elements of evidence:

1. In-service incurrence
2. Current illness
3. A causal relationship between the first two

Techniques in developing each of these elements are demonstrated by example in subsequent chapters. Chapter ten details how to go about getting military health records and helps you find supporting evidence relevant to your military duties that are the cause of your disability. Chapter ten will cover how to get records from government archives using the Freedom of Information Act. These are examples that help you focus on what you want, say, and do.

The whole purpose of this chapter and all succeeding ones is to put you in control. Put these three elements in the right context and you have a winning claim.

In-Service Incurrence

Many claims are denied because they are submitted without proof of a medical condition or of 10 percent disabling at the time of submission. Often a veteran will call the 1-800 hotline number inquiring about filing a claim for a condition he alleges occurred in the service. The VA service representative after listening to the veteran tells the veteran, "I will send you the forms you need to complete and return."

In this situation, the veteran is not aware of the responsibilities to provide proof of current medical disability, in-service incurrence, and a causal relationship between them before he mails them back to the VA. His thinking is, the "VA has my records, or they can get them; that is all the proof I need." 38 CFR §3.159(d) provides that if a claim is inherently incredible or clearly lacks merit the VA has no duty to assist in the development of the claim or if the VA determines service medical records are not relevant to the claim a denial of benefits letter will be dispatched.

STEP ONE—KNOW WHAT THE VA KNOWS

You are certain that your recently diagnosed PTSD is related to the fifteen months you spent in Iraq. File a notice of intent known as an Informal Claim announcing that you will be submitting an application and evidence for a service-related disability within the one-year period. Here is an example of the notice that should be sent to the VA.

There is one last step to take when dispatching this notice to the VA. Take it to your congressional representative or senator and request they forward it to the VA on your behalf.[2]

It is almost impossible to have a claim granted if you do not have access to the same records the VA will use to adjudicate the claim. Other records that are equally as important and that the VA might not request, such as unit history, after-action reports, and causalties reports, could establish a combat-related medical problem. Here are a couple of examples where obtaining this kind of evidence would put your claim in the category of "more likely than not" having affected your health, thus establishing a service connection:

---

100 West South Street
Barksdale, Florida 33771
813-555-1212

August 1,2005

St. Petersburg Regional Office

9500 Bay Pines BLVD

St. Petersburg, FL 33708

Please accept this letter as my intent to file an informal claim for PTSD under 38 CFR§ 3.155, <u>Informal claims.</u> Upon receipt of all evidence a formal application will be made.

John D. Rockefeller

SSN # 000-00-0000

C# 00-000-000

a. You are a helicopter crew chief during the Tet Offensive of 1968. Your Huey was running around-the-clock operations taking reserve troops to the combat zone and evacuating the wounded. When the chopper returned there was unbelievable carnage that you had to clean before the next scheduled sortie. You removed body parts, and scrubbed blood off the floor and side of the interior cabin. The unforgettable sounds of the wounded as they are moved to a waiting ambulance are still heard in your dreams. You have been diagnosed with PTSD, but the VA will not recognize direct service connection because you do not have a combat MOS, have not been awarded the Combat Infantry Badge, and have not been wounded by the enemy in a firefight and subsequently awarded the Purple Heart.

b. A former Air Force specialist is suffering from the effects from respiratory cancer. This is what we know about the veteran: He served in the Air Force from 1969 to 1973 and was honorably discharged. The veteran never served a tour of duty in Vietnam. However, he was placed on temporary duty (TDY) on three occasions for a total of twelve weeks during his enlistment. As a photo intelligence interpreter he was assigned to DaNang AFB, Cam Ranh Bay AFB, and Nha Trang AFB to support three special military intelligence operations. This is everything we know about the veteran.

He filed this claim under the provisions of 38 CFR §3.311(b) and (c) as amended on June 9, 1994, for presumptive service connection for respiratory cancer.

In example (a) the veteran must prove he did in fact witness these traumatic events. There are a host of records available for him to a build case of reasonable doubt. His DD 214 will show he was in Vietnam during the Tet Offensive and that he was a helicopter crew chief. The National Archives and Records Administration (NARA) can provide information concerning his unit's activities during the Tet Offensive. Also available are the unit's operational records from 1954 to the present. The base hospital records can show a history of causalities treated at his base.

In example (b) the veteran must provide sufficient evidence to satisfy the provisions of two regulations. The first is Presumption of Service Connection, 38 CFR §3.307(a)(6)(ii)(iii) and (b), and the second is Diseases Associated with Exposure to Certain Herbicides, 38 CFR §3.309(e).[3] Evidence for his case must include copies of the orders that placed him TDY to Vietnam and an oncologist's medical assessment that he is currently being treated for lung cancer. Since this presumed health problem carries a thirty-year delimitating date, he must establish that the disease was first diagnosed prior to the thirty-year cutoff.

In example (b) the veteran can start building his case by contacting Unit Historical Records and obtain accounts of the three missions he supported in Vietnam.[4] His DD-214 will establish his intelligence AFSC and may even include the number of days he was TDY to Vietnam. The citation for the Bronze Star lends proof that he did in fact participate in three special operations against the North Vietnam regulars during the twelve weeks he was in Vietnam. Providing copies of the Personal Duty Status (PDS) reports for the period he was TDY will show just where he was during his time in Vietnam.

Sworn Statements
Once you have the documents it is time to prepare a sworn statement tying everything together, and have it notarized. [5]

Sworn Statement by Veteran
There is no set format or form in which to initiate a sworn statement. The sworn testimony is in narrative form and if at all possible, it should be typed so that there can be no misunderstanding what you are saying. The statement should be brief, and the language should be very carefully chosen. Present information based only on the facts of the issue under consideration that are pertinent to the claim. Again, I must caution you that lay statements concerning medical issues do not carry the same weight as reports

from medical personnel. Only competent medical personnel can make statements of a factual basis regarding a medical problem.

The following illustration is offered as a guide in organizing your declaration. The contents of your declaration will depend primarily upon the facts you are able to substantiate and enter into evidence. This format is very workable and when properly executed is a valuable document. The declaration is your assessment of the facts as you know them. You are setting the stage for the VA to address the issues you raised in the context of all the evidence submitted as part of the claim. If it denies the claim, the VA must state factually what evidence they used that was superior to yours.

DECLARATION OF JOHN PAUL JONES

Now comes John Paul Jones, being duly sworn, and states as follows:

1. My name is John Paul Jones. I reside at 1421 Riverside Drive, Chicago IL 60616.

2. I enlisted in the United States Navy on October 15, 1952, and served honorably until I was medically discharged on April 20, 1954, for Anxiety Reaction and chronic depression moderate. When separated I was given disability severance pay in the amount of $7,600.

3. Following my separation I returned to the Chicago area, where I was treated at VAMC Hines Mental Health Clinic for approximately three years. The treatment consisted of one-on-one therapy sessions with a psychiatrist. I have tried for several years to retrieve copies of my clinic file for the period of 1969 and 1970 to no avail. I've been promised several times by the hospital records department that the records would be obtained from storage, copied, and forwarded to me. To date this has not happened.

4. I received additional treatment from VAMC Hines Mental Health Clinic on an irregular basis for chronic anxiety with depression from 1982 through 1990.

5. Following my medical discharge in April 1954, I have been unable to develop a stable work history. With the exception of one job lasting three years, the longest I worked for any one employer was one year. In a majority of the cases the reason I was terminated was because I could not get along with other employees or deal with the public one-on-one without experiencing a response of sudden anger for the slightest provocation. I have not been able to work for the past five years.

6. I'm unable to concentrate at times to the degree that people start looking at me when I suddenly do not respond to them appropriately. I often have a deep feeling of guilt, and in many case I am unable to determine why it is that I feel guilty. I sleep very poorly and will wake up many times during the night. I often lie awake for hours with the feeling that something terrible is going to happen. I have lost more then forty pounds since leaving the service.

7. On September 1, 1996, I was granted Social Security Disability Benefits for anxiety and depression.

8. The attached medical records from the Social Security mental health examination show the psychiatrist did in fact associate the events that occurred in the service with current disability.

9. I declare under the penalty of perjury that the above statement is true and correct to the best of my knowledge.

Date

Signature of John Paul Jones

Notary Seal and Certification Here

Sworn Statement by Spouse

The spouse of a married veteran, his or her immediate family, or close friends can provide valuable support to a claim by use of a sworn statement. The same rules that apply to the veteran also apply to spouses, family, or friends in that they cannot say for example "I know that John P. Jones has a severe anxiety condition."

Court decisions back up regulations and manuals that a lay person is not qualified to give evidence pertaining to a medical condition. However, they can give evidence as to what they observed and the circumstances surrounding the veteran at the time the observation was made.

The following is a suggested format for a spouse, family member, or friend who will give a sworn statement. Again the same basic rules previously discussed apply to preparation of the declaration.

DECLARATION OF PATTY ANN JONES

Now comes Patty Ann Jones, being duly sworn, and states as follows:

1. My name is Patty Ann Jones. I am the wife of John Paul Jones. I reside with my husband at 1421 Riverside Drive, Chicago IL 60616.

2. I have known my husband since January 1971 and married him two years later on June 2, 1973. I have been with my husband every day since 1971 and have observed the effect of his disability on a daily basis.

3. During the past twenty-five years John has had fifteen jobs, which never last more then a year. He has not been employed for the past five years. Several of the jobs he quit. The only explanation he offered was he couldn't get along with the boss. But the majority of times, he was terminated because he was disruptive in the workplace and at odds with other employees. He has no close personal friends and will not go out and join in local social events.

4. John has been taking Xanax and Zoloft for several years for anxiety and depression and has been in and out of therapy at VAMC Hines Mental Heath Clinic for the past several years.

5. Although he has never been abusive to me physically or verbally he has flared into a rage when provoked by neighbors or strangers.

6. During the past five years he would often become very depressed and would sleep twelve to fifteen hours a day. Also during these periods he would say that he would be better off if he were dead. Once I could get him back to the mental health clinic they would readjust his medication and his condition would improve.

7. John is always expressing thoughts which reveal fear and hopelessness. He has not shown any interest in participating in hobbies or attending public events; he seems to withdraw from any contact with other people and invents all kinds of excuses why he must stay away.

8. John was granted Social Security Disability Benefits about a year ago. His ward letter stated that the benefits were granted on the basis of severe chronic anxiety and depression.

9. I declare under penalty of perjury that the above is correct to the best of my knowledge.

Date

Signature of Patty Ann Jones

Sworn Statement by Employer and Former Employer

A sworn statement from an employer or former employer can influence the rating process. Compensation benefits are supposed to be determined by the degree the disability reduces your capability to be gainfully employed. At times obtaining statements from some supervisors or employers may prove very difficult. One factor that complicates the process of obtaining a sworn statement from an employer or former employer is the fear of a lawsuit or physical harm. You should be willing to give your former employer a release against any lawsuits and in no way present yourself as a danger to him or her. In many cases a third party such as a spouse, family member, or friend will be able to negotiate on your behalf.

Example of a Sworn Statement by an Employer

The following illustration will provide some guidance in preparing a sworn declaration by a former employer.

DECLARATION OF HENRY R. SMITH

Now comes Henry R. Smith, being duly sworn, and states as follows:

1. My name is Henry R. Smith and I reside at 5151 Lake Front Circle, Apartment 1121, Chicago IL 60631.

2. I am the owner of Smith Tool and Die Company, located at 304 Orange Street, Complex D, Chicago IL 60611. My company subcontracts out to many manufacturers for special machine parts for their products.

3. I hired John Paul Jones on June 1, 1991, as a metal lathe operator at a starting salary of $15.00 per hour. Mr. Jones was terminated on May 10, 1992, because of an incident which nearly cost him his left hand. Approximately six months after I hired him his work performance began to change. He had several verbal arguments with other machinists who had worked for me many years. I counseled him on his workplace behavior. Mr. Jones's attitude with other workers improved but the quality of his performance was becoming poor.

4. Mr. Jones failed to properly install a clamping chuck for the item he was going to make on the lathe. As a result his sleeve became snagged by the piece of metal that was about to be turned. His left arm was jerked into the rotating piece of metal stock. Fortunately another worker saw the incident and immediately pushed the emergency shutdown button. This saved Mr. Jones's arm from being severed.

5. I subsequently learned that the VA mental health clinic put Mr. Jones on Xanax and Zoloft, which both warn that the patient should not operate machinery.

6. I had no option but to terminate Mr. Jones for his protection and the protection of my other employees.

7. I declare under the penalty of perjury that the above statement is true and correct to the best of my knowledge.

Date

Signature of Henry R Jones

Buddy Letters

Letters from former comrades, known as buddy letters, are a very valuable source of testimonial evidence in establishing a factual background to an injury or disease. This is especially true when the injury or disease was not recorded by a medical corpsman or entered into the claimant's medical file at the time of the incident. In the past, veterans were seriously handicapped by two obstacles when trying to introduce this form of testimonial evidence.

First was the acceptance of statements from former comrades as a factual account of the event claimed by the veteran. Very seldom in the past had the local VA regional office ever accepted the statements of other former service members as factual. The statements were treated as a lie or as unverifiable.

I worked the case of a former POW in which all the surviving members of a B-17 bomber attested that the veteran received injuries to his ears as a result of a high altitude bailout when the aircraft was destroyed by flak. The squadron was ordered to put up a max effort and given that there were no spare waist gunners the claimant had no choice but to fly the mission. The flight surgeon would not ground the veteran for a severe cold and blocked sinuses. The other members of the squadron all testified that a German doctor who was a POW treated the veteran for his ear condition. He was told that he had ruptured his eardrums. The crew's statements were not accepted as a plausible reason for his hearing loss because what service medical records were available were silent as to any hearing problems. The veteran was eventually granted service connection for his hearing loss upon appeal. However, it took five years for the appeal to work its way through the system, including one remand that had to be returned to the BVA for a final decision.

The local regional office had no evidence to contradict the sworn statements of the veteran or his crew other than their own unsubstantiated opinions. As previously stated, a rating board must specifically state what evidence they have that rebuts the sworn statements by the veteran or others. Again, rating boards must accept sworn statements as credible evidence and must give the evidence equal weight with all the other evidence of record.

The second obstacle is that locating former members of your military unit who had factual information concerning your injury or disease is almost an impossible task. However, beginning in the late 1980s and early 1990s locating people no longer remained an impossible task. Success still depends a great deal on how much you remember about the individual. Thanks to giant advances in storing and retrieving personnel data technology, the doors were swung wide open in ways to locate people.

Here are some suggestions to follow if you are trying to locate a former member of your unit who might be able to provide favorable evidence on your behalf. At your disposal now are nationwide phone directories; letters forwarded to the former buddies by several government agencies; computer online searches through bulletin boards; notices placed in many of the veteran service organization monthly magazines or publications; reunions, which are now held by many military organizations; personal ads placed in newspapers in the vicinity where the veteran may have resided after leaving the service. Within the last few years many small businesses have surfaced that will find a person for a very nominal cost.

CURRENT ILLNESS

I can't say this enough: If you're saying your medical problem is service connected, *do not file a claim if the condition is in remission* or *currently not disabling*. There are two analogies that express the seriousness of ignoring this warning. The first is "shooting yourself in the foot," which is what you would be doing; the second is "faster than a speeding bullet," which is how the VA would issue a denial of benefits. Here are some important reasons why you must know the claiming process:

- ◆ The VA has no obligation to assist unless the claimed condition is in fact a currently a medical problem.

◆ Before the VA schedules you for an evaluation, make arrangements to be evaluated by a non-VA specialist who will in fact write you a full consult statement after reviewing your service medical records and examining you.

◆ It is more likely than not that your VA evaluation will be conducted by a physician's assistant or nurse practitioner. VA medical centers have been able to meet shortages of medical staffing by hiring these assistants and practitioners in place of specialized doctors.

◆ Make certain the medical person who does your evaluation has in fact received your whole claim file and that it was reviewed prior to your evaluation. The statutes and regulation do require them to review the records prior to exam.

◆ When scheduled for the C&P exam take the non-VA physician's evaluations with you. Ask if the examiner has read the evaluation. If not, or if it is not in the file, let him read your doctor's finding. Later, when the report is written, if it disagrees with your evidence, he is supposed to justify in his medical statement how he reached this conclusion.

◆ Within two weeks you can obtain a copy of this report from the Freedom of Information Office just by asking. Compare the finding with the evaluation from the non-VA physician. If the findings agree with your doctor's report you're one step closer to being granted benefits. However, if the findings do not support your claim, take the VA report back to your physician and ask how the VA examiner reached this conclusion. Ask him to write a rebuttal letter for you.

◆ Before sending your rebuttal letter to the VA challenging the C&P evaluation determine the medical credentials of the VA examiner. If he or she is second-level medical personnel such as a physician's assistant or nurse practitioner, or if the physician is not a specialist in the field, immediately send a notice that the exam was flawed and prejudiced. Your letter should read generally as follows:

100 West South Street
Barksdale, FL 33771
813-555-1212

August 1, 2005

St. Petersburg Regional Office
9500 Bay Pines BLVD
St. Petersburg, FL 33708

Please accept Dr. Smith's rebuttal letter for the reasons stated that the C&P exam of July 10, 2005, was flawed and biased. The VA examiner was a nurse practitioner and not an orthopedic specialist. I request an outside medical review if you fail to accept Dr. Smith's findings.

John D. Roche
SSN #000-00-0000
C# 00-000-000

Now the VA is on notice that you are challenging the report made by second-level medical staff. The rating board has to explain in their rating why this report by a medical technician is superior to a report by a specialist with qualifications that far exceed those of the VA examiner.

Once you have obtained all the medical evidence to send to the VA, the next step is to check to see what is the level of your disability. In the example above let's assume the injury is related to the lower back. Your doctor has diagnosed your injury as unfavorable ankylosis of the entire spine. Have him state in his letter that it is his judgment your condition is best described under rating code 5235.

Causal Relationship

What the VA is looking for is a nexus or a link associating the before and after of the facts pertaining to the injury. Your job is to show this relationship.

Our airman was in an auto accident while on active duty. At the time of the accident, he was on leave visiting his parents Minneola, New York. Airman Smith was returning home after a night out with his friends. It was 1:30 AM when a car driven by a person under the influence of alcohol ran a stoplight and broadsided him. He was taken to Nassau County hospital by ambulance, where he was treated for several broken ribs and a lower back injury. The Air Force was advised of the accident and changed his duty status to "patient hospitalized in non-military hospital." A Line of Duty Investigation was ordered by his commander. They obtained copies of the accident report and interviewed Airman Smith when he returned to duty. The final report issued by the investigating officer declares that the injuries sustained were in the line of duty. Since he could no longer work on the flight because of the injuries, he was assigned to the orderly room as a clerk. He served in this capacity until his discharge in 1999.

Here is a list of evidence necessary to support his claim:

- Copy of the Minneola police report detailing the accident.
- Copies of emergency room treatment records and inpatient hospital records along with X-Ray and MRI reports.
- Copies of all current medical records that support the residual effect of the original injury.
- Sworn statement from family and friends describing how he has functioned since returning home.
  Remember, family and friends are not to give comments of a medical opinion since they are not medically trained.

However, they can relate information such as how you can no longer walk without assistance or travel any distance in a car.

◆   Letter from physician stating that there is a direct association between the accident and current back disorder.

Chapter Five Highlights

Your whole claim is built around satisfying these three elements: 1. In-service incurrence, 2. Current illness, and 3. Causal relationship between them. To satisfy Element One you need to prove the injury or illness did in fact occur in the service. You need solid evidence that cannot be refuted or at least carry sufficient weight to tip the scales in your favor.

Element Two must establish you are currently disabled by the injury or illness. Without evidence supporting this element, the VA has no duty to assist. I have had veterans coming into the office saying they want to file the claim to get it on the record. In cases like this, the only thing that will get on the record is that your claim was denied. If the condition does not flare up within a year of the denial letter, the only way you will get the claim reopened is by providing new and material evidence. That may be a lot more difficult to deal with.

Element Three is the bridge element. In other words, on one side of the river is where the event occurred and on the other side is your current illness or disability. You need evidence that will build the span across the river. You need to make the connection obvious or the claim could be denied. If you are claiming an illness take the time to research it on the Internet. You can find out all kinds of information that would support your claim.

What was covered in this chapter would never happen if you relied on the VA to perform all the steps for you. It does not have the workforce to perform and track individual claims to this degree of development. What we discussed cannot be done in just one hour, no matter how experienced the adjudication clerks and raters are.

6 | TOTAL DISABILITY DUE TO INDIVIDUAL UNEMPLOYABILITY

It was the intent of the people of this country to provide compensation to every veteran who suffered a service-related disability or disabilities, to offset the loss of earning capacity in a civilian occupation caused by the injury or disease. Within this concept is a special provision whereby a disabled veteran who is unemployable because of a condition that is not totally disabling can be compensated at a rate of 100 percent. The controlling regulations are 38 CFR §3.340(a)(2) and 38 CFR §4.16, in addition to the numerous Court of Appeals for Veterans Claims decisions clarifying the intent of the Congress to ensure the protection of disabled veterans' entitlement. This special benefit should be one of the easiest benefits for a veteran to establish.

Unfortunately, the opposite is the norm. Without doubt, it is one of the hardest to establish and one of the easiest for the VA to terminate. At the beginning of the 1980s, there were more than 100,000 veterans in receipt of Total Disability Due to Individual Unemployability (TDIU) benefits. A movement within the VA was begun to limit entitlement for this benefit. By the early 1990s, the number of veterans in receipt of TDIU was reduced to a little more than 60,000 veterans nationwide.

The reduction process was quite simple to initiate. First a series of reevaluation examinations was ordered for veterans in receipt of TDIU. Veterans were told the results of their examination showed that the disabilities improved sufficiently to enable them to return to the workplace. Next, the central office in Washington, D.C., required TDIU claims to be approved by it. Local regional office adjudicators were instructed by the central office to disregard some well-grounded claims for TDIU benefits.

This policy changing the way claims for TDIU were treated violated the provisions of 38 U.S.C. §7722 (Outreach Services) and 38 CFR §3.103(a) (Procedural Due Process and Appellate Rights). It was reported in the *Veterans Advocate*, volume 4, no. 3, November 1992, that 200 veterans in receipt of TDIU benefits were terminated in November 1992 while the central office approved only five veterans for the benefits.

TDIU Issues and the Court

When the United States Court of Appeals for Veterans Appeals (CAVA or Court) started hearing TDIU cases it found the adjudication process was out of line with the laws and regulations in place to decide TDIU issues. The *Veterans Advocate* reported that when the Court began deciding TDIU cases, all kinds of mistakes and improprieties were found. Some ROs had created secret rules or questionable directives that could possibly be illegal; basic rules were being misinterpreted by rating boards and authorization specialists; and expert medical and vocational opinions were treated as statements of speculation. Regional offices were not requesting expert vocational opinions prior to deciding the case and when professional opinions were provided by the claimant attesting to his or her inability to be gainfully employed, rating boards ignored the value of the evidence. This type of evidence was not given the same weight as symptoms noted in a C&P Examination. It was also obvious to advocates that adjudicators were refusing to discuss in detail how they arrived at the conclusion the claimant was employable.

With decisions of the Court defining the intent of the law in TDIU cases the regional offices continued to deny claims based on former standards. It seemed to many of us that regardless of what the court instructed adjudication personnel to do in deciding a TDIU claim, local ROs continued to do business as usual.

There is an excellent example in which two cases, separated

by nearly a year and reviewed by two different panels of judges, were in a sense deciding the same issue. The two cases, *Beaty v. James Brown*, 6 Vet. App. 532 (1994) and *James v. James Brown*, 7 Vet. App. 495 (1995), were declared as nearly identical by Chief Judge Nebeker when he wrote for the court in *James v. Brown*. He wrote "This case presents a situation nearly identical to that in *Beaty* in which all the evidence supports the veteran's claim for a TDIU rating. We hold that that the Board's (BVA) decision to the contrary does not have a plausible basis. Accordingly, the Board's decision is REVERSED and the matter REMANDED." The Court has been rendering numerous TDIU decisions since 1991.

The Most Common Reasons TDIU Claims Denied

For the thousands of veterans who were turned down for TDIU or had their TDIU benefits terminated, there may be grounds to reopen their claims under 38 CFR §3.105(a) (Revision of Decisions—Errors.) This action is commonly known as a CUE (Clear Unmistakable Error) and is one of the only two ways you can reopen a claim once a decision becomes final. The VA consistently justified denial of or terminated TDIU claims for these reasons:

- Benefits were being denied for TDIU when the veteran had non-service-related medical problems in addition to service-connected disabilities. The VA would not make a determination based solely on the service-connected medical conditions. It would contend that the non-service-connected medical problem was a major factor in causing the veteran to be unemployable. Therefore, any veteran who was denied benefits on these grounds should reopen his claim and argue that a determination can only be made on the service-related disabilities. Non-service-connected disabilities are irrelevant in determining TDIU.
- Many claims were denied by the VA because a veteran dropped out of the workforce because of a non-service-

connected condition or because of his or her age. Again, these issues are totally irrelevant. The VA can evaluate only the effects of the service-connected condition as it relates to employability. Do your records show the service-connected medical problem can stand alone as a cause of individual unemployability? If so, then you need to reopen your claim and argue that the only relevant issue is your service-connected condition.

♦ Local rating boards would routinely rebut unemployability assessments by the veteran's own professional vocational evaluators with their own unsubstantiated opinions. One of the very earliest cases before the Court was *Colvin v. Derwinski*, 1 Vet. App. 177 (1991), in which the VA was told that when all the evidence in the record is in favor of the veteran's claim it cannot deny the claim based on its own opinion. It must have positive evidence to disapprove the claim. If your claim was denied on this basis reopen your claim citing *Colvin v. Derwinski* and 38 CFR §3.105(a)

♦ Another error made by the VA in TDIU issues has to do with just plain ignoring original requests for this benefit. If you ever served notice on the VA, formally or informally, that you were unable to be gainfully employed because of your service-connected condition and the VA did not rate your request then, the claim is still pending.

♦ A formal application would be the submission of a completed VA Form 21-8940 (Veterans Application for Increased Compensation Based on Unemployability). An informal claim would be any form of written notice to the VA that you were unable to work because of your service-connected condition. When the VA receives an informal request for benefits it is required to send you the proper form with which to apply for that benefit. Failure to do so is a major error. Again, there may be grounds to reopen your claim for TDIU benefits based on a Clear and Unmistakable Error if you were denied under the circumstances discussed above.

- Grounds to reopen a denied claim based on a Clear and Unmistakable Error exist if the VA did not comply with 38 CFR §4.16(b). (See subsection "Basic Eligibility for TDIU Benefits" below for details of this provision of the law.) If your records show you are in receipt of Social Security Disability Benefits for the same service-connected disabilities and there is a medical profile by your doctor stating that you are not capable of working because of your service-connected condition, the VA is going to have difficulty defending the denial of the claim. If the evidence will also show you have been evaluated by a rehabilitation vocational counselor and determined not to be a candidate for cross-training into another field because of your disability, and that you provided the VA with a history of your education and work experiences, you should file a claim to reopen your claim.

- Another group of veterans, those disabled by psychiatric disorders that were rated less than 100 percent and unable to be gainfully employed, were consistently denied a 100 percent rating due to unemployability. Psychiatric disorders as identified in 38 CFR §4.125 are psychotic disorders, psychoneurotic disorders, organic mental disorders, and post-traumatic stress disorder. The schedular rating for each of these categories is found in 38 CFR §4.132.

Further, 38 CFR §4.416(c) specifically addresses the issue of granting 100 percent rating to veterans rated 70 percent disabled when the only disability is for a psychological condition and the veteran is unemployable. The Court has issued numerous precedent-setting decisions addressing the issues of veterans who are unemployable due to a psychological disability. The VA has held in many cases before the Court that veterans with only a service-connected disability for a mental condition are not entitled to TDIU. The Court has told the VA it is wrong, and that its logic contradicts the intent of Congress and the law as written.

If you are a veteran with psychiatric disabilities and were denied benefits for TDIU, you may have very strong grounds to re-open your claim under the provisions of 38 CFR §3.105(a) and 38 CFR §4.16(b) or (c), including decisions by the Court in *Murincsak v. Derwinski*, 2 Vet. App 363 (1992) and *Gleicher v. Derwinski*, 2 Vet. App. 26 (1991).

Basic Eligibility for TDIU Benefits

The governing regulations for TDIU benefits are 38 CFR §3.340(a)(2) and §4.16(a), (b), and (c). A total disability rating is based on the premise that there is impairment of mind or body which is sufficient to render it impossible for the average person to follow a substantially gainful occupation. 38 CFR §3.340(a)(2) establishes entitlement to a total disability rating when the schedular rating for the condition or conditions is less than 100 percent disabling.

38 CFR §4.16(a) details the eligibility requirements necessary to receive TDIU benefits when the current rating is less than 100 percent disabling. Subparagraph (a) establishes where the schedular rating is less than total (100 percent), but in the judgment of the rating-board member the veteran is unable to follow a substantially gainful occupation, a total disability rating may be assigned. However, to qualify under subparagraph (a) if you have one disability, it must be rated at least 60 percent disabling. If you have two or more disabilities one disability must be rated at least 40 percent and the other disabilities' ratings will be sufficient to establish a combined rating of 70 percent

Adjudicators were told that marginal employment shall be considered substantially gainful employment, thereby providing a basis for denial. VA policy defines marginal income as annual earned income that does not exceed the poverty threshold for one person.

Subparagraph (b) addresses the needs of a veteran for whom one disability is rated less than 60 percent or for whom the combined disability rating for two or more disabilities is less than 70 percent. It was established to ensure that a veteran unable to qualify for benefits under 38 CFR §3.340(a)(2) or 38 CFR §4.16(a) would be considered entitled to Total Disability Benefits if unable to be gainfully employed because of a service-connected disability.

The regulation reads in part,

> It is the established policy of the Department of Veterans Affairs that all veterans who are unable to secure and follow a substantially gainful occupation by reason of service-connected disabilities **shall be rated to be totally disabled**. [emphasis added] Therefore, **rating boards should submit** [emphasis added] to the Director, Compensation and Pension Service, for extra-scheduler consideration on all cases of veterans who are unemployable by reason of service connected disabilities, but who fail to meet the percentage standards set forth in paragraph (a) of the section.

The reduction in the number of veterans already approved or being approved for TDIU benefits stems from several factors. First, 38 CFR §4.16(a) grants rating boards considerable leeway in deciding whether the claimant is capable of obtaining and maintaining gainful employment. This is because the rating board is allowed to exercise personal judgment in deciding the facts of the case. Allied to this factor of personal judgment, rating-board members are not specially trained to equate the medical limitations of the claimant's disability to the ability to be gainfully employed. The Court has rendered many decisions addressing the issue of TDIU. In one such case before the Court, *Gleicher v. Derwinski*, 2 Vet. App. 26 (1991), the court held the VA improperly denied a

TDIU claim because it based its denial of benefits on its own un-substantiated vocational opinion. If TDIU benefits were denied when the record provided sufficient evidence you were not capable of being gainfully employed and the VA had no evidence to refute your claim other than their personal judgment, you should reopen your claim.

Another reason many veterans experience so much difficulty in being approved for TDIU benefits under 38 CFR §4.16(b) is that local regional offices seldom follow the intent of 38 CFR §4.16(b). The veteran is notified that because the standards set forth in 38 CFR §4.16(a) are not met the claim is denied. The denial letter cites the percent of disability required to be eligible for TDIU benefits. The veteran is not told TDIU benefits are possible if the service-connected condition, regardless of its rating, is responsible for his or her inability to be gainfully employed. If you were de-nied TDIU benefits on the basis that you did not meet the provi-sions of 38 CFR §4.16(a) but you are unemployable due to a psy-chological disability rated less than 70 percent, file a claim to re-open your case based on a clear and unmistakable error (38 CFR §3.105(a)). The basis of the reopened claim would be that the re-gional office of original jurisdiction failed to comply with the pro-visions of 38 CFR §4.16(b), and forward your claim on to the cen-tral office in Washington DC.

Very few veterans and service officers for various organiza-tions know what the regulations mandate. For example when initi-ating a claim, most claimants do not provide the type of evidence that establishes that the service-connected condition is responsible for causing the inability to be gainfully employed. Veterans and many advocates do not know that VA doctors performing a C&P examination are to state in their evaluation whether the service-connected condition is responsible for the individual being unem-ployable. The rating boards know this statement is to be part of the evaluation report. However, its absence is ignored and so are the provisions of 38 CFR §4.2 (Interpretation of Examination Reports) directing a rating board to return the examination to the medical center as inadequate for evaluation purposes.

Subparagraph (c) is a special provision of the law to assist veterans with psychological problems who are rated 70 percent disabled and unable to be gainfully employed. Again the law is quite liberal in its intent, but the actual implementation of the policy by many local regional offices is quite the opposite. Before the Court of Veterans Appeals was created by Congress it was almost impossible for a veteran to be granted TDIU benefits when the schedular rating for a psychological problem was 70 percent. It is still very difficult for a veteran to be rated totally disabled under this provision of the regulations by local regional office rating boards. The only saving grace is that now the Board of Veterans Appeals (BVA) is examining each case under guidelines provided by the many Court decisions. The veteran unfortunately must wait several years to be granted TDIU benefits because of being forced to appeal the initial denial of TDIU benefits.

One of the earliest cases decided by the Court, *Gleicher v. Derwinski*, 2 Vet. App. 26 (1991), addressed what the VA was required to do when a veteran with a scheduler rating of 70 percent was unemployable solely because of his psychological problem. The VA was contending that veterans with only a service-connected psychological disability were not entitled to TDIU benefits.

Writing for the Court, Judge Holdaway held that "a veteran with a 70 percent disability rating is entitled to an 'extra scheduler' total disability rating if he is unable to secure or follow a substantially gainful occupation as a result of the disability." The Court further stated that in this case "the BVA failed to consider the 1988 VA psychiatric examination report and the 1988 VA social and industrial survey, both of which concluded that the appellant was incapable of securing or maintaining employment." There was no evidence of record to the contrary to rebut the appellant claim. This is a prime example of VA rating-board members using their own judgment, totally ignoring the law and positive medical evidence, and issuing a decision contrary to the regulation based solely on their own personal judgment.

Proving a Claim for TDIU Benefits

Always remember that the claimant has the burden to prove his claim. In one of the very earliest cases decided before the Court, *Colvin v. Derwinski*, 1 Vet. App. 171 (1991) the Court spelled out the ABCs of the VA's duty toward the claimant.

They said it was the VA's duty to: 1) obtain the evidence, 2) consider the evidence, 3) evaluate the claim, and 4) if the claim is denied, to explain how it arrived at that decision in light of expert medical and vocational opinions from professional witnesses. The VA must tell you exactly how they justified the denial of benefits based on their own unsubstantiated opinion. Local regional offices continue to this day to deny claims contrary to the finding of this case and others just like it. For this reason alone *you have to depend only on yourself to put together a winning claim*. Don't make the mistake of thinking the VA will do all the digging and searching for evidence that will grant you the benefits claimed.

Proving the merits of your claim is not a difficult task if you understand exactly what kind of evidence is needed to get the job done and what the rules are that the VA are to follow. As previously stated, this should be one of the easiest ways to be rated 100 percent disabled. TDIU claims need proof your service-connected disability alone is responsible for your inability to be gainfully employed. There are five sources of evidence you can go to in order to prepare a well-documented TDIU claim. Taking the time to put together a well-documented claim will enhance your chances of having your claim approved at the local regional office without being forced into the appeal process. You need to provide expert medical proof, vocational proof, a sworn statement by you, and sworn statements from a former employer or prospective employers who rejected your application for employment because of your service-connected disability. If you are collecting Supplemental Social Security benefits because you are unemployable send a copy of your Social Security award letter which confirms SSI benefits based on your service-connected medical problems.

MEDICAL EVIDENCE

The first requirement is to obtain an expert medical assessment from your own physician. The doctor must explain in writing exactly how your service-connected disability affects your ability to be gainfully employed. Should you have more than one disability of which one is not service connected, explain to doctor that the report must address only your service-connected condition. However, if your doctor could make a statement to the effect that your non-service-connected conditions would not or could not be the cause of your unemployability, by all means have him or her do so. Do not let the doctor lump all your disabilities together and give a generalized report, because if the report allows the slightest doubt that your service-connected condition is not responsible for your unemployability the VA will jump on this point and deny the claim.

If you are being treated solely by a VA medical service for your service-connected condition it is doubtful if the VA physician will write the kind of letter you need. They will tell you verbally that because of your service-connected condition you can't work but they are very, very reluctant to put it in writing. When working with VA doctors on behalf of clients I was never successful in obtaining the type of letter necessary to prove unemployability.

One last thought on medical evidence: You cannot afford not to have an assessment by a specialist in the field that is related to your disability. When you see the specialist state up front that you want an evaluation concerning your service-connected condition and its effects on your ability to be gainfully employed. The doctor must understand that this report must be in writing. If the doctor resists providing a written report do not invest further money or time. Say thank you, but I'll find someone who will meet my needs.

Remember you have a lot riding on this claim, $2,528 per month for life. The cost of a first-rate medical work-up should not be a reason to reject need for the examination.

VOCATIONAL EVIDENCE

The second most important step in supporting your claim is an evaluation by a professional vocational counselor. Developing an unimpeachable source of evidence requires the claimant to be dogged in the search for a professional vocational counselor. The credentials of a counselor are critical to your case.

A professional vocational counselor's educational background will range from a bachelor's degree to a doctoral degree (Ph.D.) in vocational counseling. If you have a choice, select an individual with a Ph.D. in vocational counseling. Remember, you want to impeach any negative conclusions drawn by a rating-board member who has had no special training to qualify as a vocational expert. If you are forced to go the appeal route, the higher the credentials of your vocational counselor, the greater your chances are of having the decision reversed on appeal.

If you have no idea where to start in your search for a vocational specialist, start with the closest legal service that helps indigent individuals in civil cases. Call the local bar association where you live and ask for the telephone number of the legal service that provides help to those with little or no income in civil cases. These services do a great deal of litigating on behalf of clients being denied Social Security disability benefits. They most probably will be able to put you in touch with a vocational specialist who is experienced in dealing with the government. The plus for hiring specialists with this kind of experience is they know how to prepare written evaluations that have all the right buzz words and they understand the bureaucratic obstacles you are trying to jump over.

Once you have located a specialist, your next job is to explain what you need in order to qualify for TDIU benefits. You must provide the following tools for the specialist to work with:

- Copy of your complete VA claim file
- Copies of Social Security Disability (SSD) decisions and the evidence used to grant SSD benefits
- Copies of all medical evidence from private physicians
- Copies of any sworn statements from former employers that terminated your employment because of your disability
- Copy of any special educational training you may have completed
- Copies of high school, college, or technical school transcripts
- Copies of the pertinent parts of chapters three and four of VA regulations that apply to your disability

It's important that the vocational specialist understand the VA's definition of "marginally employed" as opposed to "substantially gainfully employed." This meaning is spelled out in 38 CFR §4.16(a). It is also necessary that the vocational specialist be aware of how age and non-service-connected disabilities are irrelevant in the decision-making process. The only issue that the vocational specialist must address is a professional opinion that your service-connected disabilities alone would prevent you from being gainfully employed.

CLAIMANT'S SWORN STATEMENT

Preparing a sworn statement is not as complicated a task as it might sound. The statement should identify the individual by name, VA claim number or Social Security number, and current address and should carry a statement to the effect that the information provided is true and correct to the best of your knowledge. It should be signed before a notary public. This will ensure that your statement (evidence) complies with 38 CFR §3.200(b).

The format of the letter should be a series of direct statements of fact such as:

1. I live at 782 Lincoln Road, Boonville, Texas 11111.

2. I have not worked since January 5, 1996.

3. I am service connected for heart disease and rated 60 percent.

4. When I worked for Cooper & Sons in the shipping department I would lift packages up to fifty pounds. When I could no longer lift packages without severe angina pain I was terminated. I had no other skills or education that might let me train for another job within the company.

5. I have tried to obtain other jobs but when it was learned that I suffered from heart disease with acute angina pains upon exertion my applications were rejected. I was awarded Social Security Disability benefits because of my heart disease in May 2005.

6. Each day I have to take six different medications for my heart condition.

7. I declare under the penalty of perjury that the above statement is true and correct to the best of my knowledge.

Date

Signature of Roger P Roberts

Notary's seal and certification

LAY STATEMENT IN SUPPORT OF CLAIM

A lay statement can be from anyone who can provide information as to how your service-connected disability affects your ability to work. A sworn statement is preferable for it is in compliance with 38 CFR §3.200(b). Lay evidence can be from your wife, other family members, close friends, former employers, or prospective employers who declined to hire you because of your service-connected disability.

The VA often refers to this type of statement as a buddy letter, but it is actually lay evidence. Until Congress gave every veteran a means (Court of Veterans Appeals) of challenging BVA decisions disputed by the veteran, lay evidence was seldom given any evidentiary weight. Rating boards cannot ignore this evidence or fail to give it its proper evidentiary weight. Two cases decided early on by the Court, *Colvin v. Derwinski,* 1 Vet. App. 171 (1991), and *Cartright v. Derwinski*, 2 Vet. App. 24 (1991), held that lay evidence in and of itself may warrant service connection.

Both 38 CFR §3.200(b) and §3.307(b) dictate how the VA will treat lay evidence in determining the granting of specific benefits sought. First 38 CFR §3.200(b) instructs that all written testimony submitted by the claimant or on his or her behalf for establishing a claim for service connection will be certified under oath or affirmation. In referring to the adjudication process of deciding a claim 38 CFR §3.307(b) states in part, "The factual basis may be established by medical evidence, competent lay evidence or both."

As previously mentioned, a lay statement made under oath should be simple and direct, stating only facts, not opinions or conjecture. The same basic format that was outlined for a veteran's statement can be adopted for use by anyone.

SOCIAL SECURITY DISABILITY EVIDENCE

A veteran who has been granted Social Security Disability benefits for the same service-connected condition for which he or she is trying to obtain TDIU benefits can thank the Court for giving them a major leg up. Early on, the Court addressed the issue of veterans in receipt of SSD benefits for the same reasons that they were granted service-connected benefits. The first four cases concerning the impact of SSD benefits by the Court, *Collier v. Derwinski*, 1 Vet. App. 413 (1991), *Murincsak v. Derwinski*, 363 (1992), *Brown v. Derwinski*, 2 Vet. App. 444 (1992), and *Shoemaker v. Derwinski*, 3 Vet. App 248 (1992), clearly defined what the VA must consider and do when a veteran is in receipt of SSD benefits for the same reason he or she is receiving compensation benefits. The VA continued to dismiss the importance of receipt of SSD benefits, by giving the evidence very little value. The Court discussed the impact of SSD benefits in these subsequent cases: *Masors v. Derwinski*, 2 Vet. App. 181 (1992), *Clarkson v. Brown*, 4 Vet. App. 565 (1993), *Beaty v. Brown*, 6 Vet. App. 538 (1994), and *James v. Brown*, 7 Vet. App. 495 (1995).

These are the basic ground rules the VA must consider when adjudicating a claim where the veteran is in receipt of SSD benefits for the same conditions that granted him or her compensation benefits:

♦   An SSD claim cannot be ignored to the extent its conclusions are not accepted; the reasons should be clearly stated.

♦   A determination by the Social Security Administration (SSA) that a claimant is entitled to disability benefits is relevant to a VA determination of the severity of claimant's disability. Further, the Court holds that disability ratings by SSA are not outdated for making a determination, since SSA continuously reviews eligibility for disability benefits.

♦   When the claimant is recognized as unemployable by SSA, the VA must consider entitlement under 38 CFR §4.16(b) even if the condition is rated less then those standards required by 38 CFR §4.16(a). In theory if you had a 10 percent disability and Social Security determined you were unemployable, the VA would have to grant the benefit or prove you were vocationally and medically capable of being employed.

♦   The VA must obtain and review the claimant's Social Security records when put on notice he or she is receiving SSD benefits.

♦   The VA cannot justify the denial of TDIU benefits because it feels that SSA disability determinations are based on a different set of standards. If the VA rejects the findings of an SSA disability determination, it must state in detail exactly what evidence it has that is superior to the finding of the claimant's SSA decision granting benefits and why the SSA determination is not relevant in your case.

The initiative of ROs to request SSA records and associated medical records when advised that the veteran is in receipt of SSD benefits based on his or her service-related injuries or disease is still a losing battle for most veterans. With all the cases decided by the Court on this issue and all the remands by the BVA, the ROs are still not doing their job.

If you were denied TDIU benefits in the past because the VA did not consider the records and decision of SSA, you should re-open your claim based on clear and unmistakable error under 38 CFR §3.105(a). If you were told that because your service-connected disabilities did not qualify for TDIU benefits under 38 CFR §4.16(a), you want to reopen your claim if in fact you were in receipt of SSA benefits for the same reasons you were granted service connection. If you told the VA you were in receipt of SSD benefits but the VA did not obtain these files, you have grounds to reopen your claim under 38 CFR §3.105(a).

Informal and Formal Application for TDIU Benefits

Unless you have a completely documented claim ready for filing, do not file an original application for TDIU benefits initially. *It's a major tactical error to go into the VA with a claim that is not well documented and supported by evidence that will win you benefits.* They cannot and will not put a claim together for you. If you blow it at this point, it's all over but the cussing. Your only recourse is to appeal this action.

Two to three years later your case will be reviewed by the BVA and the only issue on appeal will be, did the VA have a duty to assist you in developing your claim? If they affirm the decision of the RO, your last recourse is the U.S. Court of Appeals for Veterans Appeals. Let's assume that nearly five years have gone by and the Court reverses the BVA. Now we go all the way back to square one and determine if your service-connected condition will entitle you to TDUI benefits based on the evidence in the record at that the time it was denied.

AN INFORMAL CLAIM

The very first step in applying for TDIU benefits is to file an informal claim. This action will:

- ◆ Protect your entitlement date
- ◆ Give you one year from the date the VA furnishes the application form (VA form 21-8490) to submit your claim for consideration
- ◆ Enable you get a complete copy of your VA claim file
- ◆ Arrange for a medical and vocational assessment to document your claim that you are too disabled to work
- ◆ Obtain a sworn lay statement, including sworn testimony by you as to how your service-connected condition has prevented you from being gainfully employed
- ◆ Obtain copies of all your Social Security Disability records to support your claim that you are unemployable
- ◆ If you have not applied for SSD benefits, you will have time to do so and have your claim for SSA benefits decided

An informal claim is a written notification to the VA that you intend to file a claim for Total Disability Due to Individual Unemployability. The statement should be short and to the point, such as,

> Please accept this action as my informal notice to apply for Total Disability Benefits Due to Individual Unemployability. My service-connected heart condition has made it impossible for me to continue to be gainfully employed. A formal application will be submitted once I receive the formal application and once I have obtained the medical and vocational evidence necessary to grant TDIU.
>
> I also request that I be furnished a complete copy of my VA claim file at the earliest possible date so it will be available to my doctors and vocational counselors.

FORMAL APPLICATION FOR TDIU BENEFITS

To claim TDIU benefits you must initiate a claim action on VA form 21-8940 and submit it to the RO that serves the area where you live. Unless you have obtained all the evidence previously discussed, do not call the VA on their toll free number 1-800-827-1000 and request the official application form.

If the VA has not provided you with the application as they are required to do by law, send them a certified letter telling them this is your second request for a TDIU application. Attach a copy of the first request putting them on notice that you are applying for TDIU benefits. Doing business with the VA by telephone is a very bad idea because any transactions you conclude with them cannot be verified or proven. It is your word against theirs and I assure you, they are not going to give you the benefit of the doubt.

The application form is straightforward and is divided into Basic Identification of Claimant and four other specialized sections. Section I, items 1 through 6 identify the claimant; Section I, items 7 through 12, focus on disability and medical treatment; Section II, items 13 through 21, deal with employment history; Section III, items 22 through 25, seeks information concerning schooling and training; and Section IV is authorizations, certifications and signature releases.

BASIC IDENTIFICATION OF CLAIMANT

The first six items on the application are for identification only. They ask for both your Social Security number and VA claim number. It is most likely the VA assigned your Social Security number as VA claim number if your original claim for benefits dates back to the mid 1970s. Prior to the change a VA claim number was an eight-digit number in the format of C-00-000-000. If you do not know your C-number you can obtain it by calling the nearest local regional office. Their identification system can cross-check name, date of birth, military serial number, or Social Security number to find your C-number.

DISABILITY AND MEDICAL TREATMENT

Items 7 through 12 require a considerable amount of information to support the claim for TDIU benefits with very little space provided. The best way to complete the form under these circumstances is to enter into each box "See Attachment 1 for Details." When recording the information on attachment 1 for item 7, for example, write, "Item 7, Lower back injury; gunshot wound to left forearm and right calf; residual damage to liver due to infectious hepatitis." Items 9 and 10 should be combined when there is more than one doctor involved. For example, "Item 9 and 10, Dr. Robert Smith, 1000 South Turner Street, Winston, OH 55441, April 2, 1986, to date; Dr. Elizabeth D. Green, 2230 N. Main Street, Winston, OH 55442, July 30, 1990, to date; Dr. Harry G. Hart, 315 Harrison Blvd., Winston, OH 55446, September 3, 1993, to date." You would follow the same format for Items 11 and 12 if you had multiple hospitalizations relative to your service-connected disabilities. Make certain that on each page you attach you print your name, VA claim number, and Social Security number. You should also note the numbers of the individual pages, as well as the total number of pages. For example, "Page 1 of 3 pages," "Page 2 of 3 pages," and so on.

EMPLOYMENT STATEMENT

Items 13, 14, and 15 could be the same date or could reflect three entirely different dates, depending on the circumstances involved. For example if the claimant was doing physical work and his shoulder, arms, and right leg caused him extreme pain to the extent that he could no longer perform his assigned tasks, this would the be the date his disabilities affected his full-time employment. He may have stayed out of work on sick leave for a month, returned to work, but soon found he could no longer perform any of his duties. His employer terminated his employment effective the end of the following month because he was allowed to use up his vacation time.

Item 17 is your employment history for the past five years.

Normally this is a one- or two-line entry, since most employees tend to work for the same employer for at least seven years before changing jobs.

Items 18 through 21 have several items that need discussing. Item 18, "do you receive/expect to receive disability retirement benefits" would normally be checked "no." The VA wants a detailed explanation in item 25 as to why your disability forced you to leave your job. Item 25 is totally inadequate to give a detailed explanation as to the reasons you had to stop working. In Item 25 add "See Attachment 1 page 2 for explanation of reasons disability caused me to become unemployable." Item 20, "have you sought employment since becoming disabled" would normally be checked "no"; however, if in fact you were in receipt of federal worker's compensation benefits, 38 CFR §3.958 prohibits concurrent payments of VA compensation benefits and worker compensation benefits after September 13, 1960.

SCHOOLING AND OTHER TRAINING
Items 22 through 24 provide the VA with some insight into your potential for being employed in another occupational field. They are really going to be looking hard at any individual with a college education or other special training with the assumption that he or she should be able to find some kind of "gainful employment." Education does figure into the formula they use in determining basic eligibility. This is why it's essential that you retain the services of a well-qualified vocational specialist who will weigh all factors of your background before making a determination as to your employability.

I have seen the VA deny TDIU benefits based on the assumption that the claimant's college degree made him or her employable. This one fact overrode his doctor's finding that he or she was unable to be gainfully employed. Remember, these rating specialists do not have any special medical, legal, or vocational training.

What they do have is the authority to use their own judgment. Your claim has to be well supported by expert evidence or it's going to be years before you might see TDIU benefits.

AUTHORIZATION AND CERTIFICATION

The authorization section of VAF 21-8940 talks about granting permission for the VA to go out and solicit information from doctors, surgeons, hospitals, or dentists who have treated you. You are giving them permission to obtain *any background information* these sources may have on you. When you sign the application, you are automatically granting them the right to contact anyone to obtain information about you.

The certification portion of Section IV has you affirming that all statements made are true and correct to the best of your knowledge. Further, it states that you certify that your service-connected disabilities do not permit you to follow *any* substantially gainful occupation. The word "any" is highlighted, and I think the only reason for this is to intimidate the claimant. It reminds one of first days of the Reagan administration, when it kicked thousands of individuals off the Social Security Disability rolls because "everyone can do something." However, the administrative law judges reinstated benefits to these individuals as fast as the cases could be processed. They did not uphold the concept that everybody can do something and is therefore able to be substantially gainfully employed.

Chapter Six Highlights

If your service-connected disability has removed your ability to be gainfully employed there is a provision in the law whereby a veteran could be entitled to benefits paid at the rate of 100 percent. In 2006 a married veteran would be entitled to $2,528 per month.

It is not absolutely required that you be at least 70 percent disabled before becoming eligible for TDIU benefits. The key that opens the door is the service-connected injury or illness does in fact preclude you from becoming gainfully employed. In theory, your disability could be rated as low as ten percent and TDIU benefits could be authorized. It is almost certain the claim would be denied and require an appeal and two trips to the BVA before the benefit was granted.

The term "gainfully employed" does not mean you can be forced to consider any kind of employment based on the opinion of the rating-board member. The measurement of your abilities can be and should be determined by a professional vocational counselor along with a physician's medical evaluation stating what you can or cannot do. For example a veteran service-connected for heart disease cannot work in an environment that requires physical strength or is mentally stressful. His performance may be drastically affected by the medication he is required to take each day.

Remember, if you are receiving Social Security benefits for the same reason you are receiving VA benefits the VA cannot ignore this fact. If you tell the VA you are receiving SSD benefits it has to get the case file from the Social Security Administration.

The quickest and best way to pursue a TDIU claim is by filing an Informal Claim and doing the legwork yourself. Have your congressional representative submit your request for records from any federal agency that might have evidence that could help your claim.

7 | CLAIMS BASED ON SECONDARY DISABILITIES

Secondary disability claims are straightforward and, if properly documented, should sail right through the adjudication process. What could be simpler? If your service-connected condition is the proximate cause for another medical problem, that condition also becomes service-connected. Then why is this benefit one of the top five most difficult to establish?[1] One reason is directly related to local VARO rating-board members and the other reason relates to the claimants. First, let's look at the VA. Within this group are several factors that account for the reason rating boards turn down many claims based on adjunct disabilities. Rating-board members have difficulty in dealing with medical opinions. Medical opinions from fully qualified doctors or specialists are not treated as statements of factual medical evidence by many rating-board members. I used to mutter bad words each time a well-documented claim based on adjunct disabilities was denied. Rating-board members, who have vast discretionary powers to determine if the medical assessment by a specialist is a fact or opinion, do so purely by speculation. These individuals, with no specialized legal or medical training, most likely with only a high school diploma and maybe ten to fifteen years of VA service, are now sitting in this position of power. They reach deep into their pocket of "experience" and pull out a decision determining that the doctor doesn't know what he is talking about. Their "experience" tells them the claimant's doctor is offering a biased opinion.

A case in point is that of a veteran who was service-connected for Buerger's disease. The condition eventually leads to arteriosclerosis obliterans heart disease and congestive heart failure, and severe ischemic cardiomyopathy. The veteran filed a claim to establish the advanced medical conditions as secondary to Buerger's disease in November 1988, and after several trips to the BVA was finally granted 100 percent service connection for these conditions in *1995*. The first time the rating board denied the claim, the justification was based on the opinion of a part-time, retired general practitioner employed by the VA who disputed the findings of the appellant's non-VA cardiologist and the findings of another VA doctor.

The Statement of the Case rationalized that the relationship between Buerger's disease and the other heart problems was a new, unsupported medical concept with no foundation. The rating board was provided with medical excerpts from a medical textbook, *A Primer of Cardiology*, written by a professor of cardiology at Tulane University in 1947, detailing the concept that the board member considered to be new. This medical publication, like the medical assessment by the veteran's doctor, did not alter the board member's decision. The claim made several trips to the BVA, and each time, the case was remanded to the VARO to have a VA cardiologist examine the client. If you guessed that the same VA fee-basis doctor conducted the rescheduled C&P Examination, you're right. A notice was immediately served on the VARO indicating that the examination was flawed because it failed to follow the specific instruction of the remand order. By protesting, we got the appeal back on the waiting list to be returned to the BVA.

Finally the BVA took the decision away from the VARO and granted the benefits. The sad part is that the veteran lived only a little more than a year after the benefits were granted. How much better his life would have been if he had enjoyed seven years of benefits instead of seven years of aggravation.

The VA was using downsizing tactics including enticing senior rating-board members, authorizers, and section chiefs into early retirement. They were replaced with individuals with shallow experience. This movement to reorganize and reduce costs included eliminating the doctors assigned to each rating board. The organization of "new VA," as it is now known, led to the denial of thousands of claims because the frontline troops were inexperienced and untrained in medicine or law. The message being sent was "If you don't like our decision, appeal it."

The "new VA" was facing increased caseloads, to be handled by less experienced decision makers. The next step was to alter the structure of rating boards. Three-member boards no longer evaluated claims. One-member boards were the new working tools of the VA. The grade levels of claims specialist were GS-9 to GS-12. This new machine was whittling away the tremendous backlog of cases—but at the expense of the veteran.

Many veterans and service officers also added to the problem. Claims were filed with no factual evidence linking the service-connected condition to the alleged secondary medical problems. Of the many appeals lost, the most frequent reason was that the veteran did not prove his or her case. The veteran must submit a well-grounded claim. Perhaps thousands of individuals have conditions that could be service-connected, if they only knew how to prove their claim.

I'm probably going to say this several more times before the end of this book: The fact that the VA has a duty to assist if the claim is possible *does not mean you can rely on the VA to make your claim*. You must take the initiative; it is your responsibility to make sure you medically link your service-connected condition to the disabilities you are claiming as an adjunct condition.

Court Findings Related to Secondary Disability

Decisions of the United States Court of Appeals for Veterans Claims provide a list of dos and don'ts, so to speak, to be followed by both the VA and the veteran if a claim is to be satisfactorily adjudicated. Using these findings of the court and following the regulations greatly increase your chances of having benefits granted.

FOR THE VETERAN

◆   When an issue involves a determination based on medical etiology or medical diagnosis, competent medical evidence is required to fulfill a well-grounded claim. A belief by the claimant that his current condition is the result of his service-connected disability can and will be denied on the basis that the claim is not well-grounded if medical evidence is not the basis for the claim. (*Lathan v. Brown*, 4 Vet. App. 269 (1993).)

◆   The claimant must present a plausible claim, one which is meritorious on its own or capable of substantiation. (*Murphy v. Derwinski*, 1 Vet. App. 78 (1990).)

◆   The burden of submitting a well-grounded claim cannot be met merely by presenting lay testimony. A layperson cannot offer competent medical opinions. (*Grottveit v. Brown*, 5 Vet. App. 91 (1993).)

◆   A service-connected claim (including one for secondary service connection) must be accompanied by evidence that establishes that the claimant currently has the medical condition claimed. (*Lynch v. Brown*, 9 Vet. App. 456 (1996).)

FOR THE VA

◆   The VA cannot ignore a well-grounded claim by neglecting to address it or acknowledge it. (*Travelstead v. Derwinski*, 1 Vet. App. 344 (1991).)

◆   The VA cannot grant service connection when the claimant's service-connected condition aggravates, but is not the proximate cause of, a non-service-connected condition. (*Leopoldo v. Brown*, 4 Vet. App. 216 (1993).)

◆   The VA cannot make unsupported medical conclusions when justifying the denial of service connection. (*Leopoldo v. Brown*, 4 Vet. App. 216 (1993).)

- When the claimant presents a well-grounded claim, the VA has a duty to assist in developing the facts pertinent to the claim. (*Murphy v. Derwinski*, 1 Vet. App. 78 (1990).)
- The VA cannot ignore its own regulation about evidence of service connection; it is required to consider all the evidence of record, including medical records and all pertinent lay statements. (*Harder v. Brown*, 5 Vet. App. 183 (1993).)
- When a claim is denied, the rating board must state its reasons for doing so and, more important, point to a medical basis other than the board's own unsubstantiated opinion. (*Paller v. Principi*, 3 Vet. App. 535 (1992).)

Filing a Claim for Secondary Benefits

A claim for benefits resulting from medical disabilities secondary to a service-connected injury or disease should be filed on VA form 21-4138, Statement in Support of Claim. There is no set format or a form that asks specific questions. The claim is in narrative form and should be typed so that there can be no misunderstanding as to what you are saying. The claim should be brief and the language should be very carefully chosen, with arguments based only on the facts that can be supported by evidence that relates the medical condition to your service-connected disability.

The evidence should include an evaluation by a specialist who will state that the disability claimed is linked to your service-connected condition. The evidence should also include copies of all relevant inpatient and outpatient treatment records. The medical evidence must also show that you are currently suffering from this claimed condition and the degree to which it is disabling as measured against VA standards as outlined in 38 CFR Part 4.

Before filing your claim, obtain a complete copy of all pertinent medical and hospital records. Evidence in this category includes:

- Hospital admission medical examination and history report
- Operating report
- Discharge summary
- Nursing notes
- Lab test results
- X-ray, MRI, and CAT scan summaries
- Complete list of all medications administered

These records are essential when trying to establish service connection for a condition that is secondary to your service-connected disability.

While you are requesting non-VA hospital records, also request the VARO custodian of your VA claim file to provide a complete copy of the claim file. Your request for these records cannot be denied, nor can it be ignored by the VA. This is a right granted under the Freedom of Information Act. Most important, you want these records before you actually file a claim. Again, let me stress, *you want these records before you file your claim.* By reviewing your claim file, you can quickly determine if the VA has all your inpatient and outpatient military health records. If you were hospitalized on active duty, your hospital records will be filed under the treating hospital at the National Personnel Records Center (NPRC). To obtain a copy of these records you must make a separate request, one that is not part of a request for outpatient records.

The success of your claim depends on the type of claim you assemble. The effort you put into preparing the claim is directly proportional to what you get out of it. You have to know what you are talking about and what you can prove, or you lose.

Next, obtain a copy of the parts of the current 38 CFR Parts 3 and 4 that are applicable to your claim. All VAROs are supposed to maintain a complete historical library of laws, regulations, VA circulars, manuals, and General Counsel opinions. Visit the VARO, if possible, and obtain a copy of every legal citation that is pertinent to your case. If travel to the VARO is not practical, consider contacting one of the service organizations that maintain fulltime staff at every VARO, such as the American Legion, Veterans of Foreign Wars, Disabled American Veterans, or the State Service Office. Tell them what citations you are looking for and that you are preparing a claim based on medical problems secondary to your service-connected disability. Emphasize that you need to know *exactly* what laws, regulations, manuals, and so on, are currently in effect, and what they require in order to file a well-grounded claim. Do not accept a condensed verbal summary from the service officer over the phone. You need to read these published rules and regulations to properly prepare your claim.

The burden of submitting evidence sufficient to justify a belief by a fair and impartial individual that the claim is well grounded rests with you, the claimant. A claim for establishing medical conditions secondary to the original service-connected condition must meet this test. The bottom line is that without medical evidence, you have no claim.

A veteran's statement attesting to service connection is not sufficient to trigger the VA's duty to assist when the issue is a medical question of entitlement. Without a well-documented claim that has strong supporting medical evidence, you will not be in control. When your claim proves entitlement based on VA regulations and standards, the VARO must dispute your evidence with more than just its own unsubstantiated opinion. The burden then rests on the VARO to prove that you're not entitled.

Your primary objective is to ensure that benefits are granted at the local VARO level without having to appeal. But, if you do appeal, you will win. It is a sorry state of affairs when the lowest level of a government agency makes it necessary for the claimant to turn to a higher authority before benefits can be approved—a step that may take another three to five years before benefits are granted.

Example of a Claim Based on Secondary Disabilities

You now have a copy of your claim file, pertinent laws, regulations, and medical evidence to support your claim. You are ready to state your case in writing. The following sample is offered as a guide to organizing your arguments to establish service connection for a secondary medical condition.

> This is a claim to establish service connection for a right shoulder disorder secondary to my service-connected left forearm amputation. The Wichita, Kansas, regional office granted service connection for a combat injury on February 10, 1969. I was rated 70 percent disabled for a minor left forearm amputation under rating code 5123.
>
> On January 10, 1997, I slipped and fell on the ice in front of my home, which resulted in a right scapulohumeral joint injury. My right arm broke the fall because I instinctively protected the left amputated arm from additional injury. The fall caused a right (major) chronic Grade 2 rotary cuff tendonitis condition secondary to instability of the dominant right scapulohumeral joint. The attached medical evidence also provides clinical evidence of moderate to marked instability with three of three positive impingement signs.
>
> Dr. Raymond Scott, my non-VA orthopedic surgeon, notes in his medical evaluation dated March 3, 1997, that the injury has resulted in a greatly reduced range of motion of the right arm. He states that the range of motion is limited to the distance midway between my side and shoulder; movement beyond this point produces severe pain.
>
> Dr. Scott's evaluation points out that based on the VA evaluation standards in 38 CFR Part 4, the injury to the right shoulder would be considered at least 50 percent disability for the right shoulder. The evaluation specifically points out

that this type of disability is consistent with an injury where only one arm was available to break the fall. He further stated that if I had a complete left arm I would not have sustained this type of injury.

I was granted Social Security disability benefits effective June 1, 1997, based on the left forearm amputation and the limited use of the right arm. Please also consider this an informal application for total disability based on individual unemployability.

In support of my claim, the following evidence is attached and made part of this claim: copies of Dr. Raymond Scott's treatment records from January 12, 1997, to June 1, 1997; Dr. Scott's complete medical assessment, dated March 4, 1997; my sworn statement detailing the circumstances of my fall on the ice and my inability to be employed; a letter from my former employer, who terminated me because I could no longer perform my duties; and a sworn statement from my wife stating I have tried to find work but have been repeatedly disqualified because I have essentially lost the use of both arms.

Chapter Seven Highlights

Knowing that rating-board members may be limited in sorting out complex medical issues, the claimant must carefully build his evidence package at a lay level of understanding. Some of the many factors affecting rating board decisions are inexperience, very little time to assess and study a claim, no medical or legal training to provide a basic level of understanding, and failure to follow regulations and procedures when reviewing a claim.

Rating-board members are permitted a great deal of discretion when deciding the merits of a claim. If they don't understand your evidence and how it links to your service-connected condition, some rating members will deny the claim. Your only alternative should this happen is to file a Notice of Disagreement. If you read the remand decisions of the BVA, you will quickly lose confidence in local VARO rating-board members. Case after case is remanded for the most basic errors. Some of these errors should have been learned in Rating Board 101: "What I should know before I decide a claim."[2]

VA medical personnel performing C&P examinations seldom follow the procedures required of them by the *Physician's Guide for Disability Evaluation Examinations*. All too often, the appointed examiner knows nothing of your problem until you walk through his door.

The examiner often does not have your claim file, or, if it was sent from the VARO, did not read it. The examination often fails to follow and report certain mandatory procedures associated with the type of examination requested. More likely than not, the examiner is not a full-time VA medical staff member.

When a flawed examination report is returned to the rating board, the board is supposed to return it for compliance with standard examining procedures. In the thirteen years I hand-wrestled with them, I never had a case in which the exam was returned to the hospital on the initiative of the rating-board member. Instead, the claims were decided on an examination that was flawed.

The usual sequence of events that followed was an appeal of the decision with an argument that the exam was flawed, and why. The appeal would make its way to the BVA after several years, when it would be remanded to the VARO with an instruction to order a *thorough and contemporaneous examination* with a specialist, which was supposed to have been done several years earlier, when the claim was first processed. Do not make the mistake of expecting the VA to make your claim for you. Yes, the law does say that if you submit a well-grounded claim, the VA has a duty to assist. Only one person can make your claim: you. You must know what is required before benefits can be granted, and then hand the VA all the necessary proof tied up in a neat package.

Make certain you get copies of all medical records associated with your claim. Obtain a copy of your complete claim file so you can provide your doctor with the medical evidence pertaining to your service-connected disability. Now when he prepares your assessment it will be based on evidence and not a hearsay account of what you, his patient, said happened. You will want to provide your doctor with a copy of the section of 38 CFR Part 4 that pertains to the disability being claimed. The report that is prepared on your behalf should state how the doctor rates your disability using VA standards. Make certain that the report states that because of your service-connected disability, the condition being claimed is secondary to that service-connected medical condition.

Remember, you have a duty to submit a well-supported claim. Unless you do this, your claim is going to be denied and you are going to have an extremely difficult task of trying to salvage it. There is only one way to win: send in a claim that contains evidence that demands the benefits be granted. There are no shortcuts.

8 | CLAIMS BASED ON TREATMENT BY THE VA

The history of this benefit goes back more than eighty years to the passage of the World War Veterans' Act of 1924, in which Congress extended service-connected benefits to any veteran who suffered a further injury or disability incurred while hospitalized by the VA. The statute, known as "Section 213 Benefits," entitled a veteran to compensation benefits whether or not the injury or disability was the result of negligence by hospital staff.

A decade later, in 1934, the VA changed the regulatory language of the implementing regulation, making benefits payable only when negligence could be proved. Congress did not amend the law in 1934 to narrow the rights of a veteran who claimed additional injuries or disabilities while being treated by the VA. The VA undertook this initiative on its own. It was never Congress's intent to place on veterans the difficult burden of proving negligence in order to receive compensation.

For the next sixty years, the VA paid benefits only when a veteran could prove negligence was the cause of his or her disabilities. Over that time, veterans who suffered injuries or disabilities while being treated by the VA were deprived of lawfully entitled compensation benefits. There is no telling how many veterans were denied service connection—thousands or even tens of thousands—until a veteran by the name of Fred P. Gardner refused to accept the VA rationale.

Mr. Gardner filed a claim in November 1988 because an operation on his lower spine in 1986 was the direct cause of nerve and muscle damage to his left leg. The VARO denied his claim on January 26, 1989, on the basis that 38 CFR §3.358(c)(3) requires the disability to be the product of an accident or mistake by the VA medical staff. The VA maintained that there was no proof of negligence or accident regarding the medical procedure performed on his spine by VA hospital medical staff. The veteran filed a timely Notice of Disagreement with this decision and the VARO of original jurisdiction confirmed the denial of service connection in September 1989. A formal appeal was filed and forwarded to the BVA. The BVA reviewed the case in January 1990 and upheld the decision of the VARO. The BVA stated, "We do not find evidence of fault on the part of the VA or of the occurrence of an unforeseen, untoward event, resulting in permanent additional disability. Accordingly, entitlement to the benefits requested is not demonstrated."

Mr. Gardner filed a timely appeal to the United States Court of Appeals for Veterans Claims, and his case was argued on August 7, 1991. A favorable decision was rendered on November 25, 1991, as amended on December 3, 1991. The case, known as *Gardner v. Derwinski*, 1 Vet. App. 584 (1991), was almost as great a landmark decision as *Gilbert v. Derwinski*, 1 Vet. App. 49 (1990). This decision blasted a hole through the VA system of "doing things our way." The order read,

> The Court holds 38 CFR §3.358(c)(3) unlawful as exceeding the authority of the Secretary and in violation of the statutory rights granted to veterans by Congress under section 1151. Accordingly, the decision of the BVA is REVERSED and the matter REMANDED for further proceedings.

Mr. Gardner won, but still waited another four years before the issue was finally closed. The VA did not give up its initiatives and power that easily. It appealed the decision of the United States Court of Appeals for Veterans Claims to the United States Court of Appeals for the Federal Circuit on March 9, 1992. The Federal Circuit issued its decision on September 13, 1993, upholding the

United States Court of Appeals for Veterans Claims decision and affirmed the decision that 38 CFR §3.3 58(c)(3) was illegal. The order read in part:

> the VA's desire to pay less compensation than that authorized by statute could not make legitimate the unlawful nature of 38 CFR §3.358(c)(3). The VA must make its regulations carry out the purposes of a statute, not amend it.

What's really interesting is one of the arguments raised by the VA to the Court of Appeals for the Federal Circuit. While the press releases were cranking out slogans about how much we owe our veterans, the secretary was in court arguing that acceptance of the VA's version of its regulation should prevail because of the cost of providing extra compensation to veterans who couldn't prove negligence or accident. If the decision of the United States Court of Appeals for Veterans Claims were upheld and the regulation invalidated, the VA would have to pay everybody whose physical condition was worse following treatment by the VA. The court told the VA, "[W]here a statute's meaning is clear, the cost of implementation is a concern for Congress, not the VA; the VA's duty is to pay benefits based on the clear language of the statute."

The secretary of the VA was determined to fight the loss of a regulation that allowed it to save millions and millions of dollars. In January 1994, the solicitor general of the United States petitioned the U.S. Supreme Court on behalf of the VA to review the finding of the Court of Appeals for the Federal Circuit decision in *Brown v. Gardner*, 115 S Ct. 552, 13 OL Ed 2~ 462. The Supreme Court agreed to review the lower appeals court's findings. On December 12, 1994, the Supreme Court released its decision. It affirmed the lower court's finding by a vote of 9 to 0. The Court held

> that the statute is quite clear and does not place any requirement on the veteran to show fault before compensation can

be paid; and that just because the VA has been improperly applying the law for more than sixty years is not grounds to legitimize a regulation that contradicts the statute.

Eight years passed from the time Mr. Gardner filed his application for benefits to the time the Supreme Court decided that the VA illegally adjudicated his claim under a regulation that denied his right to benefits and contradicted the intent of Congress. During 1996, Mr. Gardner's victory on appeal worked its way back to the original VARO of jurisdiction to be readjudicated, this time based on the medical facts of his case. I have no information as to whether Mr. Gardner was granted service connection for the residual effects of his operation to the lower spine. If his claim was denied on different grounds, I imagine Mr. Gardner is once again fighting it out with the VA using the appeal system.

What the Regulations Say

The prevailing statute pertaining to an application for compensation benefits based on medical problems resulting from treatment by the VA medical system or health problems resulting from training under the Vocational Rehabilitation Program is 38 U.S.C. §1151, and the regulations implementing the statute are 38 CFR §3.358(a), (b), and (c) as revised and 38 CFR §3.800. The portion of the adjudication manual pertinent to an 1151 claim is M21-1 Part VI, Change 42, dated December 7, 1995.

Although the Supreme Court upheld the declaration of the United States Court of Appeals for the Federal Circuit and the United States Court of Appeals for Veterans Claims that proof of negligence was not the intent of Congress when it passed the World War Veterans' Act of 1924, claims under 38 U.S.C. §1151 will always be difficult to win. The amended change to 38 CFR §3.358(c) leaves intact many of the original elements that a veteran must prove before entitlement is established.

For instance, the Supreme Court left intact the doctrine of *volenti non fit injuria*. The decision also raised two other important elements a veteran must deal with in order to establish service connection. First, the Court held that 38 U.S.C. §1151 permits service connection for all but the *necessary consequences* of properly administered VA medical or surgical treatment or an examination to which a veteran consented. The Court stated that compensation should not be payable for the necessary consequences of treatment to which the veteran consented. Claims will be adjudicated based on the interpretation that the meaning of "consent" applies to both expressed consent and implied consent.

Blacks Law Dictionary defines *volenti non fit injuria* as knowing and comprehending the danger and voluntarily exposing himself or herself to it. In doing so, he or she is deemed to have assumed the risk and is precluded from recovery for an injury resulting therefrom. A *necessary consequence* means a consequence certain or intended to result from treatment or examination.

The second element is informed consent, which is a major consideration when submitting a claim based on VA treatment. When undergoing a form of treatment or surgical procedure in a Veterans Administration Medical Center (VAMC), you are required to give your consent for this treatment. It is the physician's responsibility to provide information related to your treatment and obtain your consent. He must record your consent in the "progress notes" section of your hospital record. If you consented to the treatment and the hospital staff followed the medical and administrative procedures exactly as published, you may not have a valid claim. The theory is that you acknowledged and accepted any risks.

The final rule change to 38 CFR §3.358(c), based on the Supreme Court decision in *Brown v. Gardner*, was published in the *Federal Register* on May 23, 1996, and was amended as follows:

(3) Compensation is not payable for the necessary consequences of medical or surgical treatment or examination prop-

erly administered with the express or implied consent of the veteran or, in appropriate cases, the veteran's representative. *Necessary consequences* are those which are certain to result from, or were intended to result from, the examination, or medical or surgical treatment administered. Consequences otherwise certain or intended to result from a treatment will not be considered uncertain or unintended solely because it had not been determined at the time consent was given whether that treatment would in fact be administered.

What the rule does is narrow the VA's risk of being required to grant compensation benefits when the medical service provided may have an adverse affect. For example, suppose you gave permission for an exploratory surgical procedure for kidney problems. However, once your abdomen was opened, the exploratory procedure showed one kidney had to be removed. You cannot claim compensation benefits just because you now have only one kidney. Your kidney was removed because you gave implied consent. They were performing the procedure to determine the root of your medical problem. The permission to remove the kidney could also be justified if the doctor certifies that in his medical judgment, failure to remove the kidney might have endangered your life.

The unchanged portions of 38 CFR §3.358(c) are key to determining whether your claim under 38 U.S.C. §1151 is compensable. To satisfy the requirements of conditions outlined in (c)(1) through (c)(6) the following conditions must be met:

- You have to show that the additional disability is actually the result of such disease or injury or an aggravation of an existing disease or injury and not merely a coincidental.
- You must be able to prove that the disease, injury, or aggravation of an existing condition was suffered as a result of VA medical or surgical treatment or hospitalization, or as a result of vocational rehabilitation training.

◆ You must be able to show that the injury or disease was not the result of your willful misconduct or failure to follow instructions. With the exception of incompetent veterans, veterans will be barred from compensation benefits if their conduct in any way led to complications related to their treatment.

◆ You must be able to prove that a disability you are claiming while in vocational rehabilitation training was directly caused by the activities involved in your training program.

◆ If you are injured or contract a disease while in a nursing home under VA contract compensation, benefits under section 1151 are not payable. The VA holds that the nursing home is an independent contractor and, accordingly, it is its own agent and its employees are not to be deemed employees of the VA.

VA Tools to Skirt Entitlements

The requirement for a veteran to sign a consent statement and form SF-522, Request for Administration of Anesthesia and for Performance of Operations and Other Procedures, before treatment is administered is a catch-22 situation. If you don't sign it, the VA sends you packing; if you do sign it, it can effectively insulate itself against granting service-connected benefits because you consented to the risks. So where does that leave veterans? You've got to know the rules the VA must follow.

Historically, the VA is known for not following its own laws, regulations, manuals, and policies. When treating you it must do the following:

◆ The doctor himself or herself must inform you of the risks involved in the treatment that you are about to authorize. The physician must explain in detail the known consequences or expected consequences of the procedure you are to undergo. Possible consequences must also be discussed when the doctor knows the frequency of certain kinds of complications and there is a reasonable chance they could occur. Informed consent also means that the doctor discusses effects that are not intentionally caused, desired, or expected. It also means that alternative options are covered.

◆ The practitioner must document everything discussed in your inpatient medical record. The memo will include the date and time the consent was given, your ability to comprehend the information (were you awake and alert? confused? under some form of sedation at the time?), the fact that you were given an opportunity to ask questions, the fact that you gave your consent freely and were not under duress or coercion, and the fact that he discussed the medical treatment in understandable language.

◆ When a procedure entails use of sedation, produces considerable discomfort, has a risk of complications or death, requires injections of any substance into joint space or body cavity, or is classified as a surgical procedure, the VA *must* also obtain a signed SF-522. This release must also be made part of your inpatient hospital records.

Elements of an 1151 Claim

You may be entitled to compensation benefits based on disabilities resulting from treatment administered by VA medical staff or while in vocational rehabilitation. Your claim must be carefully crafted so that you can skirt limitations imposed by 38 CFR §3.358(a), (b), and (c). Some special areas should be zeroed in on when determining if your claim has a chance of being granted. VA medical staff must fulfill specific responsibilities; otherwise, benefits must be granted. Failure of the VA to dot the i's or cross the t's is what to look for in developing evidence to justify the granting of benefits.

The VA must grant service-connection in the face of evidence of additional disability or death through carelessness, negligence, lack of proper skill, error in judgment, or similar instances of fault. Benefits must also be granted if additional disability or death resulted from an accident that was not a reasonably foreseeable adverse event.

If procedures requiring signed consent do not show that the veteran was fully informed and that the claimed condition was a possible result of the medical procedure for which consent was given, then the claim must be granted. For example, suppose your doctor told you that if you consent to an operation, two conditions could occur. You grant your consent, but as a result of the operation you are now suffering from the complications of two conditions that were not discussed before the procedure. Your claim would have to be granted.

Another circumstance in which benefits would be granted involves fault by someone other than a VA medical staff member. Suppose your doctor prescribed a certain drug and you suffered a side effect causing an additional disability or even death. If it is determined that the pharmaceutical supplier filled the prescription incorrectly, you would be entitled to compensation.

When there is insufficient evidence to prove informed consent concerning a surgical procedure, other therapeutic treatment, or a prescribed course of treatment, the claim must be granted. Insufficient evidence in this category would include the hospital losing or failing to enter your informed consent in the records. The VA could also be challenged if someone other than your primary care physician or the doctor doing the procedure discussed the risks and possible complications associated with the procedure. *Only a doctor can review this information with you.*

Failure to properly diagnose or treat a condition can generate a claim based on acts of omission rather than acts of commission. VA policy establishes that a failure to diagnose in a timely manner or properly treat a symptom that directly causes increased disability or death may give rise to entitlement under section 1151. If a veteran is discharged prematurely from the hospital under the guidelines required by the hospital administrative process known as DRG (Diagnostic Related Groups), a possible claim action exists.[1] Eligibility hinges on whether an early discharge caused a relapse or a worsening of the disability, or whether the timing of the discharge caused the disability to be aggravated beyond the level of natural progression associated with the condition.

Compensation is payable under section 1151 for any disability caused by medication that was prescribed by VA and taken or administered as prescribed, except for the necessary consequences associated with the disease. For example, if you were taking several medications and then given a drug that is known to cause kidney failure when interacting with those previously prescribed, you would have grounds for a claim.

Another area to look into is the professional skill level of VA physicians responsible for your treatment. The VA has extreme difficulty recruiting topflight medical specialists. I recall that one VA medical center used a nurse to function in the capacity of a gynecologist because none were on staff at the hospital. It is common practice to use part-time general practitioners and foreign doctors with minimal language skills to examine and treat veterans. In this hospital medical center, resident students from a local medical school work part-time to treat and examine veterans. Here lies an area of vulnerability for the VA medical system and the basis of a valid claim.

The statute states very clearly that if someone who lacks the proper skills treats you, you have the basis of a claim under section 1151. You can obtain the medical background of any doctor by contacting the American Medical Association (AMA), 515 N. State Street, Chicago, IL, 60610 (312-464-5000), and asking for the doctor's professional profile.

Filing an 1151 Claim

A claim for benefits for complications resulting from medical treatment by the VA, or for an injury or disease sustained while enrolled in a vocational rehabilitation training program, should be submitted on VA form 21-4138, Statement in Support of Claim. The claim must be made in narrative form as there are no specific questions on the form.

If possible, type the narrative. The claim should be brief and the language carefully chosen, with your arguments based only on facts that can be supported by the evidence in your claim file, hospital records, and the regulations that apply to your case.

It's important when basing your claim on disabilities arising from treatment by the VA that your claim statement show your condition was not one that could have been anticipated or a necessary consequence of that treatment. You must scrutinize your records to ascertain exactly what consent you granted and whether the records show that you were (or were not) aware of the consequences of the intended treatment.

Before filing your claim, the first step is to obtain a complete copy of all your hospital records. These are the records you must get from the hospital in order to support your claim:

- the admission medical examination and history
- the operating report
- the discharge summary
- nursing notes
- lab test results
- X-ray, MRI, and CAT scan summaries
- a complete list of all medication administered

These records are essential if you are trying to establish service connection under section 1151.

If you believe that the VA is responsible for your disability, the next step is to take these records to a medical specialist for review and confirmation that the treatment you received did in fact cause the disability you are claiming. Your doctor's written report must also address the issue of whether or not the disability incurred was normally a condition that could or would occur with the type of treatment administered.

At the same time you request hospital records, contact the VARO who is custodian of your VA claim file and request a complete copy of the claim file and vocational rehabilitation records. The VA cannot ignore this request—it is a right granted under the Freedom of Information Act. Most important, you want these records before you announce your intent to file a claim. Let me stress, *you want these records before you file your claim.* The success of your claim depends on the type of claim you put together. You have to know what you're talking about or you will lose.

Next, obtain a copy of the current *Code of Federal Regulations* (38 CFR) that is applicable to your claim. All VAROs are supposed to maintain a complete library of laws, regulations, VA circulars, manuals, and General Counsel opinions. If you can visit a VARO, do so and obtain a copy of every legal citation that is pertinent to your case. If travel to the VARO is not practical, consider contacting one of the service organizations that maintain full-time staff at every VARO, such as the American Legion, Veterans of Foreign Wars, Disabled American Veterans, or the State Service Office. Tell them the citations you are looking for, and that you are preparing an 1151 claim and need to know exactly what laws, regulations, and manuals are currently in effect.

The claimant has the burden of submitting evidence sufficient to justify a belief by a fair and impartial individual that the evidence is sufficient to trigger the VA's duty to assist. A claim filed under section 1151 must meet this test. There is no statute of limitation in applying for service connection under this provision of the statute. You can apply even if the treatment occurred fifty years ago. However, obtaining proof may be difficult.

If the VA previously denied you benefits under section 1151 on the grounds that negligence was not shown, you may be entitled to benefits because the rule used to deny your claim was illegal. In this case, after you gather all of your evidence, reopen your claim based on a clear and unmistakable error.

Suing the VA in Federal Court

As a veteran or surviving spouse you can bring a civil suit against the Department of Veterans Affairs into federal court under the Federal Torts Claims Act for injuries or diseases resulting from medical malpractice. Actually, claims under 38 U.S.C. §1151 and the Federal Torts Claims Act can be filed at the same time if the basis of the claim is medical malpractice. The difference between these two remedies is that under section 1151, to recover for the disabilities resulting from treatment by the VA, you do not have to prove negligence. However, in federal court, recovery will hinge on establishing that disability or death was in fact the result of negligence.

If you prevail in federal court, any awards obtained under the Federal Torts Claims Act are offset by compensation benefits you might be entitled to or have received under section 1151. For example, say you are awarded $200,000 in federal court because of the disabilities incurred through medical treatment by the VA and are subsequently granted service connection at a rate of $2,000 per month. You would receive your first compensation check only after eight years and four months.

If you are denied service connection on your case and you win an appeal in federal court, you have grounds to reopen your claim based on new and material evidence. The legal and medical basis that succeeded in federal court would be the arguments used to establish service connection under section 1151.

To establish a claim in federal court, follow the basic steps outlined previously in "Filing an 1151 Claim." Because this legal

action is being decided in a court of law, you need to be repre-
sented by an attorney. Obtain the services of an attorney who spe-
cializes in medical malpractice cases and one who also practices in
federal court. If you do not know such an attorney, contact the
local bar association in your area and ask for a list of firms that
specialize in medical malpractice cases.

I am not an attorney and therefore cannot go beyond this point
in discussing the possibilities of action against the VA in federal
court. I can, however, tell you that you have only two years from
the date of the injury or from the date the injury is discovered—
whichever comes later—to bring suit under the Federal Torts Claims
Act.

Chapter Eight Highlights

For more than sixty years the VA illegally adjudicated claims based
on injuries or diseases resulting from treatment by the Department
of Veterans Affairs. The Supreme Court ruled in *Brown v. Gardner*
that a veteran or surviving spouse did not have to prove negligence
before benefits could be granted based on treatment by the VA.
The VA's action to change the statute's meaning by changing the
regulation was illegal. All prior decisions since 1934 in which benefits were denied because the claimant did not prove negligence
can be reopened based on a clear and unmistakable error. The court
decision changed only 38 CFR §3.358(c)(3), and left the remain-
der of the paragraph intact. One very important provision left intact was the doctrine of *volenti non fit injuria*.

This doctrine is now the VA' s major tactic in justifying the
denial of benefits because consent was given. Whether the consent
was expressed or implied, it will be assumed that veterans know-
ingly and voluntarily exposed themselves to the dangers and risk
of the treatment. Yet failure to consent to the prescribed treatment
means the loss of medical treatment for the problem.

Remember, only the doctor can discuss the details of the treatment plan with you and ask for your permission. During this interview he must tell you what will occur, what to expect, possible secondary disabilities, and whether the treatment will correct the problem. If success is not completely assured, you must be advised of the degree of success you could reasonably expect.

Do not sign any form or release unless a physician brings it to you. Demand that you be properly advised by a doctor, and not by a nurse, physician's assistant, social worker, or any other hospital staff member. As the VA employs the services of many foreign doctors, you may not understand what is being explained because of a language barrier. The VA still would be out of compliance with the regulations if it assigned such a physician because you must be able to comprehend the risks explained before you give your consent. Everything the attending physician discusses with you must be recorded in the progress notes. Your inpatient hospital records must also include a signed copy of your SF-522 if you are given anesthesia or undergo an operation or any other medical or surgical procedure. Failure of the VA to follow this procedure is basis for a well-grounded claim and the granting of benefits. If there is no proof that you were properly advised of the dangers involved, or if those records are missing, the VA must grant service connection for the disability claimed.

You must carefully screen all the records for evidence to establish the basis of a well-grounded claim. Even if you signed a consent or an SF-522, a claim can still be successfully argued. You must prove carelessness, negligence, lack of proper skill, error in judgment, an unforeseeable accident, an improper or delayed diagnosis, or authorized drugs that you are allergic to or that were in conflict with other medication being prescribed that resulted in additional disabilities or death.

Again, if you were not properly advised of the possible consequences of the treatment plan or if a hospital staff member other than your physician briefed you, you should file an 1151 claim. A premature discharge from the hospital resulting in medical complications that cause additional disabilities or aggravation of an existing condition is also grounds for a claim.

Taking the time to put together a well-organized claim is the only way of ensuring all the facts and evidence will be available to a rating-board member. Do not assume that all you have to do is state that an event happened and the VA will jump in and build your case for you. The duty to assist comes into play only after the VA is convinced they have a duty to assist.

Therefore, you must get copies of all pertinent medical evidence, including hospital records, doctor's outpatient records, and assessments of your condition. You need a medical statement from your doctor confirming that the problem you are experiencing is definitely related to the VA treatment. The inpatient records must show that you were not aware of the consequences of the treatment plan.

An individual who has no in-depth training in law or medicine is deciding your claim. Most likely he or she will rate the claim guided only by personal instincts of what he or she perceives as the meaning of the medical or legal evidence. In addition, the great number of claims to be decided does not allow the luxury of researching facts or reading court decisions when determining each claim. There is no time to sift through several hundred pages of medical and legal evidence to determine if the claim is well grounded or the facts are sufficient to grant service connection based on the Doctrine of Reasonable Doubt. When a rating-board member is uncertain as to what is actually involved, he will most likely deny the claim. If he errs, it will be in favor of the government. The unspoken motto of adjudication is if the claimant does not agree with the decision, let him argue it out in the appeal system.[2]

If you suffered serious injury or death as a result of treatment by the VA, you or your surviving spouse should take all the medical records to an attorney specializing in medical malprac-tice to determine if you have a winnable case under the Federal Torts Claims Act. Remember, you have only two years from the date of injury or its discovery to take action in federal court. Your evidence must be able to support a lawsuit that the VA was negligent in its treatment, and that your disability is the result of this treatment.

9 | C&P EXAMINATIONS

The Department of Veterans Affairs' Health Administration is actually a multipurpose agency, and the first weak link in the adjudication function at all VAROs. The agency has four primary functions: first, mandatory inpatient and outpatient treatment for service-related disabilities; second, treatment of non-service-related injuries and diseases based on the availability of medical services and patients' financial resources; third, conducting Compensation and Pension (C&P) Examinations; and fourth, medical research.

The purpose of this chapter is to make you aware of what the VA must do when it conducts a C&P Examination, how the exam is supposed to be done, and what you must do if the procedures prescribed by the statutes, regulations, and case law are not followed. Most important, you'll learn what to do if you are not given a thorough and contemporaneous medical examination. Millions of veterans are cheated out of lawful benefits because of flawed C&P Examinations and the flawed interpretation of these examinations by rating-board members who have neither medical nor legal training or experience.

VA Health Administration

Before we focus on the VA's responsibility to administer C&P Examinations, a general discussion of the overall operation of the VA Health Administration is in order. During the latter part of 1997, VA medical service came under the scrutiny of both Congress and the public because of abusive management styles, the condoning of sexual harassment of patients and employees, many unnecessary deaths of veterans in VA medical facilities, and congressional pressure to cut operating costs and reduce services.

Here are some newspaper headlines that captured the public's attention and weakened trust and confidence in VA medical care:[1]

♦ VA fails to diagnosis cancer in Cleveland
♦ VA uses unsupervised residents and other practices that would not be accepted elsewhere
♦ VA cardiac units suffer higher death rates
♦ VA cancer researcher convicted of lying in 2005
♦ Probe into VA deaths ends in Pittsburgh

There is a story that broke in the *Plain Dealer*, an Ohio newspaper, in 2001 by Joan Mazzolini that should have sent chills up the spine of anyone seeking medical care from the VA. It is a real horror story about how VA management's inability to recruit U.S. doctors has led it to circumvent U.S. Immigration and Naturalization laws and to hire foreign doctors on a part-time basis to meet local demands.

Contradicting VA Hoopla

To create a medical environment influenced primarily by budget considerations that dictate the degree of care available is wanton disregard of the intent of the laws authorizing medical care of veterans. VA healthcare management strives to cut operational costs without any concern for the effect on patients. For example, employing physicians who have to meet only minimum standards to practice medicine has generated great savings. In the private sector, if a doctor moves from New York to Florida, he must be relicensed in Florida in order to practice medicine. Not so with the VA. Title 38 *U.S. Code* Chapter 74, section 7402, requires only that a doctor graduate from a medical school approved by the secretary (which could be anywhere); complete an internship satisfactory to the secretary (no standards prescribed in the law); and obtain only a one-time license to practice medicine, surgery, or osteopathy in any state. Over the years the press has reported cases in which a doctor whose license was revoked by one state's medical board was now practicing medicine for the VA in another state without having to be relicensed.

No other professional standards are demanded of VA doctors. Requiring only minimum professional experience for the VA means lower salaries. The law also allows VA hospitals to hire doctors on a fee basis or a part-time basis, or hire interns and resident student doctors. These would-be doctors comprise nearly 30 percent of all doctors in the VA system.

In 2005, two events orchestrated by the administration and top management of the VA sent lawmakers scurrying about looking for answers and pointing fingers. The first was the expenditure of nearly a billion dollars for a new hospital all-purpose computer system. Test programs conducted at Bay Pines hospital revealed that the new system was unreliable and dangerous to use. One of the problems that became public was the failure of automated ordering of medical supplies to produce results, causing critical operations to be postponed due to lack of supplies.

The most serious incident in 2005 was the failure of White House, OMB, and VA Undersecretary for Health Administration for underestimating the operational funds for fiscal year 2006. They were advised by nearly every veteran's service organization that they were dangerously below budget standards. However, in June 2005 they acknowledged the budget was short nearly one billion dollars. Congress reacted with shock at such an error. This was followed in July with a new estimate to meet the 2006 health care cost. The new figure was two billion dollars. A supplemental authorization bill was rushed through Congress, as many Republican representatives were seriously concerned about the backlash that could occur in the 2006 election year.

Veterans Healthcare Eligibility Reform Act of 1996

In September 1997, the VA Health Administration announced an-other new healthcare strategy that discreetly further distanced it-self from promises made for medical care to veterans who served their country. Veterans seeking medical care after October 1998 were (and still are) required to apply annually for enrollment in the VA healthcare program, at which time they are assigned to one of seven priority groups. Failure to apply makes the veteran ineli-gible to receive medical treatment.[2] Exactly what care you receive is determined by the group to which you are assigned. The career bureaucrats and tax-cutting politicians were looking for a way of limiting medical support for a very large aging veteran population. Bureaucrats will never earn the brownie points necessary to enjoy the favor of some politicians and the administration unless they can cut the cost of operating the VA so the money can be spent on other projects.

It's not a big stretch to relate this program to the story of Robin Hood. Only, in this version, "Robin VA" takes from those in need of help and returns millions of dollars to the king's coffers so the monies can be used for more important projects that do not deal with the needs of people.

There is another feature of this new healthcare program veter-ans should know about. The veteran's eligibility status is evaluated annually by the primary care center to determine if they will re-main in their current priority group, be assigned to a lower priority group, or be terminated from the program. For example, let's as-sume you were assigned to Priority Group 2 when first enrolled because you have a 30 percent service-connected disability. How-ever, the VA rating board reduced your current rating to 0 percent based on their interpretation of the results of a recent C&P Exami-nation. You have now been identified as Priority Group 6 eligible, which translates to continued priority care for your service-related condition only. For unrelated, non-service-connected medical problems, you are dropped to almost the lowest level of care. Don't despair, for there is a bright side to this demotion: if you do get care for a non-service-related medical problem, the VA will not charge you a copayment fee for the treatment.

Veterans Millennium Healthcare and Benefits Act of 1999

On November 30, 1999, the Veterans Millennium Healthcare and Benefits Act (PL 106-117) was signed into law. The act addressed long-term care healthcare issues along with day-to-day adult healthcare needs. This new statute adds subsection 1710A and 1710B to *U.S. Code* Title 38, Part II, Chapter 17 to spell out who is eligible for long-term nursing home care. Briefly, eligibility is extended to any veteran who requires nursing home care for a service-related injury or disease and to any veteran who needs such care for any reason if he has a service-connected disability rated 70 percent or more. This new entitlement dealing with granting benefits for any condition may be very narrow in scope depending how the term "disability rated 70 percent" is interpreted. There are two ways a veteran could be rated 70 percent disabled by the VA: A single disability could be rated 70 percent or multiple disabilities could collectively qualify for a 70 percent rating.

C&P Examinations

Almost all service-connected benefits extended to veterans rely on some degree of disability that was incurred in the service, aggravated in the service, or resulted from treatment in a VA facility by VA medical staff. Veterans wishing to apply for non-service-connected pension benefits must also prove they are sufficiently disabled to be rendered unemployable. The claim process for service connection requires the VA to obtain original service medical records, medical records from VA treatment centers (hospitals or clinics), copies of records from private physicians, and hospital records before deciding the merits of the claim.

38 CFR §3.326(a) states that where a reasonable probability of a valid claim is indicated, a Department of Veterans Affairs examination will be authorized. However, the regulation also permits the rating board to decide the claim based on the findings of a private physician if the report meets certain standards. The specialist's report must include clinical manifestations and substantiation of diagnosis by findings of diagnostic techniques generally accepted by the medical authorities. Pathological studies, X-rays, and laboratory tests must be part of the specialist's assessment.

If the records are not sufficient to determine the current degree of disability, or if the rating board elects not to accept the specialist's report for any reason, a C&P Examination will be scheduled. Herein lies a major unfairness to veterans. The medical expertise of the examining physician is left to the discretion of the medical service. In my thirteen years working with veterans as an advocate, I don't recall a single case in which a board-certified doctor specializing in the condition being evaluated examined the veteran. All C&P Examinations were administered by non-VA-staff doctors who were recruited from the ranks of retired doctors. Many of the doctors I inquired about through the AMA (American Medical Association) headquarters in Chicago were identified as family practice physicians or general practitioners. A while back, using Prodigy's "Veteran's Bulletin Board," I asked if it was a common practice throughout the United States for veterans to be examined by these fee-basis general practitioners. The responses were not surprising: C&P Examinations by non-specialist doctors is a common practice of VAMCs.

The only time a general practitioner cannot conduct a C&P Examination is when an appeal is remanded to the VARO and the remand order instructs that the claimant be examined by a board-certified specialist. VA manual M 21-1 Part 4, Change 38, dated

August 30, 1995, mandates this procedure be followed. Yet the VA assigns whomever it pleases, not necessarily a board-certified doctor. In many cases, the same doctor did the initial evaluation. And I've yet to see a document in a claimant file showing that the rating board refused to accept the examination and mandating the medical center assign a board-certified specialist.

This is why it's important for you to know the medical specialty of the examining physician; it's the basis for an appeal if benefits are denied. The court has held many times that the VA has a duty to provide you with a thorough and contemporaneous examination. When you have a complex medical problem and are examined by a retired general practitioner, a physician assistant, or a nurse practitioner, a red flag should go up.

Inside the C&P Examinations

The process starts when a claim is filed for any benefit involving a disability or disease that was incurred in the service. Your claim and medical evidence are forwarded to the adjudication division, where the medical evidence attached to your claim and service medical records are reviewed. By law, the rating board can rate your claim just on this evidence if it deems it adequate for rating purposes.

If the evidence does not suggest that the claim is plausible, meritorious on its own, or capable of substantiation, the VA does not have a duty to assist in its development. If this decision is rendered, the veteran will spend the next three to five years arguing only one point: Did the evidence trigger the VA duty to assist?

Assuming the claim meets this standard, the law mandates that the VA has a duty to assist the veteran from this point forward. When the rating board cannot make a rating based on the medical evidence submitted with the claim and the service medical records, it must request a C&P Examination from a VA medical facility. The veteran should be scheduled for a *thorough and contempora-*

neous examination, more commonly referred to as a C&P Examination, by the medical facility closest to his home.

The rating board tells the medical facility what kind of examination to conduct. The request is forwarded electronically through the Automated Medical Information Exchange (AMIE). In most cases the rating board orders only a general evaluation with no request for a specialist.

Even if the rating board requested a specialty examination, the hospital is not obliged to assign a specialist. It has complete freedom to assign whomever it chooses. Through the years I have seen hospitals assign only fee-basis doctors or resident student doctors from a local medical school to evaluate complex medical problems claimed by veterans. Physician's assistants and nurse practitioners are used to conduct many of these C&P exams. Downsizing of hospital staffing and tightly controlled fiscal budget restraints make the practice of contracting fee-basis physicians an ideal choice. As for the requirement that veterans receive an examination that is actually thorough and contemporaneous, the best that can be said is that it is a farce.

Never forget this: The VA Benefits Administration and VA Health Administration are like two families who have the same last name but are unrelated. Each function is not accountable to the other for its actions and no real central authority exists to control these two agencies.

However, 38 CFR §4.2, "Interpretation of an Examination Report," requires the rating specialist to return the examination report when the diagnosis is not supported by the findings or if the examination report does not contain sufficient details. Rating boards seldom if ever return C&P Examinations unless the veteran or the advocate has protested that the examination was inadequate and thus flawed. Rating boards can easily deny benefits when the exam protocol fails to follow the examining procedures outlined in VA Medical Manual lB 11-56, *Physician's Guide for Disability Evaluation Examinations*.[3] I have never seen a rating-board member study the results of a C&P Examination to ensure that the report submitted was in full compliance with VA Manual lB 11-56. There are several reasons for this, one of which is that because of the shallow level of medical knowledge, they fail to detect the flawed nature of the examinations. All you have to do is look at the remand and reversal rate of appeals reviewed by the BVA (between 70 percent and 80 percent nationwide) to know that rating boards are extremely deficient in the interpretation and application of the concepts related to law and medicine.

AMIE C&P Examination Program

AMIE is a multipurpose electronic system used to exchange information between medical centers, outpatient clinics, and regional offices. One program within AMIE is the AMIE C&P Examination Program. The program is designed to electronically transmit examination requests to medical centers. After the medical center prints the requests and schedules specific examinations, standardized examination worksheets are printed. The printed request and worksheet now become the official record between the VARO and medical center.

It is important for veterans to know all about the examination process. When your claim is denied, a major part of your appeal will involve proving that the VA did not follow regulations, manuals, statutes, and case law. Obtaining copies of the records generated during the examination process is absolutely essential should you have to go head-to-head with the VA in a dispute challenging its decision. Briefly, the program is as follows:

- The VARO office clerk electronically inputs the request to the VAMC.
- Upon receipt of the request the medical center clerk schedules the exam.
- Worksheets are printed and the examination is scheduled.

+ Using printed worksheets, the examiner conducts the examination.
+ The examiner dictates the report using the worksheet format.
+ The transcriber enters the results into the systems and routes a printed copy to the physician for review and signature.
+ The examination report is electronically dispatched to the VARO.
+ The report is printed by the VARO clerk and forwarded to the rating board for action.

A copy of the following records should be requested from the VARO: initial request for C&P Examination transmitted to the medical facility; the doctor's report furnished to the VARO; and any lab reports, X-rays, and special tests performed and sent to the VARO. From the VA medical facility performing the C&P Examination, you will need copies of the following: the worksheet used by the examining physician, the dictated report of the examination, test results, radiological reports, lab results, and a statement from the medical facility of the physician's qualifications.

C&P Protocol

The Physician's Guide for Disability Evaluation Examinations (lB 11-56) provides the VA examiner with very specific instructions as to how an examination should be conducted when evaluating a veteran. All physicians and dentists are issued this manual to provide current guidance in examining claimants for disabilities being claimed. The policies set forth in this manual apply to all VA physicians, staff doctors, fee-basis physicians, part-time doctors, and resident student doctors training at a VAMC.

There are four important reasons why it is absolutely necessary to obtain a copy of the pertinent chapters of this manual before you are examined. First, you want to know if the examining VA physician is in fact following the procedures set forth to ensure every aspect of your condition is evaluated. Second, when you read the report forwarded to the rating-board member by the examining physician, you must be able to determine if the physician did in fact conduct all the required tests and evaluation procedures associated with your particular medical condition. Third, the report as filed must include very specific medical findings and opinions by the examining physician. And fourth, if you arrange for a private specialist to evaluate your condition or review the results of the VA examination, he will have to know what is supposed to be reported in terms of medical findings or interpretation of test results. The reason I stress these four reasons can best be illustrated by this analogy: if you were injured in an automobile accident and sustained a lifetime disability, would you take the word of an insurance company doctor as to how disabling your injuries were? The only interest of any insurance company is to see how cheaply it can settle the claim. The magnitude of your lifetime limitations, pain, or loss of income does not enter into the equation.

PHYSICIAN'S GUIDE HIGHLIGHTS

In most cases the C&P Examination is not conducted by a board-certified specialist. Hospital administration is given full discretion as to who will be assigned duties of evaluating veterans for determining entitlement to benefits. The central office in Washington, DC, has quietly authorized the use of physician's assistants, nurse practitioners, and residents from one of the local teaching hospitals and of retired general practitioners hired on a part-time basis. The *Physician's Guide for Disability Evaluation Examinations* (hereinafter called the *Physician's Guide*) does not reference the use of this type of medical staff, who are at the bottom of the totem pole of medical specialists. The manual refers to physicians only.

When a veteran is evaluated for a service-connected disability, the regulations and manuals specifically require the use of a physician to perform the evaluation. When you are scheduled for a C&P

Examination, do not assume that because the examination is being conducted in a VAMC the examiner is a specialist trained in the area being evaluated. The veteran must ask the doctor what his qualifications are and if he is board certified. If not, immediately following the examination notify the VARO *in writing* that you did not receive a thorough and contemporaneous examination because the hospital failed to provide a specialist for the condition being evaluated. When putting the VA on notice that your evaluation was not in compliance with published directives, make certain you mail your complaint to the VA by certified mail with return receipt. Failure to do so could cost you thousands of dollars down the road.

The *Physician's Guide* is a general introduction to what is expected of VA examiners. It is an outline of VA hospital administration policy, which every examining physician is required to follow. Every physician who examines claimants should be familiar with the material contained in this guide and in the VA rating schedule. Failure to follow the policies and procedures set forth is grounds to appeal a denial of benefits or a rating that is below the true level of severity experienced by the claimant.

Schedule for Rating Disabilities

Part 4 of 38 CFR is the official guide for converting clinical findings to standardized diagnostic codes and grades of severity. The purpose of furnishing the VA Schedule for Rating Disabilities (38 CFR Part 4) to VAMCs and clinics is to familiarize physicians performing disability examinations with the principle and practices of rating boards in the application of the rating schedule. The *Physician's Guide* presents explanations and techniques for performing examinations that will meet the specific requirements of the rating schedule. Joint conferences between examining physicians and adjudication personnel staff are declared necessary to provide the highest quality of medical services relating to disability evaluations.

Importance and Purpose of Reports

Physicians are told that the purpose of these examinations is to establish the presence or absence of disease, injuries, or residual conditions and to record findings indicative of the severity of the disabling conditions so that they may be evaluated. An inaccurate examination, or an incomplete or biased one, may deprive a veteran and his family of benefits to which they are entitled. Examinations that are not in compliance with policies and procedures outlined in the *Physician's Guide* or AMIE are strong grounds for an appeal.

COMPLETENESS OF REPORTS

The examining physician is responsible for making a complete and detailed report, including correct diagnosis of the disabling condition and a description of the effects of the disability on the veteran's ordinary activity. The correct diagnosis is of great importance. The reports should include the clinical and laboratory findings as well as all other evidence that will substantiate the diagnosis and severity of the disability.

The exact findings recorded are just as important as the actual diagnosis itself in meeting the needs of a rating-board member. Similarly, the findings and clinical evidence demonstrating the severity of the disability should be reported, because in most claim actions for compensation benefits, the rating-board member never sees the veteran. Clarity of description, legibility of notes, accuracy of dates, identification of normal ranges for tests reported, and other details are very important.

You need to obtain a copy of the C&P Examination and carefully review it to make certain the C&P examiner did in fact convey this detailed information in the report. If this type of information is missing, the rating-board member is required under 38 CFR §4.2 to return the examination report as inadequate for evaluation purposes. However, I assure you that rating-board members do not routinely return evaluations unless the claimant starts hollering that benefits were denied because the report was inadequate. Failure to check for missing information is one reason why so many claims are denied. The claimant has absolutely no idea what was reported, the significance of the information reported, or the conclusions of examining physician.

Scope of the Examination

A request for a C&P evaluation from a rating-board member lists all service-connected disabilities—active, static, or alleged. It has been the practice of rating boards to ask for a general medical examination only, instead of a specific examination that is directly related to the conditions being claimed. The manual states the scope of the examination should be broad enough to cover all diseases, injuries, and residuals that are alleged by the veteran. Examinations should be made by a specialist where indicated by the disabilities claimed. In *Irby v. Brown*, 6 Vet. App. 12 (1994), the court held that the VA failed in its duty to assist by not ordering a thorough and contemporaneous psychiatric examination (specialty examination) and the report therefore did not give a specific finding.

The way the system works, if you have a serious back disorder with radiating pain, a general practitioner instead of an orthopedist or neurologist will most likely evaluate you. It is totally feasible for the VA to operate by this system because it keeps the cost of care down. However, it is a breach in the doctrine decreed by this country to care for veterans who became disabled while serving the interest of the country.

If the claim was denied based on a C&P Examination administered by a fee-basis general practitioner, file a Notice of Disagreement citing that the VA failed in its duty to assist by not providing a thorough and contemporaneous examination. In addition, cite either *Sklar v. Brown*, 5 Vet. App. 140 (1993)[4] or *Irby v. Brown*, whichever is more applicable. Make certain that you state very clearly the reasons why the C&P Examination was flawed and why the case law is applicable.

General Medical and Surgical Examination

When the examiner finds specific abnormalities, all necessary studies should be made to arrive at a correct and complete diagnosis, including, if indicated, general medical and surgical examinations. Following the initial general postdischarge physical examination, when only one system is requested, only that system will be examined unless a reason for further study becomes apparent during the visit.

When you obtain a copy of your claim file, look for a copy of the order to the medical center requesting that an examination be scheduled. If the rating-board member asked for nothing more than a general physical examination and you are claiming a cardiac disorder, for example, challenge any decision denying benefits based on the fact that because you were evaluated by a non–cardiac specialist, you were not afforded a thorough and contemporaneous examination.

The C&P evaluation unit considers a general examination to include information about the patient's age, height, weight, personal appearance, nutrition, muscular development, posture, gait, right- or left-handedness, pulse rate, respiratory rate, temperature, and blood pressure. The *Physician's Guide* also directs that an exercise test should be conducted on all conditions that are manifested by general weakness, easy fatigability, or shortness of breath (dyspnea), unless such a test is inadvisable. If an exercise test cannot be performed, the reasons should be reported.

Of the hundreds of C&P Examinations I have reviewed over the years, most did not focus on the primary medical problem or detail what tests were administered that supported the diagnosis for which the examination was scheduled. The findings reported by these C&P examining physicians were loaded with basic background facts such as age, height, and weight. The doctor's narrative provided very little insight as to what was found, the degree of the disability caused by the condition, or how the disability affected the veteran's ability to work. The evaluation did not indicate what tests were administered or what medical facts led to the diagnosis. I do not ever remember reading a report in which the claimant was given an exercise test because he was exhibiting symptoms of weakness, fatigability, or shortness of breath upon exertion.

Severity of Disability

When reporting the finding of a C&P evaluation, The *Physician's Guide* emphasizes that "the essential duty of the examining physician is to record a full, clear report of the medical and industrial HISTORY, THE SYMPTOMATOLOGY and PHYSICAL FINDINGS. [Emphasis added.]" The purpose is to permit a rating-board member to compare the medical findings reported by the examining physician with the disability percentage evaluations contained in the rating schedule. For a client who intended to obtain a medical assessment from a private specialist of his choice, I always made a copy of the rating schedule for the private doctor. This provided the framework for the report to be compared against the VA rating schedule. Thus if the examination report determined the veteran was 60 percent disabled based on solid medical evidence, and the VA rated the claim at 40 percent disabling based only on its own unsubstantiated conclusions, the veteran had a winnable appeal.

Review of Claim Folders

The law requires that the veteran's claim file be available to the C&P examiner and be reviewed by the examiner before the examination. This important policy is violated and ignored by C&P physicians and rating-board members alike. The United States Court of Appeals for Veterans Claims and BVA have remanded case after case to local VAROs because they refuse to follow this policy, thus violating the veteran's rights to a fair decision.

The *Physician's Guide* states in part,

> Much of the material in the claims folder is of no use to the examining physician. However, some material *is of utmost importance* [emphasis added] in orienting the physician. Particularly important are medical, social, and industrial historical data; physical and laboratory findings of previous examinations (including those made while in active military service); and rating forms showing previous diagnosis and disability ratings. These data must be considered chronologically in order to obtain a true picture of the progress of the disorder. In some cases, the examining physician will find incomplete examinations, unsupported diagnoses, and misuse of terminology. It will be necessary for the examining physician to integrate the situation with the information available by constructing an overall picture that matches the facts available.

If the claim file is not present when you are examined, or if the examining physician has not read the file before the examination, grounds exist to appeal the denial of any benefit sought, because the VA has failed to provide you with a thorough and contemporaneous examination. If you do not see your claim file when being examined, ask the attending physician if he has it. If you see the file, ask the doctor, "Have you read the claim file in its entirety?" In either situation, if the answer is no, advise the local VARO immediately in writing that you did not receive a fair and contemporaneous examination because the examiner did not have your file present or was not aware of your case medical history. Make a copy of your letter before sending it by certified mail with return receipt requested.

Preparing for the Examination

The best way to maintain control throughout the entire claims process is to take the initiative. Do not file a claim until you have built a winnable case.

The first step in building a winning case is to file an informal claim. By doing so, the entitlement date is protected and you have up to one year to prepare your claim and obtain all evidence necessary to prove entitlement. For example, let's say that you sustained a back injury in the service that has now been diagnosed as intervertebral disc syndrome. Your condition is characterized as severe recurring attacks with persistent symptoms compatible with sciatic neuropathy. You can no longer be gainfully employed. Physical activity is limited because of the severe chronic pain.

The second step is obtaining copies of all VA regulations, manuals, and pertinent case law that may pertain to your circumstances. Copies of VA regulations (38 CFRs) can be found in your local county law library or on the VA home page on the Internet. Copies of United States Court of Appeals for Veterans Claims decisions can be found at the law library (look for West Publishing Company's *Veterans Appeals Reporter*). The *Physician's Guide for Disability Evaluation Examinations* can be found at all VAMCs, state service officer locations, and county veteran's service offices. You will need to copy chapter one and the chapter that is pertinent to your condition.

The third step is to arrange an appointment with your personal medical specialist requesting an assessment of your condition. He should have a copy of the 38 CFR Part 4 regulation, chapters from the *Physician's Guide*, copies of any service medical records, and a copy of any lay statements from people knowledgeable about the injury or disease. If others have treated you for these same conditions, obtain copies of these records.

If you do not have a specialist to work with, the local AMA chapter or hospital referral service will provide the names of doctors whose specialty covers your condition. To save yourself grief and unnecessary expense, first determine if the doctor will give you a written assessment of the findings. Without a written report, an evaluation is useless for VA purposes.

The fourth step is to develop a lay statement to support the authenticity of your claim. Unless you file a claim within the first year following your separation, the VA has a nasty habit of denying benefits based solely on the fact that service medical records are silent as to your condition. If the event that caused the injury to your back was not documented in your service records, you can bet the decision will be "claim denied." All lay statements should be in the form of a sworn deposition so that these statements become evidence.

Remember, a statement from family or service friends will not be accepted as valid evidence if the statement is giving a medical opinion. A lay statement can give sworn testimony as to what was witnessed or the limitations observed subsequent to the injury. It is important that before filing the claim, veterans give a sworn detailed statement as to what occurred, where they were treated, and how often they were treated. If the injury occurred during combat with the enemy, then your statement alone is sufficient to establish service incurrence.

The fifth step is to prepare all the supporting evidence to be appended to your claim.

After taking these steps, you will be ready to file your official claim and to take any scheduled C&P Examinations within the following few months.

Taking the Examination

Once you are scheduled for a C&P Examination, you must comply with the order and report to the medical center or clinic or risk being denied benefits.[5] Failure to report can complicate and bias your claim. However, if the condition you are being evaluated for is cyclical—having inactive and active stages— you must contact the medical center and advise them of this fact so you can be re-scheduled and evaluated when the condition is active and can be observed by a physician. Failure of the VA to evaluate your condition during an active stage is grounds for a reversal if the claim is denied.[6]

Medical examiners assigned to the C&P unit are notorious for spending only five to twenty minutes with a patient. The evaluation may be flawed because the examination was all or in most part performed by a physician's assistant, nurse practitioner, or resident student doctor. However, precautions can be taken to reduce the ineffectiveness of an examination by an examiner with limited medical skills:

- Take someone with you if at all possible. This person can attest in a sworn statement that you were in the examining room only "x" number of minutes. Your companion can also testify if you were sent to other medical services at the clinic, and if so, which ones. Try to get your witness into the examining room with you so he or she can attest to whether your claim file was in fact available at the time of the evaluation and whether the doctor was knowledgeable about your medical history.

- Determine the examiner's credentials. Is he a cardiologist, orthopedist, or neurologist, for example? Find out if the doctor is board certified in a specialty and whether he is currently licensed in the state where the examination was conducted. After the examination, write the AMA at its national headquarters in Chicago and obtain a background report on the doctor or doctors who examined you. All this information is necessary if you have to refute the examiner's ability to administer a thorough and contemporaneous examination.

- List your medical problems and describe all the symptoms

you are experiencing for each medical condition. If you are on medication, list each drug used to treat your problems, along with the dosage. If the medication has resulted in side effects that are responsible for other medical problems, record this information and make it known to the examiner.

◆ Give the examiner a copy of the credentials of and the medical assessment by your own private specialist. In many cases this will intimidate or influence an examiner of a lesser medical background. When the VA uses minimally qualified examiners to medically evaluate complex injuries or diseases, a veteran will be able to counter this breach of faith.

Don't Make Assumptions

If your claim is denied, you should not accept the results of a VA medical evaluation as conclusive and absolute. A lot is riding on the results of a C&P Examination, and to assume that the VA administered a *thorough and contemporaneous examination* is a grave mistake that could deprive you of lawful entitlements and care. Do not assume that the VA examining doctor is an expert in the field related to your disability problems. The services of a recognized private specialist should be obtained to refute the medical findings of any VA physician if benefits are denied. This is the only way to protect your interests.

Chapter Nine Highlights

The entire VA system is undergoing a transformation that is not necessarily in the best interest of veterans. The VA Health Administration has been engaged in two very ambitious programs that will downsize the VA healthcare system and drastically cut costs.

Undersecretary for Health Dr. Kiser claims his program "Prescription for Change," subtitled "The New VA," will work wonders. The goal is to reduce hospital beds to fewer than fifty thousand nationwide; adopt an ambulatory care system, thus minimizing inpatient care for the twenty-six million veterans; expand services to include treatment for nonveterans such as Medicare patients and Medicaid patients based on contract agreement with other government agencies; and employ more nonphysician caregivers, further reducing the level of skilled care for the very ill veterans. His doctrine tells us that these major changes are about to surface. Every VAMC is preparing to reduce the number of employees across the board. This is the reason they are opening what is known as "Employee Transition Offices." This is where they send the about-to-be-fired employee to suggest other employment opportunities.

The second initiative designed to reduce access to healthcare programs from veterans across the board was made part of the Veterans' Healthcare Eligibility Reform Act of 1996. Veterans desiring medical treatment from the VA had to enroll in the VA healthcare program by October 1998. At the time of enrollment, a veteran was assigned to one of seven priority groups. This program requires every veteran who is not rated at least 50 percent disabled to register annually. The priority group to which a veteran is assigned is not permanent and can be adjusted up or down the priority ladder.

When both programs are implemented and fused into a single purpose, the VA has the structure to limit healthcare to those with service-related conditions. With the exception of veterans having disabilities rated 50 percent or higher, the only treatment available to a veteran who is rated less than 50 percent will be for the actual condition that is service related. Once this goal is achieved, billions of dollars can be redirected to more satisfying political goals totally unrelated to the needs of the citizenry.

Most VA medical examinations are performed by minimally

trained examiners. Doing so is cheaper than providing the kind of specialist required to properly evaluate a serious injury or complex disease. The VA is also resorting to using nurse practitioners and physician's assistants to conduct C&P Examinations. Even though they allegedly work under the supervision of a physician, an examination by one of these nonphysician caregivers can be worthless.

It is an absolute necessity for a veteran to consult with a private medical specialist before being examined by the VA. You must provide your specialist with medical records of your condition, VA regulations, and manuals that are applicable to your situation. Your specialist's assessment of your condition must show a clear diagnosis, the limitations it imposes upon you, and how it relates to your contention that it is service incurred. The doctor's closing remarks should contain a statement similar to this:

> Based on a review of Mr. Smith's service medical records and my examinations and tests, it is my opinion that this condition did in fact occur while he served in the U.S. Army between 1945 and 1955. Using the standards published in 38 CFR Part 4, Mr. Smith is 60 percent disabled.

By law, the VA must provide you with a *thorough and contemporaneous examination* if the medical evidence submitted with your claim and your service medical records are not sufficient to rate your claim. You cannot afford to sit back and expect the VA to adjudicate your claim like King Solomon. To be successful you must know exactly what the VA must do when you are examined. Remember that 38 CFR Part 4 and the *Physician's Guide for Disability Evaluation Examinations* are the tools the VA examiner must work with when he evaluates your condition. Know what should be checked, and if he does not follow the manual ask why he is not following the procedures mandated in the *Physician's Guide.*

Make certain when you are examined that you ask the examiner for his credentials and whether he read and reviewed your claim file before this examination. Don't let him ignore the question; get an answer. Failure to review your file is a violation not only of the *Physician's Guide* but also of federal law. Make this fact known to him even if he gets huffy because of your question. You cannot afford to be passive in these matters. As soon as the examination has been concluded, go to the waiting room and record everything that was discussed and checked. Record the total time you were with the examiner. If you don't make certain that they dot every "i" and cross every "t," it may cost you three to five years trying spent trying to resolve your claim.

10 | PROVE IT OR LOSE IT

Properly supporting a well-grounded claim requires facts that cannot be rebutted or dismissed as pure speculation by a rating-board member. Failure to substantiate your case will result in an almost immediate denial of the claim. Nothing would suit the VA more than to have a claim based on an unsubstantiated premise that an injury or disease was incurred on active duty. The claim would be denied as not being well grounded.

For the next three to five years, if you persevere, your claim will slowly wiggle its way through the appeal process, and the only issue under consideration would be whether the initial claim would lead a reasonable person to believe that it was *possible* that the condition could be service related. Always remember that you have the burden to show a reasonable possibility that your injury or disease occurred on active duty. Until you establish that the claim is well grounded, the VA does not have to lift a finger to help you. The VA is required by law to take a veteran aside and say, "If you want to get this claim approved, you must prove these points by providing the following types of evidence." With limited time, a limited number of adjudication personnel, and a massive number of new cases each day the VA cannot become your personal counselor. It is all up to you.

You must stop a moment and ask: "What does the VA require before it will grant benefits for this condition?" "What must I prove?" "What kind of proof do I need?" and "Where do I find this proof?" Then you must assemble a case based on facts that will allow the rating board only one option: to grant the benefit claimed. The goal is to have benefits granted without being forced into a three- to five-year appeal contest. If your claim has to be appealed, make certain the BVA or the Court of Appeals for Veterans Claims will reverse the VARO. You will never win a claim if it's based solely on your own unsubstantiated opinion that your disability is service related.

Knowing What the VA Wants and Where to Look for It

The first step in winning your claim is to determine exactly what the VA requires in order to grant benefits. You must look in 38 CFR Parts 3 and 4 for instructions that pertain to your claim. You need a copy of all pertinent CFR paragraphs and rating schedules relating to your medical problem. These regulations, statutes, and manuals will tell you exactly what must be established before benefits can be granted. This is an easy but absolutely necessary step in the process of building your case.

LIBRARIES
Libraries are a rich source of information for a veteran seeking supportive references necessary to the preparation of a claim. Many specialty libraries are available to veterans searching for facts: law libraries, public libraries, the Library of Congress, major university libraries, city libraries such as New York Public Library, and medical school libraries such as Harvard University Library. And don't forget the Internet. A veteran can collect a lot of information if he is determined to dig for facts.

Law Libraries
Every county law library nationwide subscribes to the complete annual printing of the Code of Federal Regulations. The volumes are numbered sequentially, and the regulations pertaining to the Department of Veterans Affairs are found in volume 38 CFR. Law school libraries also have current copies of these publications.

Four other publications found in law libraries should be researched and supportive information copied. The first is U.S. Code 38 and the second is United States Code Annotated (U.S.C.A.) volume 38. The third is the *Federal Register,* the daily publication of changes of government policy and procedures. The fourth is the decisions of the United States Circuit Courts, Federal Courts of Appeals, and United States Court of Appeals for Veterans Claims published in documents called *Reporters*. They include the published decisions for the various federal courts. West Publishing Company is one of the publishers of the federal court system's decisions.

For specific decisions concerning veterans' issues, consult West's *Veterans Appeals Reporter*, published one to two times a year. Here you will find all the final decisions of the United States Court of Appeals for Veterans Claims that have become case law and are binding upon the VA and veterans. If the VA or the veteran appealed the court's decision to a higher court, then you must follow the trail all the way through the judicial system to the United States Appeals Court or to the Supreme Court.

Title 38 *U.S. Code* is the actual statute that governs the operation of the Department of Veterans Affairs. The annotated version, privately published by the West Publishing Company, is extremely valuable because it simplifies the legalese of the statute. This publication is vital to the researcher as it offers many special services such as cross-referencing to CFRs and the legislative history of that section of the statute. Also available are references to certain court cases that may have been a factor in clarifying the meaning of a particular sector of the statute.

Law libraries also carry the *Federal Register*, released daily. This is a very important source of information as it contains current changes the VA put into effect or changes they are proposing to implement in the near future.

University Libraries
Many university libraries throughout the United States have been

designated as depositories for government publications and documents. As a citizen you are entitled access to this information on deposit by the government without being a member of the faculty or student body. Available will be all current CFRs and U.S. statutes (Title 38, for example). You will be able to find changes to VA policy and procedures, published in the *Federal Register*. You will not be charged for accessing this information. However, there is usually a nominal charge for copying the documents.

Public Libraries

Many public libraries maintain a complete set of federal regulations and statutes. The extent and availability of the information will depend on the size of the community supported by the local library system. However, many library systems are now linked in a network. Although a particular library may not have 38 CFR or Title 38 *U.S. Code* in house, it may be able to request it from a library within its network.

VA REGIONAL OFFICES

Every VARO has a reference library reading room that is available to the public for research. In addition to having current copies of Title 38 *U.S. Code* and 38 CFR Parts 3 and 4, they are a rich source of other valuable information that could support your claim. On file will be the VA Manual M-21; VA circulars released by the central office in Washington, D.C.; specific public announcements of policy changes and procedures printed in the Federal Register; a complete set of opinions released by the General Counsel; the *Physician's Guide for Disability Evaluation Examinations* (IB 11-56); and decisions rendered by the Court of Veterans Appeals printed in *Veterans Appeals Reporter* by West Publishing Company.

In the event the local regional office will not provide a means for you to copy the information you need, there are other options. First, make an accurate list of each document you want a copy of, making certain to identify the pages, paragraphs, subject titles, and document name and number. Then go to your congressional representative's office and request assistance in obtaining copies of the information you require. This is public information available under the provisions of the Freedom of Information Act. In preparing this book, I had to use my congressional representative's office several times because I was being stone-walled. Do not be timid about using the services of an elected official, as this is one of the important functions they perform.

VA MEDICAL CENTERS AND CLINICS

If you live within a reasonable distance of a VA medical center or clinic, you can obtain a copy of chapters of the *Physician's Guide* that spell out in detail exactly what the C&P examiner must check and report on.

If you have a patient file at either a VA hospital or clinic, ask for a copy of the entire file. It will support your statement that you are currently being medically treated for this problem. Remember, when the application is filed you must be currently suffering from the residual effects of the injury or disease to have a valid claim. Veterans often came into my office wanting to file a claim for, say, a bad back. They would describe an incident that happened which could account for an injury to the back. However, when I asked the $64,000 question—"What does your doctor say about your condition now and what kind of treatment is being administered?"—I would get an answer such as "Well, I'm not being treated now for it, I just want to get it on the record now so if it starts hurting again I will already be service connected for it." If you file a claim while the condition is not actively causing medical problems, you will lose. You cannot prove entitlement.

More important, you will handicap yourself in the future. The VA will have denied your claim as insufficient to trigger the duty to assist. To reopen your claim the only option available is to introduce medical evidence that is new and material. This is evidence that was never previously considered and would justify a belief that the current medical problem is directly linked to the back in-jury on active duty. The more years between the original incident and the current flare-up, the steeper the climb up the face of the mountain.

VETERANS SERVICE OFFICES: STATE AND COUNTY
The availability of these publications at your local county veterans service office depends upon several factors, one of which is the support the office receives from county commissioners. If the com-missioners understand the importance of this service to the com-munity, and if the budget is sufficient to properly run an advocacy program, the office will most likely have the publications discussed.

The second factor is whether the individuals who are employed as advocates are aware of these publications. If they have not been trained in the use of these publications, it is most likely they will not have the regulations, statutes, *Federal Register* releases, or court decisions available. In some counties, commissioners and admin-istrators give only lip service to the needs of veterans and will do just enough to avoid negative public opinion.

Each state funds and operates a Department of Veterans Ser-vices that may be a good source for obtaining copies of the infor-mation needed to support your contention that the medical condi-tion in question is service related. However, in many states the state veterans service agency coexists with the VA in the regional office. I would suggest you first visit the regional office reading room before trying to obtain the information from the state office.

INTERNET
If you have access to it, the Internet is a great way to copy the required information needed to perfect your claim. You will find 38 CFR and Title 38 *U.S. Code*, the *Federal Register* for the past several years, and decisions by the United States Court of Appeals for Veterans Claims. The VA has also posted decisions of the BVA

for 1995 and 2001. By surfing several of the university law libraries on the Web, you will find decisions concerning veterans' cases
that received an appellate review.

You can find *38 CFR* at the following Web addresses:

http://www.access.gpo.gov/naralcfr/waisidx_01/ 38cfrvl_
01.html

http://www.access.gpo.gov/nara/cfr/waisidx_01/ 38cfrv2_
01.html

http://thomas.loc.gov

The *Federal Register* is available at:

http://www.webopedia.com/TERM/g/gopher.html.

Title 38 *U.S. Code* can be found at:

http://uscode.house.gov/title38.htm (Follow the link to the information you are searching for)

http://www.law.cornell.edu/uscode/38

Case law can be found at these Internet addresses:

http://www.fedcir.gov (U.S. Court of Appeals for the Federal
Circuit)

http://www.va.gov/vbs/bva (Board of Veterans Appeals)

http://www.vetapp.uscourts.gov (U.S. Court of Appeals for
Veterans Claims)

OTHER SOURCES

A complete list of all federal government Web servers can be found
at http://www.sba.gov/world/federal-servers.html. For easy reference, print this sixteen-page list of all government servers and book-
mark pertinent sites. This index provides direct links to almost three
hundred servers. For example, if you want to go to the U.S. Army
server, scroll down the alphabetical listing of server addresses until you reach U.S. Army, and then click on it.

To purchase a copy of 38 CFR Volume I and Title 38 *U.S.
Code*, contact the Government Printing Office (GPO) via the
Internet. The GPO also offers BVA decisions from 1993 through
1999, on CD-ROM, as well as an annual subscription service pub-

lished quarterly on CD-ROM. For the location of the closest government bookstore, go to http://bookstore.gpo.gov/.

Although BVA decisions are not precedent setting, they do provide the basis for a strong supportive argument if your claim is denied for the same reason as a similar denied claim that was appealed and reversed. The second reason to research this database before filing a claim is to determine some of the most common reasons local regional offices deny claims.

Developing the Basic Elements of a Claim

The next step in the claim process is the gathering of evidence that will substantiate the claim. You must establish four facts:

- that you were in active service;
- that an injury or disease did occur on active duty and that the condition was not considered acute and transitory;
- that you are able to show a direct link between the incident that occurred on active duty and your current medical problem;
- that you are currently suffering from the residuals of this service-related medical problem.

Until you can address all four elements, the claim is not ready to be submitted.

ELEMENT ONE: PROOF OF SERVICE

When an original claim is filed, the very first task the VA will do is to verify military service. It will want to know the type of discharge granted, the length of your service, and the branch of service you were in when the alleged injury or disease occurred or was discovered. The veteran is responsible for providing a certified document that verifies his active-duty status at the time of discharge.

The time at which you were separated from the service will determine which document will be required to support your claim.

During and following World War II (WWII), many service members were issued a document that bore a formal certificate of discharge on one side and a summary of the individual's military service on the reverse side. Starting in the early 1950s, individuals were issued two documents upon separation: one a formal certificate of separation and the other a narrative document attesting to the details of the individual's service and known as a DD-214.

The DD-214 is the document the VA wants appended to the original claim. A box can be checked on the formal application for compensation or pension benefits (VA form 21-526) if a certified copy of a Report of Separation is not appended to the claim. The VA will request a copy of your Report of Separation from the NPRC in St. Louis, Missouri, which will add months to the adjudication process.

A request for a copy of the Report of Separation for each period of service should be filed on an SF-180 and mailed to the National Personnel Records Center, 9700 Page Avenue, St. Louis, MO 63132-5100. The NPRC will provide a certified copy of your DD-214 or Report of Separation at no charge. If the NPRC is unable to provide a certified copy of your DD-214 or separation record it will provide a Certificate of Service that is acceptable for all VA purposes. However, this document will not contain a summarized account of your military service.

Once you receive a certified copy of the document, take it to the clerk of the county court or equivalent in your state and have it entered into the public records. The clerk will photocopy it and enter it into the county archives, where it will become a permanent record. The original will remain safe, and any copies made from the original will automatically be certified. The clerk will then return the document provided by the NPRC along with a certified copy. The VA will accept this copy. Do not send an original document to the VA if it can be avoided.

If your records were a casualty of the 1973 fire at the NPRC, the NPRC will provide a certified statement based on information obtained from secondary records such as unit morning reports, pay records, and unit records. This document will be satisfactory for VA purposes.

There are several sources for obtaining blank SF-180s. Most state and county veterans service offices maintain a supply. Or you can call the local VARO (1-800-827-1000) to request one. If you have access to a computer, the form can be downloaded from http:/ /www.nara.gov/regionall mprsfl8O.html. If none of these sources are available, you can write a letter requesting a copy of your DD-214. The letter must contain the following information: your name as recorded on service records; your service serial number; your date of birth and place of birth; your Social Security number; the branch of service in which you served and organization assigned to when separated; your rank on separation; date entered service; and date of separation.

ELEMENT TWO: PROOF OF SERVICE OCCURRENCE

The whole claim pivots on several important points. First, it must establish that an injury or disease did in fact take place on active duty as alleged. Next, it must show continuity of treatment for the residuals of the injury or illness from the date of separation to the date the claim is filed. However, if the condition is chronic, then proof of continuity of treatment is not an issue. Last, it must establish that the condition is currently being treated. Detailed discussion of chronicity and continuity of treatment can be found in Chapter 1.

ELEMENT THREE: CONTINUITY OF SYMPTOMATOLOGY

As briefly outlined in chapter three, a claim for service connection becomes extremely difficult to establish under the rule of continuity of symptomatology when you have been separated from the service for many years. The greater the span between separation from the service and the claim date, the harder it is to successfully satisfy this third element. 38 CFR §3.303(b) states that "continuity of symptomatology is required where the condition claimed is shown not to be chronic or where the diagnosis of chronicity may be legitimately questioned."

To prove continuity of symptomatology, a record of continuous medical treatment must be introduced into evidence showing you were under continuous care for the disability claimed. The key factors you must keep in mind are that an injury or disease must have occurred in the service and that since leaving the service you have been treated for this condition. When a claim is initiated many years after leaving the service, the VA usually assumes that the condition you experienced on active duty was acute and transitory, or that the injury healed with no residual effects and that, therefore, your current condition was not service incurred.

You have another obstacle to deal with: determining how many times you must be treated for a condition before the VA accepts there is continuity of treatment. The regulations are totally silent on this point; thus, it is left up to the individual adjudicator to determine how many times he thinks you should have been treated. Along the same lines, the adjudicator has considerable latitude in deciding whether the first available record is a record of postservice treatment of the alleged disease or injury or whether it is a record of treatment of an unrelated service condition.

Many factors will determine your success in providing proof of continuous treatment for your medical condition. Before filing a claim, answer these questions: Have you moved around a lot since leaving the service? Is your doctor still alive? Did the doctor keep your records or were they destroyed? Did your doctor retire from private practice and, if so, were your records destroyed? Did your doctor sell his medical practice and transfer your records to someone else? How often were you treated for this condition? Does your condition go into long periods of remission between episodes?

Physician Search
We are talking about how long it has been since you were last
treated by your physician. If it was within the past five years, your
chances of locating your doctor are excellent. However, if you are
trying to find a doctor who treated you fifteen or twenty years ago,
the task becomes much more difficult. Yet there are several methods of finding a physician. Here are some ways to locate a former
doctor:

Reference Books Reed Reference Publishing Company publishes annual editions of the *Directory of Board-Certified Medical
Specialists*. This reference source contains the names of all practicing physicians and is cross-referenced by last name, medical
specialty, and geographic location. Almost all public libraries have
this reference source. The book can be found in medical school
libraries as well.

AMA Website The AMA maintains a physician locator service available to the general public via the Internet. There are several ways to search the database. The two primary methods are by
name and by medical specialty. It is quite easy to use and contains
information on more than five hundred thousand physicians. To
access this site, go to http://ama-assn.org.

Department of Professional Licensing Every state requires
its physicians to be licensed to practice medicine. Unfortunately,
the name of the agency that monitors physician licenses is not consistent from state to state.

State AMA Chapter If your former physician is a member of
his local state AMA organization, locating him should be easy.
However, physicians do not have to belong to the AMA.

Internet White and Yellow Pages If you know where a doctor lives or where you were last treated, try using InfoSpace, a free
service on the Internet that furnishes address and phone numbers
for more than two hundred million individuals. Go to http://
www.infospace.com. I successfully ran several tests on both white

pages and yellow pages. It's a great way to look up someone's phone number or address without dragging out a twenty-pound phone directory.

ELEMENT FOUR: PROOF CURRENTLY DISABLED

This is a very important element in establishing service connection for a condition that has become disabling years after you left the service. Before service connection will be granted, you must prove that the disease or injury is currently disabling. If the condition being claimed is in remission or not causing a disabling condition, do not file your claim; you cannot satisfy the fourth element. Your claim will be denied and you would not be able to win an appeal.

Seldom will the VA adjudicate a claim based solely on a non-VA physician's medical assessment. It has the authority to evaluate your claim without scheduling you for an official VA C&P Examination. If you have a condition that is in remission when you are scheduled for a C&P Examination, notify the VA medical facility and the local regional office of this fact and tell them you want to be examined when the condition is active. Make certain this notice is in writing and that you have taken steps to prevent them from claiming they were never notified of your situation. Read chapter eight for the best procedures to follow to protect your interest when dealing with the VA.

VA regulations require the medical centers to schedule an evaluation when the condition can be properly evaluated. The United States Court of Appeals for Veterans Claims has issued several binding decisions on this issue. You are entitled to a thorough and contemporaneous evaluation before a decision is rendered.

Sources of Evidence: NPRC

Service health records maintained by the NPRC are divided into two categories. The first group is those health records that are maintained and archived with Official Military Personnel Files (OMPF).

The second group is those inpatient hospital records that are maintained and archived separately in files allocated for hospital records.

OUTPATIENT MEDICAL RECORDS

OMPF files are composed of personal records generated during your period of active duty and outpatient health records, which include all sick call entries and notations, test results and lab findings, radiological reports, entry physical examinations, annual physical examinations, and separation examinations. These medical records are stored with your service record and personnel file. All these records should be requested from the NPRC using form SF-180.

However, beginning on October 16, 1992, the Department of the Army transferred all active duty outpatient medical records of recently separated personnel directly to the VA Records Management Center, St. Louis, Missouri. The Navy followed suit on January 31, 1994, the Marine Corps and Air Force on May 1, 1994, and the Air Force Reserve and Air National Guard on June 1, 1994, for personnel discharged, retired, or separated from active duty. Members of the U.S. Coast Guard continue to request copies of their health records from the NPRC in St. Louis.

If your health records (outpatient) are located at the NPRC, mail a request for copies to National Personnel Records Center (MPR), 9700 Page Avenue, St. Louis, MO 63132-5100. For health records transferred directly to the VA Records Management Center or one of its regional storage depots, call 1-800-827-1000 for the exact location of your health records and request current instructions for requesting copies. Warning: do not get talked out of obtaining copies of health records by a VA counselor advising that the VA will obtain the records after the claim is filed. The sole purpose of obtaining health records in advance is to determine what evidence is available to support your claim. This is the evidence you must take to your medical specialist for review and evaluation.

INPATIENT HOSPITAL RECORDS

Inpatient hospital records are stored separately from OMPF and outpatient health records. To get a copy of these records you must submit a special request to the NPRC, preferably using NA (National Archives) form 13042, Request for Information Needed to Locate Medical Records.

If you are unable to obtain this form, the following information is essential for the NPRC to help provide a copy of your hospital records: name, serial number, Social Security number, military hospital where treated, period of hospitalization, and medical problem for which you were hospitalized. When identifying the military hospital, identify the branch of service that administers the hospital care. The National Archive and Records Administration (NARA) archives hospital records under the name of the military hospital where treatment was offered and the branch of service of the patient. If you were hospitalized more than once, in different military hospitals, each hospital must be identified and pertinent information provided for each period of hospitalization.

TEN MILLION MEDICAL RECORDS DISCOVERED

In 1988, it was announced that a collection of computer tapes containing ten million hospital and treatment facility admissions was discovered by the National Academy of Sciences in one of its storage sites. These records were turned over to the NPRC (MPR) and for the next two years, the archivist decoded the contents of these records. When the decoding process was completed, nearly 7.8 million individual admission records were transcribed. The transcription of nearly three-fourths of these coded records is a major supplementary source of information available to some veterans whose health records were destroyed by fire in 1973 (the remaining one-fourth could not be transcribed).

The admission records are not specific or detailed medical documents, but are simply a summarization of medical information indexed by military service numbers. They contain only limited medical treatment information, but diagnosis, type of operation, and dates and places of treatment or hospitalization are frequently included. The information contained in these files would be sufficient for a veteran to reopen a claim that was previously denied.

The U.S. Army Surgeon General conducted a statistical study on active duty Army and Army Air Corps personnel in service between 1942 and 1945. Also included were active duty Army personnel and a limited number of Marine, Air Force, Navy, and military cadet personnel who served between 1950 and 1954.

If you were hospitalized during any of the periods mentioned above, request a copy of the medical information recorded from these files from the NPRC (MPR) on an SF-180. In Section II, provide your serial number, the name of the hospital and dates of confinement if possible, and the reason you were hospitalized.

1973 FIRE AT THE NPRC—RECORDS DESTROYED
On July 12, 1973, a disastrous fire at the NPRC (MPR) destroyed sixteen to eighteen million OMPF. The primary area of destruction was Army and Air Force records. Those individuals in the Army who were discharged or separated after November 1, 1912, and before January 1, 1960, suffered an approximately 80 percent loss. Air Force personnel who separated or were discharged between September 25, 1947, and January 1, 1964, experienced a 75 percent loss of records. The NPRC determined that the Air Force files that were destroyed started after the name James E. Hubbard.

The real tragedy was that the NPRC neither maintained duplicates nor kept microfilm versions of those records destroyed by fire. The problem was further compounded by the fact that an index of the records had never been compiled before the fire. However, the NPRC (MPR) will attempt to reconstruct basic service information by using secondary or alternate sources of information when requested by a veteran. It is not able to reconstruct medical information that was destroyed by the fire.

Case Law Concerning Lost or Destroyed Records

In *O'Hare v. Derwinski*, 1 Vet. App. 365 (1991), and *Sussex v. Derwinski*, 1 Vet. App. 526 (1991), the United States Court of Appeals for Veterans Claims ruled that when records entrusted to the government are lost or destroyed, special consideration is required. Associate Judge Steinberg, writing for the court in *Sussex v. Derwinski*, states, "bare conclusions [sic] as was stated here, that the 'benefit of doubt' doctrine does not apply, is inadequate" (*Gilbert v. Derwinski*, 1 Vet. App. at 59). This inadequacy is more pronounced in light of the BVA's heightened obligation to carefully consider the "Doctrine of Reasonable Doubt" because of the unavailability of the veteran's service medical records. Judge Steinberg, writing in *O'Hare v. Derwinski*, stated,

> Here the BVA decision treats the "Doctrine of Reasonable Doubt" rule standard in only the most conclusory terms: "[t]he Doctrine of Reasonable Doubt has been considered, but the evidence is not found to be so evenly balanced as to warrant allowance of the claim." That is not enough. *This is especially so in a case where the service medical records are presumed destroyed* [emphasis added]. In such a case, the BVA's obligation to explain its findings and conclusions, and to consider carefully the "Doctrine of Reasonable Doubt" rule is heightened.

Getting Copies of Health Records from the NPRC

Requests for military service and health records from the NPRC (MPR) should be submitted on an SF-180. The veteran must state in detail exactly what he is requesting. The NPRC has at times furnished a complete copy of a veteran's service record on microfilm, requiring the records to be photo-processed before they be evaluated and possibly used as supporting evidence. Inpatient hospital records are requested on a separate SF-180. Failure to provide sufficient information to allow a search of archive records will result in excessive unnecessary delays and archivists sending you NPRC NA form 13042 to identify the records requested.

WHAT YOU MUST ASK FOR
When requesting copies of service records or medical records from the NPRC (MPR) in St. Louis, use the prescribed form SF-180. The information you are requesting should be stated in Section II, Information and/or Documents Requested, as briefly as possible. For example, "Please provide a copy of all military outpatient health records and a copy of all those records that comprise my personnel file." The other entries on the form will provide the NPRC with all the facts necessary to locate your records.

When requesting inpatient hospital records, an SF-180 should be used. However, a second sheet will probably be necessary to include all the required information. Unlike outpatient records, which are filed with service records, hospital records are archived separately. The searchers must know which hospital you were in, the month and year you were admitted and released, and the nature of your illness, injury, and treatment. When identifying the hospital, the name, numerical designation, and location are essential. Here is an example of a request for copies of records for multiple inpatient hospitalizations:

> 1. I was admitted to 354th Field Hospital, Columbia, South Carolina, on January 1, 1990, for suspected heart disease. I was discharged from the hospital on January 20, 1990. A triple bypass surgery was performed on January 2, 1990.
> 2. On August 15, 1993, I was hospitalized at MacDill Air Force Regional Hospital, Tampa, Florida, for acute angina pains. I underwent double bypass surgery on August 16, 1993. I was released on September 10, 1993. Dr. Raymond Jones, Major, USAF, followed me for six months as an outpatient in the cardiology clinic.

Sources of Evidence: VA

You must consider several factors before requesting the VA to provide copies of medical records. The first question you must ask yourself is, "Where were my active duty medical files sent after I left the service?" The second question is, "How do I get copies of my health records?" The third question is, "What do I ask for?" The answers to the above questions will determine which functions within the VA to contact.

WHERE ARE THE RECORDS?

If you filed a previous claim with the VA, request copies of records from the VARO that adjudicated your last claim action. If you were discharged, separated, or retired from the Army after October 1992, or the Navy, Marines, or Air Force after 1994, contact the VA at 1-800-827-1000 for the location of your records within the VA archive system.

If your claim is an original claim, your medical records may be in one of two locations. First, if during out-processing it was indicated a compensation claim would be filed, the outpatient health records would have been sent to the VARO closest to the address given as a postservice residence.

Next, if no claim action after separation was indicated, the records would be forwarded to one of two places (and you would be notified during out processing where they were sent). For separations before October 1992 for Army personnel and January or May 1994 for Navy, Marines, and Air Force, the health records were sent to the NPRC (MPR) in St. Louis, Missouri, for storage. For separations after these dates, health records were transferred to the VA Records Management Center, St. Louis, Missouri, or one of its satellite storage facilities.

A claim action for any other purpose requires you to contact the VARO that was custodian of the claim file. This is a very important step for any veteran who is going to request an action to reopen a previously denied claim, amend the original claim to include additional disabilities, or request an increase to an existing disability rating. This is a step that must be taken. Preparing a claim without knowing exactly what evidence the VA has in your file is inviting a denial of benefits.

When a request is made for a copy of the claim file under the provisions of the Freedom of Information Act, ask for a copy of all the documents, medical records, rating decisions, C&P Examinations results, AMIE instructions to the C&P examining facility, VA Forms 626 (Remarks by Accredited Representatives), and military health records that comprise your file. To plan a winning strategy, you must know what the VA knows and what new or additional evidence will be necessary to support a claim.

HOW DO I GET COPIES OF VA RECORDS?

Military health records maintained by local VAROs are requested on VA Form 21-4138. It is important to spell out exactly what you want. For active duty health records forwarded to the VA Records Management Center, St. Louis, Missouri, first contact the center by phone at 1-314-263-2800 to find out if your records are located at the St. Louis storage site or at one of the other federal storage depositories.

Outpatient or inpatient medical treatment records stored at a VA medical center or clinic should be requested using VA form 21-4138. Make certain that the request clearly states exactly what you want. No justification is required to be given before copies of the records will be released. Do not make the assumption that treatment records or inpatient hospital records are automatically forwarded to the local regional office's adjudication division to be placed in your claim file. This does not happen. Adjudicators will not ask medical facilities if they have any hospital or treatment records pertaining to your medical problems unless the veteran has advised them that they exist.

WHAT TO ASK FOR

When requesting copies of records from the Department of Veterans Affairs, the most acceptable way is to state your request on VA form 21-4138. This form may be used when requesting copies of information from your claim file or when requesting copies of treatment records from a VA medical center or clinic.

I would suggest wording similar to the following when requesting copies of records from a regional office:

> Under the provisions of the Freedom of Information Act, I request a copy of my claim file to include all rating decisions, C&P Examinations, AMIE request to the C&P coordinator at the VA hospital, VA Form 626 filed by my accredited representative when he reviewed the rating decisions, military health records, and all responses from my private physicians.

When requesting copies of medical treatment records from a VA medical center or clinic, follow this example:

> Please provide me with copies of all inpatient and outpatient medical records currently on file at Grand Junction VAMC, Colorado, to include outpatient treatment records, admission history and physical exam reports, operation reports, discharge summaries, progress notes, nursing notes, consultation sheets, lab reports, radiological and imaging reports, and a list of medication prescribed by VA physicians. This information is requested under the provisions of the Freedom of Information Act.

Finally, make a copy of all requests to the VA and NPRC for records. Chapter eight discusses the safest way to transmit your request for records. You must back up everything when dealing with these agencies. If the VA loses your request, it may claim that it was never sent and you could lose thousands of dollars if you cannot prove it lost your correspondence. I've had several cases in which the NPRC (MPR) advised a veteran his health records were destroyed in the 1973 fire, but the same request was resubmitted through our local congressman's office and soon copies of records allegedly destroyed by the fire magically appeared. Don't always accept responses at face value. Check and recheck.

Sources of Evidence: Military Medical Facilities

The medical facility's records administrator will advise you whether the records are still under its control or were transferred to the NPRC (MPR) and, if so, when. Retired military personnel who received outpatient or inpatient treatment from one of the many military hospitals or clinics around the world have a valuable source of medical evidence to support their claim. Remember that records stored at the NPRC (MPR) in St. Louis are active-duty records. Medical records generated at a military installation after a veteran leaves active duty are archived by the military until the file has been inactive for several years. Some record collections date back to the 1940s and 1950s, but more comprehensive information was archived beginning in the 1960s. Retiree health records are sent to the NPRC (MPR) from facilities of all military services after one to three years of inactivity and are retained by the NPRC (MPR) for fifty years from the last patient activity. If the date of last treatment at a military facility was less than three years ago, the retiree's first inquiry for copies of health records should be to the facility that provided the treatment.

Sources of Evidence: Nonmedical

Nonmedical evidence can tip the scales in your favor. It includes information abstracted from official military historical records, sworn statements from individuals who have personal knowledge of an injury or disease that now is disabling you, BVA decisions,

United States Court of Appeals for Veterans Claims decisions, published medical theses by specialists in a specific field of medicine, and VA doctors' qualifications made available by the AMA. In addition, spouses, family, and friends can offer testimony as to your well-being before and after leaving the service.

Three quick points should be made: a sworn statement is evidence and has to be weighted with all the facts of the claim; lay statements cannot relate medical opinions but they can relate observations; to rebut these statements, the VA has to have evidence to the contrary other than its own unsubstantiated conclusions. The Internet is also a great place to seek out supportive evidence to build a winning claim. Look in chat rooms, veteran's bulletin boards, and government servers such as those of the Army, Navy, Marine, and Air Force, as well as the Centers for Disease Control and the National Science Center.

NATIONAL ARCHIVE RECORDS

A significant portion of historical documents concerning military information is housed in the National Archives Building on Pennsylvania Avenue in Washington, D.C., and at the National Archives at College Park, Maryland. Tracking vital information that would support your claim does not require you to go to the nation's capital to visit the National Archives. Since 1969, NARA has managed a system of regional archives that hold valuable federal records of regional origin and significance. Federal records may also be found in each of the presidential libraries managed by NARA and in a few non-NARA repositories that, by special agreement with the archivist of the United States, are affiliates in the federal network. Contact can be established by mail, telephone, or e-mail in most cases.

The NARA system of archiving documents and records for all government agencies is based on a numerical system of categories. There are more than five hundred primary groups, and within each primary group are one hundred subgroups that are further subdivided into twenty or more separate topics. Each of these secondary divisions may have hundreds of actual records. The master index and subdivision index for each record group can be searched on the Internet at. http://www.archives.gov/.

The following example demonstrates how historical records might prove a veteran's entitlement to VA benefits for diagnosed posttraumatic stress disorder (PTSD). By obtaining copies of key organizational documents from NARA that substantiate the events that caused the PTSD, the veteran increased by 1,000 percent the probability of being granted benefits.

Let's say our veteran has access to a computer with a modem. He searches for proof that he suffered a psychological trauma by contacting the NARA gopher site. He is looking for organizational records to substantiate his claim that he experienced a psychological experience so terrible that he is now totally disabled by PTSD.

First, here are the personal facts the VA has on Veteran Jones who served in the Army Air Force during World War II. Sergeant Jones was assigned to 343d Bomb Group, Eighth Air Force, in England, between 1943 and 1945 as an aircraft mechanic. The service information obtained by the VA does not show that on September 19, 1944, he volunteered to fly a B-17 combat mission over Germany, nor do his service medical records reflect that he had any injuries or illnesses while in England. Because the assigned flight engineer/gunner was injured on the previous mission, a temporary engineer/gunner replacement was needed for the forthcoming mission. Military personnel service records of Sergeant Jones do not note any combat duty during his two years overseas.

Veteran Jones logged on to the NARA site at http://www.nara.gov/ and clicked on "The Research Room." He scrolled down the next page and clicked "More," which took him to "Research by Selected Topic." He clicked on "World War II: Selected Finding Aids." This took him to "Finding Aids Across NARA Relevant to World War II Records." He then scrolled down and clicked "Military Agency Records Groups." Then he scrolled down to and clicked "Army Air Force (1903-64) RG-i3." "Records of the Army

Air Force (AAF) Record Group 18, 1903–1964," a general index
of files related to the Air Force, opened. He scrolled down the list
and clicked on "18.7.1. Records of the Office of the Commanding
General." This took him to a screen that lists all the records maintained for this group.

The veteran mailed his request to Textual Archives Services
Division, National Archives, 8601 Adelphi Road, College Park,
MD 20740-6001. He also could have called in his request (301-
713-7250) or e-mailed it (inquire@nara.gov).

MILITARY HISTORICAL ARCHIVES
Special records on each branch of service are kept by the Department of Defense. Each service branch maintains a military history
center. They are an excellent source of information about the history and mission of each organization within a branch of service.
For a starting point in collecting information concerning a former
organization you may have served in, contact one of the following:

Department of the Navy
9th and M Streets S.E.
Washington, DC 20374
202-433-3396 (Personal Papers Collection)
202-433-3439 (Archives Section)
http://www.history.usmc.mil/

U.S. Army Center of Military History
ATTN: DAMH-MD
103 Third Avenue
Ft. McNair, DC 20319-5058
202-761-5373
202-761-5444 (fax)
http://www.armyhistoryfnd.org/info.htm

Air Force History Support Office
AFHSO/HOS

Reference and Analysis Division
200 McChord Street, Box 94
Bolling AFB, DC 20332-1111
http://www. airforcehistory.hq.af. mil

Naval Historical Center
Washington Navy Yard
805 Kidder Breese Street SE
Washington Navy Yard, DC 20374-5060
http://www.history.navy.mil/

U.S. Marine Corps
Reference Section
Marine Corps Historical Center
Building 58
Washington Navy Yard
Washington, DC 20374-5060

U.S. Army
Attn.: DAMH-ZAX
U.S. Army Center of Military History
103 Third Avenue
Ft. McNair, DC 203 19-5058

U.S. Air Force
Air Force Support Office
500 Duncan Avenue, Box 94
Bolling AFB, DC 20332-1111
202-404-2264

U.S. Navy
Naval Historical Center
Washington Navy Yard
901 M Street SE
Washington, DC 20374-5060

Let me give you an example of why knowing where and how to find collaborative evidence is important in the preparation of a claim. Let's assume for the purpose of this illustration that our veteran was a former Navy fireman, serving on the destroyer USS *Macky* during World War II. In 1992, Veteran Smith was diagnosed with lung disease caused by asbestos forty-five years after he was discharged from the Navy.

Historical facts about the USS *Macky* are needed to build a claim that is plausible and not speculative. These are the facts about the ship's combat history obtained from the U.S. Navy Historical Center: The USS *Macky* was severely damaged by a Japanese kamikaze attack. Below decks, where our veteran was stationed, many of the steam and electrical wire pipes were destroyed, spewing asbestos dust and particles in all the work and berthing areas aboard ship. For more than three weeks the crippled ship slowly made its way back to Pearl Harbor for repairs. For the next two months the crew worked with civilian ship workers making internal and external repairs. Asbestos particles filled the air as the damaged areas below decks were gutted.

The veteran's personal service records do not mention that the enemy damaged his ship or that the entire crew was exposed to large concentrations of asbestos fibers. Yet fifty years later, the veteran is seriously disabled by asbestosis. The USS *Macky* combat damage can be confirmed by official naval combat records at the Navy Historical Center. Information about the use of asbestos as protective wrapping of piping and fireproofing aboard ship can also be authenticated.

By appending this unimpeachable evidence to his claim, to deny the claim the VA has to prove that such an event did not happen and that nearly three months' exposure to high concentrations of asbestos particles was not sufficient to cause the veteran's disability. This claim is very winnable and is a good example of what doing your homework beforehand and taking charge mean.

Special Military Archive Searches

HERBICIDE EXPOSURE RECORDS

Morning Report If you are trying to establish proof of an assignment in which exposure to herbicide agents is alleged, copies of the unit morning report should be requested if you served in Vietnam prior to 1974. Any change in a person's duty status is recorded in the daily morning report, including temporary duty assignments, school assignments, changes in occupational specialty, hospitalization, and departing or returning from leave status. Each day through 1974, military personnel, regardless of branch of service, were accounted for by means of the morning report. Subsequent reporting of these data was on personal data cards (PDC5). Both forms of information are in the custody of the NPRC.

Unit Historical Records, 1939–1954 Military Unit Operational Records between 1939 and 1954 and between 1954 and the present for units that served in Southeast Asia are located in Archives II Textual Reference Branch, National Archive and Records Administration, 8601 Adelphi Road, College Park, MD 20740-6001.

Unit Historical Records 1954 to Present Unit Operational Records from 1954 to the present for units that did not serve in Southeast Asia and Organizational History Files 1955 through 1979 are located in the Freedom of Information Act and Privacy Division, Hoffman Building I, Room 1146, 2461 Eisenhower Avenue, Alexandria, VA 22331-0301.

Organizational History Files 1980 to Present The organizational history of a military unit is available through the U.S. Army Center of Military History, 103 Third Avenue, Ft. McNair, DC 20319-5058. Unofficial material such as unit histories, personal papers, diaries, and photographs including certain select official papers can be obtained from the U.S. Army Institute of Heraldry, 9325 Gunston Road, Room S-112, Fort Belvoir, VA 22060-5579.

RADIATION EXPOSURE RECORDS

A copy of service personnel records confirming unit of assignment, location and dates of assignment, military service number, and military occupational specialty when exposed to radiation is necessary to initiate a search of radiation exposure records. Another source of supportive evidence confirming the same information found in service records is the unit morning report.

OUTPATIENT MEDICAL RECORDS

Copies of outpatient medical records should be obtained as a possible source of evidence of radiation exposure. Copies can be requested by submitting an SF-180 to the NPRC (MPR), 9600 Page Avenue, St. Louis, MO 63132-5100. Send a separate request for each record group as various archival departments are involved.

DEFENSE SPECIAL WEAPONS AGENCY

The Defense Special Weapons Agency (DSWA), formerly the Defense Nuclear Agency, manages the Nuclear Test Personnel Review (NTPR) program for the Department of Defense. Through the NTPR program, veterans may learn the details of their individual participation and their radiation doses, obtain documentation about the tests, and learn their organization's mission in atmospheric testing or occupational duty.

This agency has extensive archival records about various Army, Air Force, Navy, and Marine Corps organizations' participation in U.S. atmospheric tests conducted from 1945 to 1962. The agency has identified nearly 210,000 individuals who were participants in atmospheric testing. DSWA has also identified another 195,000 individuals who were members of occupational forces of Hiroshima and Nagasaki, Japan. Another key function of this agency is to collect and analyze sources of recorded dosimetry and radiation data. DSWA will provide calculated doses in cases where recorded doses are unavailable or incomplete.

All requests for documents establishing proof of participation
in a foreign government's nuclear tests must state that the request
deals with non-U.S. test participation. Proof of participation can
be obtained from the following Department of Defense sources:

U.S. Air Force
Commander, Nonflight Duties
Department of the Air Force
Armstrong Laboratory
AL/OEBS, Bldg. 140
Brooks AFB, TX 78235-5500
210-536-2378

U.S. Air Force
HQAFTAC/ICO
Flight Missions
1030 South Highway A1A
Patrick AFB, FL 32925-3002
407-494-6867

U.S. Army
Chief, U.S. Army Ionizing Radiation Dosimetry Center
Attn: AMXTM-SR-D
PO Box 14063
Lexington, KY 40512-4063
606-293-3646

U.S. Coast Guard
Commandant (G-KSE)
U.S. Coast Guard
2100 2nd Street SW
Washington, DC 20593
202-267-1368

U.S. Navy and U.S. Marine Corps
Officer in Charge

Naval Dosimetry Center
Navy Environmental Health Center Detachment
Bethesda, MD 20889-5614
301-295-5426

IONIZING RADIATION RECORDS

Morning Report If you are trying to establish proof of an assignment in which exposure to ionizing radiation is alleged, copies of the unit morning report should be requested from the NPRC (MPR).

Unit Historical Records 1939–1954 Military Unit Operational Records between 1939 and 1954 and between 1954 and the present for units that served in Southeast Asia are located at Archives II Textual Reference Branch, National Archive and Records Administration, 8601 Adelphi Road, College Park, MD 20740-6001.

Unit Historical Records 1954 to Present Unit Operational Records from 1954 to the present for units that did not serve in Southeast Asia and Organizational History Files from 1955 through 1979 are located at the Freedom of Information Act and Privacy Division, Hoffman Building I, Room 1146, 2461 Eisenhower Avenue, Alexandria, VA 22331-0301.

Organizational History Files 1980 to Present The organizational history of all branches of military service is available through the Army Center of Military History, 103 Third Avenue, Ft. McNair, DC 20319-5058.

Unofficial Unit Records Unofficial material such as unit histories, personal papers, diaries, and photographs, including certain select official papers, can be obtained from the U.S. Army Institute of Heraldry, 9325 Gunston Road, Room S-112, Fort Belvoir, VA 22060-5579.

EXPOSURE TO RADIATION DOCUMENTS

Each branch of service maintains a record of occupational radiation exposure. If your request for a copy of DD-1141, Record of

Occupational Exposure to Ionizing Radiation, from the NPRC is not fruitful, follow up with a request to the appropriate branch of service. The following identifying data must be included in your request for a copy of DD-1141: name, current address and telephone number, Social Security number, VA claim number if one is assigned from a previous claim, service number, period of service, date and place of birth, and nature of your disability. The addresses for the branches of service are as follows:

U.S. Air Force
Department of the Air Force
USAF Occupational Health Laboratory (AFSC)
Brooks AFB, TX 78235-5501

U.S. Army
Chief, U.S. Army Ionizing Radiation Dosimetry Center
Attn: AMXTM-CE-DCR
Lexington, KY 40511-5102
606-239-3249

U.S. Coast Guard
Commandant
U.S. Coast Guard
Attn: Mr. James Veazey
2100 2nd Street SW
Washington, DC 20593-0001

U.S. Navy and U.S. Marine Corps
Officer in Charge
Naval Dosimetry Center
Navy Environmental Health Center
Bethesda, MD 20889-5614
301-295-5426

OFFICE OF HUMAN RADIATION EXPERIMENTS
The Office of Human Radiation Experiments (OHRE) is a function assigned to the secretary for Environment, Safety and Health under the Department of Energy. This office has located, identified, and uncovered nearly four thousand human radiation experiments by the federal government between 1944 and 1974.

Direct your inquires to
Department of Energy-OHRE (EH-8)
1000 Independence Avenue SW
Washington, DC 20585
202-586-8800

Sources of Evidence: Witnesses

Sworn statements from you, family, friends, and former "buddies" are hard evidence that the VA must consider and weigh during the adjudication process. A statement from a third party (lay evidence) when properly executed is very important in the adjudication process. It is just as important as service medical records, postservice doctor's assessments, or any other form of evidence for building a well-grounded claim.

Until the United States Court of Appeals for Veterans Claims became a reality on October 16, 1989, such statements, for all practical purposes, were worthless. In most cases the VA adjudicators simply ignored sworn statements and in others they refused to explain why a sworn statement was not relevant and supportive of the veteran's claim. It can be safely assumed that the VA considered these statements as self-serving and of questionable veracity. However, the court, in deciding *Caluza v. Brown*, 7 Vet. App. 498 (1995), again narrowed the powers of the VA in deciding issues involving lay evidence. The decision reminded the VA that 38 U.S.C.A. §5107(a) states, "Truthfulness of evidence is presumed in determining whether a veteran's claim is well-grounded."

In 1991, the court decided several more similar cases in favor of the veteran. In *Hamlets v. Derwinski*, 1 Vet. App. 164 (1991), the court stated that the BVA *must* explain why it did not accept the credibility of the appellant's personal sworn testimony as evidence. *Cartright v. Derwinski*, 2 Vet. App. 24 (1991) followed this decision in December 1991, stating "the Secretary cannot ignore the appellant's testimony simply because the appellant is an interested party." The decision went on to point out that the VA *cannot* treat a veteran's sworn statement only as part of his contention; "[I]t must account for and explain its reasons for rejecting the testimony."

WAYS TO SEARCH FOR WITNESSES
Finding people is no longer an impossible task, especially if you have certain basic facts. To get started you need minimum background information about the individual such as complete name, where they were from, military unit you were both assigned to, rank, and military specialty. The more personal information you have about an individual, the quicker your search will turn up your witness. In today's world you have at your disposal many different government archives, the Internet, veterans organizations, and commercial research businesses that for a price will find anyone. Finding a witness is no longer an impossible task, even if fifty years have passed since your last meeting.

Computer Search for Friends and Buddies
The Internet is an excellent place to start your search for a former friend or relative. Almost all public libraries make computers available to their patrons. Three separate search services can be used: bulletin boards, the Web, and newsgroups.

Some bulletin boards are specifically dedicated to veterans and military such as Prodigy, America Online, and MSN. To access these bulletin boards, you must pay a monthly fee for service from one of these providers. Regarding Internet newsgroups, several sites can be used to locate individuals:

- sci.military.naval
- sci.military.moderated
- soc.veterans
- soc.history.war.world-II
- soc.history.war.vietnam

Another valuable source on the Internet is search engines. These search services make available more than two hundred million telephone numbers and addresses. Many services supply the individual's e-mail address as well. There is no charge for the use of these search engines. The primary search engines are:

- Yahoo's People Search (http://www.yahoo.com)
- Excite's People Finder (http://www.excite.com)
- Big Yellow's Find People (http://wp.bigyellow.com)
- Google (http://www.google.com/advancecLsearch)
- WhoWhere? (http://www.whowhere.com)
- Anywho (http://www.anywho.com)
- Netscape's People (http://www.netscape.com; click on White Pages in header)

In addition, commercial services on the Internet specialize in locating individuals for a fee. One such service (http://www.1800ussearch.com) uses the Social Security number to provide all current and past addresses for the past seven to ten years. In addition to providing telephone number, date of birth, any known aliases, name variations, and state and year this Social Security number was issued, this service responds within 24 hours by e-mail or fax. The cost is $40 per name, and $12 to $100 for various other searches.

If you kept a copy of all orders issued throughout your service period, you might have a source of vital information that will help you locate a former comrade. You will have a complete name and either a service number or Social Security number to start your search.

Government Agencies

U.S. Air Force The Air Force provides a locator service only for officers and airmen on active duty, retirees, reservists, and guardsmen. Other former members of the Air Force or Army Air Corps must be researched using alternate methods. To use this locator service, write Air Force Worldwide Locator, AFPC/ MSIMDL, 550 C Street West, Suite 50, Randolph AFB, TX 78150-4752. You can speak to a live person at 210-565-2660. The Air Force will not release the location of someone stationed overseas or in a sensitive position. However, it will forward a letter to the individual if the correct postage is on the envelope and any required fee has been paid.

U.S. Army The Army's policy concerning the release of the last known address of former Army members is strictly prohibited by the Privacy Act of 1974. However, it will assist your search by forwarding your letter to the service member's last known address. To use this service, follow these steps:

1. Place your letter in a sealed, stamped envelope and write your return address in the upper left corner.

2. Write a letter to the NPRC requesting its assistance and provide as much of the following information as possible: the veteran's full name, serial number and/or Social Security number, and date of birth.

3. Place your sealed envelope to the veteran and the letter to the NPRC in a second envelope and mail to National Personnel Records Center, 9700 Page Avenue, St. Louis, MO 63132-5100.

U.S. Marine Corps The Marine Corps does not offer a formal way of contacting former marines. However, it does provide three alternatives. The Corps publishes a monthly magazine entitled *Leatherneck* that offers a special service for locating former marine buddies. Your locator request is similar to the personal columns found in most daily newspapers. At a minimum, the information should include the veteran's full name, the unit you both served in, how long you were assigned together, a reason for trying to locate him, and your complete return address.

The second contact method is a website known as "Lost Buddies" (http://www.vetfriends.com). Here you can post a message on the Web requesting the location of a former marine. As you read through the messages by other marines, you quickly get the drift of how to look for a lost friend.

The third method available to you is the Marine Guest Book at http://www.thefew.com. A search engine is built into the Web page so you can search for a former buddy by last name.

U.S. Navy Like the Air Force, the Navy has two separate programs, one for individuals on active duty and another for those who have retired. Family members, active duty personnel, and retirees may use the Navy's World Wide Locator. To do so, you need the service member's full name, Social Security number, grade, or rank, and, if possible, last known duty station. Address your letter to World Wide Locator, Bureau of Naval Personnel, Per-312, 5700 Integrity Drive, Millington, TN 38053-3120.

When trying to locate a Navy retiree through the World Wide Locator, follow the same four steps outlined under the section on the U.S. Army but send your letter to the address given in the preceding paragraph.

Department of Veterans Affairs You may be able to locate a former comrade using the VA. The first step is to call the local regional office servicing your state at 1-800-827-1000 to determine if the veteran is in its database. If so, the VARO will likely have a valid address for the individual. The telephone counselor will instruct you in the proper way to prepare the letter you wish to have forwarded on your behalf. The method used when working through the VA is similar to that outlined above for the remailing service offered by the U.S. Army. In this case, you address your cover letter to the local regional office asking that it forward your unaddressed letter to the veteran. Again, being able to provide a service number or Social Security number will increase your chances of a successful contact.

Department of State A source often overlooked in a search for a former friend is the U.S. Department of State. Many former service personnel reside in foreign countries after leaving the military. An American citizen residing in a foreign country must register with the U.S. Embassy or Consulate. U.S. embassies and consulates help locate U.S. citizens overseas for relatives or friends. The Department of State estimates that it handles over two hundred thousand such requests each year.

Persons in the United States inquiring about the whereabouts of a citizen abroad may contact the Department of State, Overseas Citizens Services, by phone at 1-202-647-5225. If you wish to write for assistance in locating a former service member residing overseas, address your letter to Overseas Citizens Services, U.S. Department of State, 2201 C Street NW, Washington, DC 20520. In your letter or conversation with a representative of the Department of State, tell them you need to locate your friend so he can provide testimony that will have a positive effect on the outcome of a claim pending before the VA.

Newspapers and Magazines

Newspaper Classifieds This is an excellent method to use if your former comrade was from a large metropolitan area such as New York, St. Louis, San Francisco, Los Angeles, Detroit, Chicago, Houston, or Dallas. Each of these cities has more than one daily paper. Obtain the name of the paper, mailing address, and phone numbers through your local library's reference department. Placing a short message in the classified personal section may lead to a contact. The ad should be brief and contain just enough basic information so the individual would recognize that he is being sought.

If you are trying to locate an individual who is still on active duty, place a classified ad in any one of the service newspapers.

The Times Publishing Company publishes four special weekly editions of its newspaper, one for each branch of service: the *Army Times*, *Air Force Times*, *Navy Times*, and *Marine Corps Times*. The *Stars and Stripes*, a 130-year-old newspaper, is published overseas for American military personnel stationed outside the continental United States; the domestic edition is dedicated to veterans of all wars. The *Stars and Stripes* is an excellent newspaper means of locating individuals stationed overseas or veterans in the United States.

To contact these newspapers, write to the following addresses:

Army Times Publishing Company, Inc.
Classified Department
6883 Commercial Drive
Springfield, VA 22159
703-750-8915
http://www.atpco.com

Stars & Stripes
Business Office
PO Box 187
Thurmont, MD 21788
http://www.estripes.com

Here is an example of how such an ad might read:

Looking for Henry B. Wall, a former marine Sgt. from VFM 126, aboard the USS *George Washington* between April 1, 1990, and August 3, 1994. Urgent! Please reply to: John Paul Jones, Box 2210, Shreveport, LA 37802-2210.

You might want to rent a mailbox through the post office or a private business to forestall annoying mail predators who load you with uninvited junk offers. This way you can throw away all the junk mail at the post office and your actual address will be protected.

Magazines Monthly and bimonthly magazines published by the various service organizations may offer a better opportunity to reach a former service person if you have no idea where he may reside. On the other hand, newspaper classifieds are an excellent search tool for locating someone if you have a general idea of where to look.

Veterans service organizations have millions of members who receive their monthly magazine as part of their membership package. Many of these same organizations have their own website and offer various online services to both members and nonmembers.

Dozens of monthly or bimonthly magazines are dedicated to veterans and active duty personnel. Most associations formed during the 1970s, 1980s, and 1990s, as well as those whose roots go back before the turn of the twentieth century, publish their own organizational magazine for the benefit of their membership. The service organization magazines are too numerous for all to be included here. Here are just a few of the organizations whose memberships reach into the millions:

American Legion Magazine
Advertising Editor Assistance
PO Box 1055
Indianapolis, IN 46206
http://www.legion.org/publicationslpubs_mag_index.htm
317-630-1200

V.F.W. Magazine
Advertising Editor
Veterans of Foreign Wars Building
406 West 34th Street, Suite 219
Kansas City, MO 64111
http://www.vfw.org
816-756-3390

DVA Magazine
PO Box 14301
Cincinnati, OH 45250-030 1
http://www.dav.org

NCOA Journal
Noncommissioned Officers Association
1065 IH 35N
San Antonio, TX 78233
http://www.ncoausa.org
1-800-662-2620

Editor
Military Officer Association of America
201 N. Washington Street
Alexandria, VA 22314
703-683-1480
http://www.moaa.org
http://www.moaa.org/Locator/Default.asp

Naval Affairs
Attn: Editor
Fleet Reserve Association
125 N. West Street
Alexandria, VA 223 14-2754
http://www.fra.org

Leatherneck
Mail Call Editor
PO Box 1775
Quantico, VA 22134
http:/www.mca-marines. org/Leatherneck/lneck.html

Air Force Magazine
Air Force Association
1501 Lee Highway
Arlington, VA 22209-1198
703-247-5800
http://www.afa.org/magazinelmagz.html

Miscellaneous Sources
In tracking a former service member, include state or local government agencies in your search plan. Most states will provide a current address based on a registered driver's license. The more information you provide, the better your chances of receiving helpful information.

Your likelihood of success increases if the individual does not have a common name such as Smith, Jones, Brown, or Green. Can you imagine how many Smiths live in New York State? Try to provide the agency with the individual's full name, approximate location of residence, age, and sex. For example, if you knew that your buddy entered the service from Westbury, Long Island, New York, send the initial request to the Department of Motor Vehicles, Empire State Plaza, Albany, NY 12228. Your letter should provide his or her full name, age, gender, and the city, town, or county he lived in before entering the service.

You can find the correct mailing address and telephone number of the auto licensing agency in your public library's reference department. As most states charge a small fee for this service, call first for the costs and the information they will need.

Several books provide some practical insight as to where to start looking for a lost friend or family member and how to go about it.

- *How to Locate Anyone Who Is or Has Been in the Military: Armed Forces Locator Guide* (8th ed.), by Richard S. Johnson and Debra Johnson Knox. (Spartanburg, SC: Military Information Enterprises, 1999.)

◆ *Find Anyone Fast: By Phone, Fax, Mail and Computer*,
    by Richard S. Johnson and Debra Johnson Knox.
    (Spartanburg, SC: Military Information Enterprises, 2001.)
◆ *How to Find Almost Anyone, Anywhere*, by Norma Mott
    Tillman. (Nashville, TN: Rutledge Hill Press, 1995.)

Consult your local librarian for other titles that would assist
you in your efforts to locate a former buddy.

Sources of Evidence: National Archives

Most people never need to use the services offered by NARA. Yet
it is one of the most valuable sources of obtaining primary and
secondary evidence to support a claim for compensation benefits.
The secret is to know what information to ask for and where to
address your inquiry.

In most cases, large agencies such as the Department of Defense store their historical records first by branch of service, then
subdivided by various commands, headquarters, and organizational
units. NARA has two primary storage facilities and twelve regional
centers. Most military information is stored in one of three locations: National Archives I, 700 Pennsylvania Avenue NW, Washington, DC 20408, and National Archives II located at 8601 Adelphi
Road, College Park, MD 20740-6001. The third primary location
of interest to veterans is the National Personnel Records Center,
9700 Page Avenue, St. Louis, MO 63132-5100. Personnel service
records, outpatient health records, and military hospital records are
stored at this facility.

Information from the NARA could help you obtain compensation benefits when there are no primary records or documents to
support your claim. A case can be built using secondary sources of
evidence so that the doctrine of reasonable doubt is triggered in
your favor. Background facts of our imaginary case are as follows:
You injured your back and hip in March 1974 when you fell off the
wing of a KC 135 aircraft you were working on while stationed at

MacDill Air Force Base (AFB), Tampa, Florida. The hospital records could not be located and your outpatient records are silent as to any back or hip problem.

By obtaining a copy of the morning report for your unit for the period you were hospitalized, you can establish that you were in fact hospitalized. The morning report will not explain why you were in the hospital, only that you were a patient. Next, you will need to get a copy of the Line of Duty Investigation initiated to investigate the incident. This investigative report shows that your injury was in the line of duty and that you did indeed fall off the wing of an airplane. Next, you want to support this information with a sworn statement from a friend who was with you when you were injured and who visited you several times during your hospitalization. A nurse told Airman Blackburn the extent of your injuries. You located your friend through the NPRC in St. Louis. Your letter was forwarded to him at the address he gave when being discharged. Airman Blackburn, now Mr. Ronald Blackburn of Tampa, Florida, furnished you with a sworn affidavit. You also prepared a sworn statement detailing the events of the injury, your hospitalization, symptoms you experienced, when they started, and all postservice medical treatment for your back and hip.

The final step involves showing continuity of treatment for the injury to your hip and back. Give your orthopedic specialist a copy of all the evidence and a copy of rating schedule 38 CFR §4.71(a)(5250) and (5293). Request that your doctor write a detailed medical assessment based on the material you gave him. In assessing your current level of disability, your doctor also noted that your condition is common for injuries that occurred many years ago. He should further state that according to the VA rating standards outline in 38 CFR Part 4, your hip injury is 70 percent disabling and your back injury is 60 percent disabling.

The VA would be hard pressed to deny this claim because to rebut your evidence it must have substantial evidence to the contrary. All it would have is its own unsubstantiated opinions. A claim carefully crafted like this, even though all the evidence is of a secondary nature, has everything in its favor.

I am not saying that the local regional office might grant benefits based on a first-time review of the evidence and facts. You have to remember that the individual reviewing the claim is not medically trained to comprehend the complexities of any given illness or injury or to apply the concepts of law the case is being based on. Furthermore, the rating-board member will devote no more than an hour to your claim. He or she will not spend time researching medical issues he or she knows very little or nothing about, will not review the file in its entirety, page by page, or spend time trying to decipher scribbled medical information written by some VA doctor.

You put together a well-grounded claim that will eventually win. If you are satisfied that your claim is based on facts and that the evidence you based the claim on supports your contentions, *never, never back off and quit in frustration. Appeal! Appeal! Appeal!* Sooner or later your claim will reach a level where an individual is capable of adjudicating it based on the laws and medical facts.

Sworn Statement by the Claimant

[Note: The following examples are repeated from chapter five, but they are important enough to your claim to bear repeating.]

When filing an original claim or a claim for increased benefits, amending an original claim, or reopening a previously denied claim, a sworn statement by the claimant should be part of the package. Nowhere in statutes, regulations, or manuals does it state that the VA will ask for a narrative statement detailing the circumstances and limitations imposed by your disability. Yet the records provide only limited facts.

Medical records and service records provide very little insight as to the actual circumstances surrounding the events responsible for the injury or disease. The records will not provide a clear picture of the everpresent pain and limitations imposed by the injury or disease. The records the VA will work with will not reveal how the current medical problem affects your ability to earn a livable wage, why your employment was terminated, or that you had to quit your job because you could no longer function in the workplace.

The problem is further complicated by the fact that the VA maintains a nationwide adjudication force of employees who may have no more than a high school education and yet decide complex medical and legal issues. They receive no extensive training in injury or disease medicine so as to properly comprehend the complexities of reported medical problems, nor are they provided with formal legal training to enable them to apply the concepts of law created by decisions of the court.

With the VA using single-signature rating by individuals with no formal medical or legal training, you cannot afford to be casual and assuming. You need to submit a claim that is well documented so that if the benefits are denied at the local regional office level and you are forced to appeal, your benefits will eventually be granted.

Until a major change takes place in the adjudication process, background information reported by a physician evaluating your medical condition will be treated as hearsay evidence and dismissed as unsubstantiated. The VA justifies the exclusion of your physician's remarks on the assumption the doctor has no factual knowledge of the event and is only reporting what you said. However, with the introduction of sworn testimony as evidence, the VA must now evaluate and weigh these affidavits with all the other evidence and facts related to the claim; it cannot dismiss them as not factual.

EXAMPLE OF CLAIMANT'S SWORN STATEMENT

There is no set format in which to initiate a sworn statement. The sworn testimony should be in narrative form and typed. The statement should be brief and the language carefully chosen. Base your information only on pertinent facts of the issue under consideration. Your statement should be sworn and signed before a notary public.

I must caution you that a lay statement will not carry the weight of a factual opinion concerning a medical issue. Only competent medical personnel can make statements of a factual basis regarding a medical problem.

The following illustration is offered as a guide in organizing your declaration. The contents of your declaration will depend primarily upon the facts you wish to have considered as evidence. This format is very workable and when properly executed is a valuable document.

Declaration of John Paul Jones

1. My name is John Paul Jones. I reside at 1421 Riverside Drive, Chicago, IL 60616.

2. I enlisted in the U.S. Navy in October 1952 and served honorably until I was medically discharged on April 20, 1954, for anxiety reaction and moderate chronic depression. When separated, I was given disability severance pay in the amount of $7,600.

3. After my separation I returned to the Chicago, area where I was treated at VAMC Hines Mental Health Clinic for approximately three years. The treatment consisted of one-on-one therapy sessions with a psychiatrist. I have tried for several years to retrieve copies of my clinic file for the period of 1969 to 1970, to no avail. I've been promised several times by the hospital records department that the records would be obtained from storage, copied, and forwarded to me. To date this has not happened.

4. I received additional treatment from VAMC Hines Mental Health Clinic on an irregular basis for chronic anxiety with depression from 1982 through 1990.

5. After my medical discharge in April 1954, I have been un-

able to develop a stable work history. With the exception of one job that lasted three years, the longest I worked for any one employer was one year. In a majority of the cases the reason I was terminated was that I could not get along with other employees or deal with the public without having response of sudden anger at the slightest provocation. I have not been able to work for the past five years.

6. I'm unable to concentrate, at times to the degree that people start looking at me when I do not respond to them appropriately. I often have a deep feeling of guilt, and in many cases I am unable to determine why I feel guilty. I sleep very poorly and wake up many times during the night. I often lie awake for hours with the feeling that something terrible is going to happen. I have lost more than forty pounds since leaving the service.

7. On September 1, 1996, I was granted social security disability benefits for anxiety and depression.

8. I declare under the penalty of perjury that the above statement is true and correct to the best of my knowledge.

Date
Signature of John Paul Jones
Notary Seal and Certification Here

Sworn Statement by Spouse, Family, and Friends

A spouse, immediate family, or close friends of a veteran can provide valuable support for a claim supported by a sworn statement. The same rules that apply to the veteran also apply to spouses, family, or friends; for example, they cannot say, "I know that John P. Jones has a severe anxiety condition." Court decisions back up regulations and manuals in declaring that a layperson is not qualified to give evidence pertaining to a medical condition. However, they can give evidence as to what they observed and the circumstances at the time the observation were made.

EXAMPLE OF A SWORN STATEMENT BY A SPOUSE
The following is a suggested format for a spouse, family member, or friend who will give a sworn statement. Again the same basic rules previously discussed apply in preparing the declaration.

Declaration of Patty Ann Jones

Now comes Patty Ann Jones, being duly sworn, and states as follows:

1. My name is Patty Ann Jones. I am the wife of John Paul Jones. I reside with my husband at 1421 Riverside Drive, Chicago, IL 20616.

2. I have known my husband since January 1971 and married him two years later on June 2, 1973. I have been with my husband every day since 1971 and have observed the effect of his disability on a daily basis.

3. During the past twenty-five years John has had fifteen jobs, which never last more than a year. He has not been employed for the past five years. Several of the jobs he quit; the only explanation he offered was he couldn't get along with the boss. But the majority of times he was terminated because he was disruptive in the workplace and at odds with other employees. He has no close personal friends and will not go out and join in local social events.

4. John has been taking Xanax and Zoloft for several years for anxiety and depression and has been in and out of therapy at VAMC Hines Mental Health Clinic for the past several years.

5. Although he has never been abusive to me physically or verbally, he has flared into a rage when provoked by neighbors or strangers.

6. During the past five years he often was very depressed and

slept twelve to fifteen hours a day.

Also during these periods he said that he would be better off if he were dead. Once I could get him back to the mental health clinic, they would readjust his medication and his condition would improve.

7. John is always expressing thoughts that reflect fear and hopelessness. He has not shown any interest in participating in hobbies or attending public events; he seems to withdraw from any contact with other people and invents all kinds of excuses for why he must stay away.

8. John was granted social security disability benefits about a year ago. His award letter stated that the benefits were granted on the basis of severe chronic anxiety and depression.

9. I declare under penalty of perjury that the above is correct to the best of my knowledge.

Date
Signature of Patty Ann Jones
Notary Seal and Certification Here

Sworn Statement by Employer

A sworn statement from an employer or former employer can influence the rating process. Compensation benefits are supposed to be determined by the degree the disability reduces your capability to be gainfully employed. Unfortunately, obtaining statements from some supervisors or employers may prove very difficult. An employer or former employer may be reluctant to provide a statement of reasons for the veteran's termination. For example, if the veteran had a severe psychological problem the employer may fear for his own and his employees' wellbeing. An employer who terminates a veteran for physical disabilities risks being sued under the Americans with Disabilities Act. You should be willing to give your former employer a release against any lawsuits and in no way present yourself as a danger to him. In many cases a third party such as a spouse, family member, or friends will be able to negotiate on your behalf.

EXAMPLE OF A SWORN STATEMENT BY EMPLOYER

The following will provide some guidance in preparing a sworn declaration by a former employer.

Declaration of Henry R. Smith

Now comes Henry R. Smith, being duly sworn, and states as follows:

1. My name is Henry R. Smith and I reside at 5151 Lake Front Circle, Apartment 1121, Chicago, IL 60631.

2. I am the owner of Smith Tool and Die Company, located at 304 Orange Street, Complex D, Chicago, IL 60611. My company subcontracts to many manufacturers for special machine parts for their products.

3. I hired John Paul Jones on June 1, 1991, as a metal lathe operator at a starting salary of $15 per hour. Approximately six months after I hired him his work performance began to change. He had several verbal arguments with another machinist whom I had employed for many years. I counseled him on his workplace behavior. Mr. Jones's attitude with other workers improved but the quality of his performance was poor.

4. Mr. Jones was terminated on May 10, 1992, due to an incident that nearly cost him his left hand. Mr. Jones failed to properly install a clamping chuck for the item he was going to make on the lathe. As a result, his sleeve became snagged by the piece of metal that was about to be turned. His left arm was jerked into the rotating piece of metal stock. Fortunately another worker saw the incident and immediately pushed the emergency shutdown button. This saved Mr. Jones's arm from being severed.

5. I subsequently learned that the VA mental health clinic had put Mr. Jones on Xanax and Zoloft. Both of these medications indicate that patients should not operate machinery.

6. I had no option but to terminate Mr. Jones, for his protection and the protection of my other employees.

7. I declare under the penalty of perjury that the above statement is true and correct to the best of my knowledge.

Date

Signature of Henry R. Smith

Notary Seal and Certification Here

Sworn Statement by Former Comrades

Letters from former comrades, or buddy letters, are a very valuable source of testimonial evidence in establishing the factual background of an injury or disease. This is especially true when the injury or disease was neither recorded by a medical corpsman nor entered into the claimant's medical file at the time of the incident. In the past, buddy letters were not seriously considered as evidence. The statements were treated as a lie or not having credibility.

I worked a case of a former POW in which all the surviving members of a B-17 bomber attested that the veteran received injuries to his ears as a result of a high altitude bailout when the aircraft was destroyed by flak. Even though the veteran had a severe cold and blocked sinuses, the flight surgeon had refused to ground him. The squadron was ordered to put up a maximum effort and because there were no spare waist gunners, the claimant had no choice but to fly the mission. His buddies all testified that a German doctor treated the veteran for his ear condition. He was told that he had ruptured his eardrums. The crew's statements were not accepted as evidence of his hearing loss because available service medical records were silent as to any hearing problems. The veteran was eventually granted service connection for his hearing loss upon appeal. However, it took five years for the appeal to work its way through the system.

The local regional office had no evidence to contradict the sworn statements of the veteran or his crew other than its own unsubstantiated opinion. As previously stated, a rating board must specifically state what evidence it has that rebuts the sworn statements by the veteran or others. Rating boards must accept sworn statements as credible evidence and must give the evidence equal weight with all the other evidence of record.

Formerly, locating former members of your military unit who had factual information concerning your injury or disease was almost an impossible task. However, beginning in the late 1980s and early 1990s, locating people was no longer an impossible task. Success still depends a great deal on how much you remember about the individual. Thanks to giant advances in storing and retrieving personnel data, locating people is much easier.

At your disposal now are nationwide phone directories; letters forwarded to former buddies by several government agencies; online computer searches through bulletin boards; placement of notices in many of the veterans service organization monthly magazines or publications; reunions held by military organizations; and personal ads in newspapers where the veteran may have resided after leaving the service. Plus, within the past few years many small businesses have surfaced that will find a person for a nominal fee.

EXAMPLE OF A SWORN BUDDY LETTER

Declaration of Ronald Blackburn
Now comes Ronald Blackburn, being duly sworn, and states as follows:
1. My name is Ronald Blackburn and I reside at 4551 Swan Avenue, Tampa, FL 33603.
2. I served with Sergeant Henry Miller at MacDill Air Force Base, Tampa, FL, between July 1, 1970, and June 30, 1974. We were both assigned to the 301st Air Refueling Wing's maintenance squadron. Sergeant Miller was discharged in June 1974, and I retired from the Air Force on August 31, 1995, as a Chief Master Sergeant E-9.

3. We were both performing inspections on the upper surface of the left wing of a KC-135 when Sergeant Miller slipped and slid off the leading edge of the wing. When I looked over the edge of the wing, he was lying on his back. He fell approximately twelve feet before striking the cement ramp. The accident happened in early March 1974. The line chief sergeant immediately sounded the alarm for medical care and the base hospital dispatched an ambulance. I recall that Sergeant Miller was hospitalized for nearly two weeks.

4. I visited him several times while he was hospitalized. I was told by the duty nurse during the first visit that although he did not break any bones he did injure his hip and lower back quite seriously. For more than a week they had him heavily sedated because of the pain.

5. When Sergeant Miller was released from the hospital, he was assigned to limited duty status until his discharge on June 30, 1974. He performed no duties that involved lifting or twisting. He was assigned to work in the squadron orderly room running errands for the sergeant major and commander.

6. I declare under the penalty of perjury that the above statement is true and correct to the best of my knowledge.

Date
Signature of Ronald Blackburn
Notary Seal and Certification Here

Chapter Ten Highlights

Knowing what the VA will require in the way of evidence is an absolute must if you expect to submit a winning claim. You cannot protect your interest in the decision-making process if you do not know what the regulations dictate. You cannot win if you are unable to submit a claim that is supported by evidence. You cannot win if you do not know how to collect this evidence. You cannot win if you do not know why the VA denies valid claims. You cannot win if you assume the VA is an all-knowing agency and that you can rely upon its skills to adjudicate the facts of the case accurately and fairly.

What do the regulations say about your claim before benefits can be granted? To answer that question you need to obtain a copy of pertinent sections of 38 CFR Parts 3 and 4. The CFR is available online and in local law libraries, VARO reading rooms, and university libraries designated as federal depositories.

Always keep in mind you have the burden of submitting a well-grounded claim. Equally important is your responsibility to satisfy the four basic elements of a claim for compensation benefits.

First, you must prove you were in the service. Second, you must demonstrate that an injury or illness did in fact occur while you were on active duty. Third, if the claim is not filed within one year after leaving the service or the medical condition is not universally accepted as being medically chronic, evidence must be introduced of treatment that satisfies the continuity of symptomatology rule. Fourth, the medical condition that you are claiming as service related must be active when the claim is filed. Failing to satisfy each of these elements before submitting your claim will result in a denial of benefits.

Proof of Service The VA requires an original Report of Separation (DD-214) or the equivalent. Its regulations allow for the acceptance of a certified copy from the clerk of the court where the original document was recorded. Do not send the VA an original discharge record; always send a certified copy. If you have lost your original Report of Separation, a certified copy can be obtained from the NPRC.

Proof of Service Occurrence Where do you look for this evidence? Start by requesting copies of all your outpatient and personnel records from the NPRC. Remember that inpatient hospital records are not stored with your personnel records. If you were hospitalized, submit a separate request for these documents providing specific information as to the hospital name and location, period of hospitalization, and reason for hospitalization.

Evidence of Treatment When primary evidence cannot be located, you must then focus on building a claim based on secondary evidence. Copies of unit historical records often provide details of unit casualties that can substantiate a combat-related injury. Unit morning reports or PDCs will provide duty status for any given day. If you were hospitalized, the records will show the period of hospitalization but not why you were hospitalized. An official line of duty investigation is an excellent way to substantiate an injury.

If you were one of the service personnel used as human guinea pigs for the purpose of determining effects of biological agents, exposure to radiation, or various types of mind-controlling drugs, you can request records from government agencies under the provisions of the Freedom of Information Act. The number of individuals who never realized they were unwilling participants in these tests is probably in the thousands. If you were one of them and you can prove it, you could be entitled to compensation benefits for the health problems created by the tests.

The VA must accept and treat sworn statements as it would any other form of evidence. A sworn statement from a former comrade is an excellent form of secondary evidence. The statement should reflect only observations, not unsubstantiated opinions. Your friend cannot give a medical opinion because he is not a physician. However, he can describe the observable symptoms and how they were affecting you.

As the claimant, you should always give a sworn statement. Detail all the events leading up to the injury or illness, how the illness has affected you, and what you cannot do now that you could do before you became disabled. A sworn statement should be straightforward and follow the examples above. Your goal is to get pertinent information into the record that would not normally be included.

You are now ready to file a claim for a service-related disability, ask for an increase in benefits, amend a claim to include additional service disabilities, reopen a previously denied claim, or claim that your medical condition is considerably worse following treatment by a VA medical staff member. Once you've completed the appropriate form for the type of claim being filed, the next step is to organize all the evidence pertinent to the claim in a logical sequence.

Try to think of this process as if you were a Pre-Determination Team member. In what order would you look at all the supporting documents and evidence to decide the merits of the claim and what action to take next? Remember these people cannot and will not spend hours looking through all the evidence to search for confirmation of the facts that are alleged. As I have stated many times throughout this book, your claim will more than likely be reviewed by one individual who has only basic skills in medicine and law. The adjudication process is further complicated by the fact that the person deciding the claim will not have their decision reviewed in detail. If the team member ignores favorable evidence, for whatever reason, no one will perform an in-depth review prior to the decision being finalized to determine if all the facts were considered and properly interpreted.

It has been my experience in the past on many occasions that team members ignore what they do not understand. They then deny the claim based solely on their own unsubstantiated conclusions. If they are not sure, they deny. The message they are sending out is, "If you don't like it, take it up with the BVA. You will get a decision in two or three years." In the meantime, they are easing the backlog of cases.

The organization of your claim must tell the whole story from beginning to end. When you have all this evidence, what do you do with it? Stuff it all in an envelope and send it to the regional office? No! Do not jeopardize all the effort put forth during the development phase by doing this.

You need to stay in control by forcing the VA to focus, in a logical manner, only on the facts supported by the evidence. Do not give the VA a chance to decide what is relevant. Prove that the claim is valid when it is submitted. Make the VA prove that the evidence is not valid and justify the denial of benefits. Always submit a claim knowing that it is grantable and that if it is denied at the local regional office level, it will be reversed on appeal. However, your real goal is to present the case so the adjudicator will be able to connect dots of evidence, like a child connecting dots to draw a picture. You want the benefits granted now, not in five years.

Organizing the Claim

Let me explain what I mean by organizing your claim. You want your evidence to tell a story and you want the adjudicator to follow it to only one conclusion: benefits approved. Sometimes this is easier said than done. The assembly process should allow the evidence to flow in one direction only, proving your entitlement to benefits.

To demonstrate the assembly process, I'll use the following example. A veteran submitted an original claim in 2002 for service connection based on two medical conditions alleged to be service related. One condition is lung cancer and the second condition is a back injury.

The veteran served in the Air Force from 1969 to 1973 and was honorably discharged. The active duty outpatient health records show the veteran was treated for neck pain resulting from a whiplash injury when the jeep he was traveling in rear-ended another vehicle. The LOD of the accident stated that the veteran was a passenger in the jeep and was not at fault for the accident. It also showed that he was taken to the base hospital emergency department for treatment. He was admitted to the base hospital for three days, and the discharge diagnosis was severe cervical sprain resulting from whiplash. The service health records were silent as to any symptoms normally associated with lung cancer. The veteran is not a smoker and, following his discharge, worked in an office as a claims adjuster for an insurance company. He suffered no physical injuries following his discharge.

The veteran married twice after leaving the service. His first marriage took place in 1977 and ended in a divorce two years later. In 1980 he remarried, and two children were born of this union—a son in 1983 and a daughter in 1987. The veteran was never assigned a Permanent Change of Station to Vietnam. However, he was placed on temporary duty (TDY) on three occasions for a total of twelve weeks during his enlistment. As a photo intelligence interpreter he was assigned to DaNang AFB, Cam Ranh Bay AFB, and Nha Trang AFB to support three special military intelligence operations. This is everything we know about the veteran.

A table of exhibits should be the first appended enclosure following the formal claim application. This table is very important because it outlines the evidence and sequence of events pertinent to your claim. The format is quite simple.

A Statement in Support of Claim (E-8 and E-15) tells the VA what is being claimed and why. There is no specific format. It should be brief and to the point and typed. It is best if the statement is made using VA form 21-4138.

In our hypothetical claim, the veteran injured his neck in a jeep accident. The accident happened in 1972, a year before he was discharged, and the claim was not filed until 1998, twenty-five years after he left the Air Force. The veteran needs to protect himself against a premature VA conclusion that the active duty

TABLE OF EXHIBITS

injury resulted in no permanent disability and that the cause of the current problem occurred after leaving the service.

Because of the twenty-six-year lapse between the time of the injury and the filing of the claim, the veteran must show continuity of treatment. The veteran's statement focuses VA attention on the evidence concerning this injury:

> In 1972 I was a passenger in a jeep that rear-ended another army vehicle. I was hospitalized at McCord AFB for three days and was under outpatient care until my discharge. Following my release from the hospital, I was given a permanent physical profile change restricting my duties to administrative tasks only. I have been treated for chronic pain and limited motion of my neck for nearly twenty-five years.

Each exhibit number should be prominently displayed on the lower left corner of each page. If there is more than one page for the exhibit, identification should be expressed in this format: E-10, page 5 of 35. It is very important to place your Social Security number in the lower right corner of every page.

> My wife of eighteen years has provided a sworn affidavit that during our marriage I was never injured or in an accident that would cause the medical problems I have endured. I am no longer able to work because of this injury and my lung cancer. My orthopedic specialist states that the neck injury is old and that the type of accident I was involved in is typical of the type of cervical spine problems currently diagnosed.

The Statement in Support of Claim concerning lung cancer should address several points concerning lung cancer resulting from exposure to Agent Orange. This is one of the disabilities that are presumed to be service related if they have manifested to a degree of 10 percent disability within thirty years from date of exposure. Here again the statement should be brief and to the point.

Between 1970 and 1972 I was placed on TDY status to the Republic of Vietnam to support special military exercise for a total of three months. I file this claim under the provisions of 38 CFR §3.309(e) as amended on May 8, 2001, for presumptive service connection for respiratory cancer. My evidence includes copies of orders that placed me TDY in Vietnam and my oncologist's medical assessment stating that I am currently being treated for lung cancer.

Assembly Process

By preparing a table of exhibits, you present your case in an orderly manner and force the VA to focus only on the key issues involved. You minimize the danger that vital evidence will be overlooked. Arrange the evidence by date, starting with the earliest record and advancing to the most recent record. This is especially important when medical treatment records are a major part of the evidentiary package. If you are claiming more than one disability, this sequence should be repeated for each disability being claimed.

With medical records, review each page and highlight those sections that specifically support your claim. Look for and highlight every relevant diagnosis you find in your records. One reason this step is important is that it can establish chronicity or continuity of treatment. Remove from the copies of medical records any treatment records that are not directly related to the conditions being claimed. You do not want to provide them with any information other than what will support your claim.

Submitting the Claim

Before you submit the claim application, look over all VA forms, making certain only those items applicable to your claim are answered. If VA form 21-4138, Statement in Support of Claim, is handwritten, make certain it is readable. When completing a formal application, remember to write "N/A" for all those item numbers and sections not requiring a written response. Answer all required questions accurately and completely.

With this task completed, have your entire application photocopied. You will always need to back up any information you provide the VA. If you are able to hand-deliver the application to the regional office, do so. Have the contact office representative who accepts your claim application package date-stamp your copy of each document and form. Among the millions of documents and files circulated within the VA, records and evidence get lost every day. Without proof that you actually submitted a claim or submitted evidence, the burden is on you to prove you filed a well-grounded claim and that you submitted supporting evidence.

When a claim is unable to be delivered directly to the VARO, the only alternative is to send the application and all supporting evidence by certified mail with return receipt requested. Before taking your complete claim package to be copied, obtain and complete Postal Service form 3811 (Domestic Return Receipt) and Postal Service form 3800 (Receipt for Certified Mail). Write the number found on the Receipt for Certified Mail form on the upper right-hand corner of each page of your claim package. Record this number in box 4a on the Domestic Return Receipt form as well. Now have copies made of the entire package.

The post office will date-stamp form 3800, affix the lower portion to the envelope with your claim, and give you the top portion with the date stamped on it. When the Domestic Return Receipt is returned, you will have a copy of the original Postal Service forms 3800 and 3811 dated and signed, a copy of your complete claim package with the certified mail number on each page, and the Receipt for Certified Mail date-stamped by the post office. You now have absolute proof that the VA accepted your claim package in its entirety. If a claim or any evidence is lost, the VA has the burden of proving that it did not lose your documents. This little procedure could save you thousands of dollars that might be lost if you cannot positively show when you submitted your claim.

The last step before mailing or hand-carrying your claim to the local regional office is to make sure the claim forms and all evidence will remain together. The VA secures all hardcopy forms and evidence in claim folders with a two-prong fastener located on the top of the file cover. Using a two-hole punch, centered, punch holes at the top of each form and document. Secure the claim with all its supporting evidence with a two-prong metal fastener. They can be purchased in any office supply store.

Chapter 11 Highlights

Although this is one of the shortest chapters in the book, it is by no means unimportant. Actually, how you put your claim together and the method used in filing the claim will have a direct bearing on the outcome. The VA is *not user friendly* and will not spend hours reviewing every document to ensure that you receive all benefits due. The law says it is supposed to, but do not count on it doing so.

The VA is always looking for ways to disallow a claim for not being "well grounded." This is why you should organize all your evidence and provide a table of exhibits so that you can lead the VA to a favorable decision. You cannot take shortcuts and hope the VA either won't notice a missing link of evidence or will sort through everything to grant benefits. Remember, it is up to you to prove the claim is well grounded.

The assembly of your claim and all its supporting evidence must follow a logical path. Each piece of evidence must link to the next and so on. For each disability claimed, I suggest preparing a Statement in Support of Claim (VA form 21-4138) as illustrated above. It is important that you tell the VA what you are claiming and even the authority under which the claim should be granted. By making the VA look specifically at that one authority, it must, if denying your claim, explain exactly why your contentions and evidence do not qualify.

Once you're ready to send in your claim, take the time to properly identify every piece of paper that is attached to the claim. If you hand-deliver your claim to the regional office and the clerk will not date-stamp every page of your copy, *do not leave the claim.* Mail the claim and documentation by certified mail with return receipt requested, using the technique discussed in this chapter. It is no exaggeration to say that the VA loses documents, forms, statements, and evidence every day. Don't let them be yours.

The claimant's understanding of the VA's duty to assist is as important to the success of the claim action as submitting a well-grounded claim. Knowing what the VA must do and what it will not do is essential. In preparing a claim you cannot assume the evidence is sufficient or that the VA will develop all relevant facts before the issue is decided. You must know exactly what is involved in the adjudication process before the rating board is permitted to decide the case. The Department of Veterans Affairs published a summary of significant holdings by the United States Court of Appeals for Veterans Claims for the benefit of all adjudication personnel. This case law has had significant impact on the adjudication of claims for veterans' benefits. By the end of 1995, the Veterans Benefits Administration had reviewed more than 7,500 court decisions and prepared nearly seven hundred decision assessment documents. The results of this effort have brought about recommendations for more than one hundred changes to VA regulations, policies, or procedures. Yet despite all this guidance, we see very little change in the number of claims being granted without being forced into the appeal process.

What the VA Must Do to Satisfy Its Duty to Assist

Although the VA has a statutory obligation to assist a claimant in developing facts pertinent to a well-grounded claim (38 U.S.C. §5107(a)), a limited duty exists even when a claim is not well grounded. The denial letter must inform the claimant what evidence is required to make the claim well grounded. The claimant then has one year to get this evidence and submit it to the VA. If the denial letter does not clearly indicate what evidence is needed to establish a well-grounded claim, file a Notice of Disagreement citing *Robinette v. Brown*, 8 Vet. App. 69 (1995). The notice to the VA can be quite simple: "Your letter of denial has failed to comply with the precedent-setting ruling of the court in *Robinette v. Brown*, 8 Vet. App. 69 (1995). I was not advised exactly what evidence was required in order to satisfy the requirements of a well-grounded claim."

By law, the VA's duty to assist includes requesting any information from other federal departments or agencies that may be needed to determine eligibility and entitlement or to verify evidence (*38 U.S.C. §5106*). Federal regulation 38 CFR §3.159 requires adjudication personnel to request other records such as hospital reports or copies of doctor's records when a release is provided.

Case Law: Defining "Duty to Assist"

Duty to assist obligations generally involve development of all relevant facts from all identified sources, both government and civilian (including lay evidence). The VA must request all historical medical records in service-connected disability claims. In addition, Social Security Administration (SSA) records must be obtained to consider claims for increase, individual unemployability, and disability pension. The VA is also obliged to obtain and consider SSA records when there is evidence that they may be relevant to a finding of service connection. The court found in *Lind v. Principi*, 3 Vet. App. 493 (1992) that the VA should have developed SSA records to consider presumptive service connection for multiple sclerosis because there was a possibility that the documents might show onset of the disease within the presumptive period.

In fulfilling its duty to assist, the court ruled in *Douglas v. Derwinski*, 2 Vet. App. 435 (1992) the VA must consider all issues.

By this, they meant issues inferred from a liberal reading of an appeal and the evidence. An issue may not be ignored or rejected merely because the veteran did not expressly raise the appropriate legal provision for the benefit sought. In *Douglas v. Derwinski* the court concluded that evidence implicating military sun exposure as a cause of basal cell carcinoma raised a well-grounded claim for direct service connection even though the appellant's contention focused on ionizing radiation instead.

When the claimant references or describes specific private medical records, VA medical records, or other records he believes may be relevant, the duty to assist requires the VA to attempt to obtain the records cited without prejudging their relevance. A good example would be obtaining vocational rehabilitation counseling and evaluation records because they may contain relevant information regarding the degree of employability.

If a veteran tries to reopen a denied claim, the VA must develop the facts pertinent to the issue being sought, even though the evidence may ultimately prove insufficient to reopen the claim when it is finally decided. The court ruled in *Ivey v. Derwinski*, 2 Vet. App. 320 (1992) that complete development is required if there is some legal or factual basis for potential allowance.

The duty to assist is heightened when there is no opportunity for personal contact (such as in the case of incarcerated veterans) or when complete service medical records are not available (such as with POW records or the service records destroyed by the 1973 fire at the NPRC). This diligent effort to obtain records is required when the records are in the control of a government agency or when only official copies of records from government sources would be reliable or relevant. This special effort must also be made when searching for records associated with disabilities incurred or aggravated in combat.

The affirmative duty of the VA to assist is also triggered when a veteran appears before a local VA hearing officer. These officers *must* explain the issues to the veteran and suggest what evidence is needed to support the claim. A hearing officer is required to request all evidence that is alleged to exist that might support the veteran's claim. The court held in *Weggenmann v. Brown*, 5 Vet. App. 281 (1993) that while VA regulations provide that a claimant may request a physical examination during a hearing, an official reexamination is required only if the prior examination was inadequate.

There is a duty to assist any time a potential claim for possible benefits exists. The VA is obliged to inform the claimants about the application requirements for unclaimed benefits if there is a potential claim. An example would be if during a records review the VA discovered the veteran suffered a serious acoustic trauma while in the service. The potential for establishing a service-connected hearing loss is possible; therefore, the VA must inform the individual of the right to file for this disability.

In *Connolly v. Derwinski*, 1 Vet. App. 566 (1991), the duty to assist was further clarified. The court held that the VA must respond to a specific request for assistance by initiating appropriate development or by explaining why the requested assistance has been denied. If a veteran does not wish to undergo further VA examination, the VA must explain the importance of the examination that was ordered so that the veteran may make an informed decision.

The VA has often failed in its duty to assist claimants when it requests the veteran be scheduled for a C&P Examination at a VA hospital or clinic. In *Hayes v. Brown*, 5 Vet. App. 60 (1993), the court held that the duty to assist is not met when a prescribed duty is overlooked, such as if a VA physician fails to render a required medical opinion, by completing a thorough and contemporaneous examination, or the VA fails to develop pertinent medical evidence despite a specific request. More generally, the VA's access to necessary information, efforts to obtain relevant information, and the claimant's cooperation are all factors for determining whether or not the VA has fulfilled its obligations in a particular case.

VA medical examinations have been mandated by the court based on duty-to-assist considerations when there is evidence of a significant change in a veteran's condition affecting pension entitlement.

- A thorough and contemporaneous examination, including review of prior medical treatment records, may resolve diagnostic questions pertinent to service connection.
- Medical records are received after an examination that may have been pertinent to the examiner's findings.
- An opinion concerning possible medical relationships between past and present disorders may be relevant to a finding of service connection.
- Verification of current disability is necessary in order to establish service connection.
- Increased disability is claimed and the record does not adequately show the current level of impairment due to service-connected disability.
- A prior VA examination was inadequate.
- A VA examiner recommends supplemental or specialist examinations.
- A plausible claim for service connection is filed within an applicable presumptive period even though a prior claim during that period for the same condition was finally denied.
- In a service-connected death case, an advisory medical opinion is required in lieu of VA examination, when necessary to resolve medical questions pertinent to service connection.

The VA's Duty to Assist Is Limited

The duty to assist is not unlimited. The VA has no duty to assist unqualified applicants or develop inherently incredible (not well-grounded) allegations. The extent of VA assistance may be limited if the claimant fails to notify the VA of all relevant records or fails to cooperate with the VA during the development process.

In *Owings v. Brown*, 8 Vet. App. 17 (1995), the court held in regards to notification requirements that the VA is not re-quired to notify former recipients of Dependency and Indemnity Compensation benefits who lost their status as surviving spouse because of changes in the law regarding DIC benefits. Along with that, a similar 1994 decision, *Harvey v. Brown*, 6 Vet. App. 416 (1994), affirmed that the VA's duty to assist does not include an obligation, prior to discharge from active duty, to assist in preparing a claim for certain education benefits that the veteran indicated to the VA that he wanted to take.

The duty of the VA to search for documents is limited to those that have been specifically identified and which by their description would be relevant and material to the claim. The VA has stated that its policy is to consider the merits of each claim as fully and as expeditiously as possible. However, all adjudication personnel have been advised that because of the potential probative value of records, they should not be prejudged.

The duty to assist ends when all relevant evidence has been obtained or cannot be obtained despite reasonable efforts, or when benefits are granted. While the VA must consider evidence that can confirm entitlement, there is no duty-to-assist requirement to develop additional records when entitlement can be established on the evidence of record.

Chapter 12 Highlights

The court has issued numerous decisions regarding the duty to assist. Not only have these decisions been very specific with respect to defining "duty to assist," but they also have been interpreted very liberally to benefit the claimant. It is important to remember these points any time a claim action is filed:

- A claim must documented to the point the VA believes it is possible before duty to assist kicks in.
- If the claim is denied as not well grounded, the VA must indicate what evidence is needed to qualify the claim. The claim remains open for one year from the date of notification.
- If another federal department or agency has evidence that is pertinent to the claim, the VA is required by law to contact this source and retrieve this information if it has been duly notified of its existence.
- The duty to assist means the VA must develop all relevant facts from all identified sources, both government and civilian, including lay evidence.
- The VA must request all historical medical records in service-connected disability claims.
- Social security records *must* be developed in considering claims for increased benefits, individual unemployability, and disability pension, or when the claimant is receiving social security benefits for the same disability for which VA benefits are being claimed.
- The VA may not ignore or reject a claim merely because the veteran did not correctly raise the appropriate legal provision for the benefit sought.
- The VA must completely develop a claim if there is some legal or factual basis for possible benefits.
- When searching for records related to disabilities incurred or aggravated in combat, the VA must make a special effort.
- If the VA loses the records, the claimant is a POW, or the fire at the NPRC destroyed the records, the duty to assist is heightened.
- If the claimant appears before a VA hearing officer, the duty to assist is triggered, requiring the hearing officer to

explain the issues and suggest the evidence necessary to support the claim.

♦   The VA must respond to a specific request for assistance by initiating appropriate development or explaining in writing why the request is being denied.

♦   The duty to assist is not met if the VA overlooks a pre-scribed duty, for example, when it accepts a VA medical examination for which the doctor did not comply with the *Physician's Guide for Disability*.

13 | DOCTRINE OF REASONABLE DOUBT

The last statement added to every rating decision by the rating board is a certification that the Doctrine of Reasonable Doubt was considered in deciding the issues of the claim. This is without a doubt one of the most important concepts written into the law governing veterans benefits. Failure of a rating board to correctly apply this provision of the law when rating a claim is grounds for remand or reversal on appeal. A claimant or advocate needs to understand this concept to ensure that benefits justified are benefits granted.

The most common statement I've seen on rating decisions denying entitlement is "Granting of the benefits sought due to reasonable doubt under 38 CFR § 3.102 was considered but the rating board concluded that the *fair preponderance of evidence* [emphasis added] was not in the veteran's favor and the rule had no application." Yet this statement as written is not in compliance with the guidance and definition provided by the court in *Gilbert v. Derwinski*, 1 Vet. App. 49 (1990).

The court stated that when, after consideration of all evidence and material of record, in cases before the Department of Veterans Affairs, there is an approximate balance of positive and negative evidence regarding the merits of an issue material to the determination of the matter, the benefit of doubt in resolving each such issue shall be given to the claimant. Therefore, a veteran need only demonstrate that there is an "approximate balance of positive and negative evidence" in order to prevail; entitlement need not be established beyond a reasonable doubt, or by clear and convincing evidence, or by a reasonable doubt, or by a fair preponderance of evidence.

The court further stated that the secretary agreed at oral arguments that the preponderance of the evidence must be against the claim for benefits to be denied. Unless the evidence offered by the VA is more compelling, the veteran must be granted benefits.

It's obvious that the rating board did not grasp this concept when they rated the claim from which I gave the quote. The VA has to show a preponderance of evidence against the claim. The guidance from the court in *Gilbert v. Derwinski* provided a definition for "approximate balance of positive and negative evidence." Simply, the phrase means evidence that does not satisfactorily prove or disprove the claim; there is one other requirement for a rating board when it denies a claim. It must explain exactly what evidence tipped the scales against the claim. It cannot simply say, "Granting of the benefits sought due to reasonable doubt under 38 CFR §3.102 was considered, but the rating board concluded that the fair preponderance of the evidence was not in the veteran's favor and the rule had no application." If your claim is denied and the only reference to the Doctrine of Reasonable Doubt is ambiguous, appeal the denial. The law requires the VA to give detailed reasons and bases for any action it takes.

Case Law: Defining the Concept

Numerous cases in which it has been alleged that the VA has failed to adhere to the Doctrine of Reasonable Doubt have been before the United States Court of Appeals for Veterans Claims. In addition, the BVA remanded or reversed local regional offices seventy-eight times during 1994 and 1995 on this very issue. Regional offices have considerable difficulty understanding the doctrine. It would be an understatement to say that if every veteran were knowledgeable of this doctrine when the claim was submitted and decided, the VA would be overwhelmed with appeals. A veteran who files a well-documented claim needs to know what the VA must prove by way of negative evidence before it can deny the application for benefits.

GILBERT V. DERWINSKI, 1 VET. APP. 49 (1990)

The Gilbert decision was a landmark case decided by the court because it considered three statutory provisions of the law. The court addressed the following issues: when it could set aside a BVA finding of material fact as clearly erroneous; the intent of giving the veteran the benefit of the doubt as written into the law; and whether the VA was in compliance with the statute when it failed to provide a written statement of the reasons or bases for its factual findings and conclusions of law.

Mr. Gilbert filed a claim for service connection alleging an in-service back injury of which he was currently suffering the residuals. The BVA upheld the denial of his claim, finding that he had not demonstrated that any back injury occurred during military service and that even if such an injury had occurred it was "apparently acute and transitory in nature and resolved without leaving any residual disability." The BVA then concluded that in view of this finding he was not entitled to the benefit of the doubt.

On review the court found that the BVA decision did not include an analysis of the credibility or probative value of the evidence submitted by and on behalf of the veteran in support of the claim. The BVA failed to provide any explanation for the bare conclusion that "the Board (BVA) does not find that the doctrine of reasonable doubt would warrant allowance of the benefit sought on appeal." The court concluded that the decision failed to comply with 38 U.S.C. §4004(d)(1) (1988) (now §7104(d)(2)), which requires that a written statement of reasons or bases for its factual findings and conclusions of law be provided to the veteran. Thus the court remanded the case to the BVA with instruction to comply with the law.

WILLIS V. DERWINSKI, 1 VET. APP. 63 (1990)

The Willis case is another example of the VA denying benefits in spite of considering the Doctrine of Reasonable Doubt in which there was no evidence in which to grant benefits under the doctrine. In actuality, the BVA ignored the principles of the doctrine by failing to provide reasons or bases for its conclusion that the veteran was not entitled to the benefits of the doctrine.

Mr. Willis filed a claim to establish schizophrenia as a service-connected disability based on the argument that his nervous condition was misdiagnosed on active duty. Six months after filing his claim Mr. Willis was examined by the VA and found to be suffering from chronic paranoid schizophrenia. He was reexamined six months later and the medical diagnosis was the same. Fifteen months after he filed his original claim, the VA notified him that his claim file, VA examinations, and service medical records had been lost and could not be located. Three months later he received a letter of denial stating that his claim for a nervous condition had been denied ten years earlier. The letter went on to say, "It must be assumed that service connection for a nervous condition was disallowed in 1979 and that you were informed of this decision."

When the case finally made its way to the United States Court of Veterans Appeals it was remanded back to the BVA. The court noted "Given the loss of the veteran's service medical records (the "contemporaneous medical record") and his claims file by the VA, this statement [VA doctors report] serves only to state the obvious; it does not refute the evidence in favor of the claim. . . . His [VA doctor's] conclusion that the veteran's psychosis was misdiagnosed by the Air Force as a personality disorder, if not refuted, would appear to establish the veteran's claim." In its remand order the court ruled the VA failed to articulate "reasons or bases" for the apparent dismissal of evidence of record favorable to the veteran, and the "reasons or bases" for its conclusion the veteran was not entitled to the benefit of doubt under 38 U.S.C. §5107 (b).

O'HARE V. DERWINSKI, 1 VET. APP. 365 (1991)

O'Hare is an example of an original claim denied by the local regional office and affirmed by the BVA that involved records destroyed in the 1973 fire at the National Personnel Records Center, St. Louis, Missouri. Mr. O'Hare filed a claim for chronic right knee disability that he alleges happened in the service. The injury occurred during a hike in the snow at Ft. Sheridan between November 1944 and February 1945. Mr. O'Hare maintains that he sought medical care for this injury at the base hospital and that he has been treated for this impairment throughout the past forty-five years. In support of his claim, the veteran submitted letters from his private physician and his two sisters. His doctor described "persistent problems with pain in the right hip and knee . . . [that] required local physical therapy, anti-inflammatories and joint injections . . . [and bother the appellant] on a fairly regular basis." His sisters stated that "when the veteran went into the army he had no leg problems and when he came out he had hurt his leg and thigh, went to doctors the last forty-five years [and] takes pain pills."

The court held that the BVA decision did not meet the requirements of 38 U.S.C. §4004(d)(1) (1988) [now 38 U.S.C. §7104(d)(1) (1992)] in that the BVA's findings and conclusions are not accompanied by reasons or bases adequate to explain both to the veteran and the court its factual findings and its conclusions, including identifying those findings it deems crucial to its decision and accounting for the evidence which it finds to be persuasive or unpersuasive. The BVA decision here fails to meet this prescription in two important respects.

First, the decision fails to include an analysis of the credibility or probative value of the evidence submitted by or on behalf of the veteran in support of his claim. The BVA made no express credibility determinations regarding the statements of either the veteran or his sister, or the letter from his physician. Such determinations are required.

Second, the reason or basis requirement of 38 U.S.C. §4004(d)(1) [now §7104(d)(l)] applies to the BVA's conclusion that the veteran is not entitled to the "benefit of doubt" under 38 U.S.C. §3007(b) [now §5107(b)]. Here the BVA decision treats the benefit-of-the-doubt standard in only the most cursory terms.

"The doctrine of reasonable doubt has been considered, but the evidence is not found to be so evenly balanced as to warrant allowance of the claim. *That is not enough* [emphasis added]."

"This [the Doctrine of Reasonable Doubt] is especially so significant in a case where the service medical records are presumed destroyed; in such a case, the BVA's obligation to explain its findings and conclusions and to consider carefully the benefit-of-the-doubt rule is heightened."

FLUHARTY V. DERWINSKI 2 VET. APP. 409 (1992)

In Fluharty's case, the VA failed to consider the Doctrine of Reasonable Doubt as it applies to a reopened claim for a total disability rating due to individual unemployability. Mr. Fluharty served eighteen months in the U.S. Army before he was given a medical discharge for a fractured right ankle in 1963. During his enlistment he injured his lower back and right thumb.

The VA initially granted the veteran a 40 percent rating for the residual of his injured right ankle and 0 percent for his fractured thumb. In 1980, his lower back injury was granted service connection and 20 percent disability rating. A claim for individual unemployability was filed in 1980 and subsequently denied.

Mr. Fluharty applied for increased benefits because of the severity of his back condition and was awarded 40 percent in 1985. Two years later the VA granted service connection for a right knee condition and rated it 10 percent disabling and gave a zero percent rating for sexual impotence due to a loss of a creative organ. He now had a combined disability rating of 70 percent.

In 1988, the veteran filed an action to reopen his claim for total disability due to individual unemployability and for an increased rating for all service-connected disabilities. Mr. Fluharty had not worked since his medical discharge in 1963. When his claim for increased benefits was denied in late 1988, the veteran filed a Notice of Disagreement and initiated the appeal process. He was called in for two VA examinations while his appeal was under consideration.

The orthopedic physician diagnosed a fractured right ankle with fibrotic ankylosis and severe arthritis of the right ankle. This report also pointed out that the "Patient is unable to work. He has a stiff right ankle and it is a severe disability. He will not improve in the future. He is not employable. There is no treatment that would improve his condition. [I] recommend that the patient have a total disability." The other VA examiner stated the appellant's unemployability was a combination of both his service-connected and non-service-connected disabilities. His report stated, "This patient has multiple medical problems along with low back pain and right leg pain. He also suffers from significant depression. He has angina and uses six to eight nitroglycerine tablets every week. When I see him at the office, he has a hard time walking from the waiting room to my examining room. He is unable to get on and off the examining table. I consider him totally disabled."

The BVA upheld the local regional office denial of benefits in April 1990. The veteran filed a timely appeal to the United States Court of Appeals for Veterans Claims.

The case was decided two years later on May 18, 1992, by a three-judge panel. The court vacated the denial of benefits based on individual unemployability and remanded the case to the BVA. The court made these points when it sided with the veteran:

- Total disability rating "will be considered to exist when there is present any impairment of mind or body which is sufficient to render it impossible for the average person to follow a substantially gainful occupation."

- The appellant has a combined disability rating of 70 percent from December 17, 1985, plus special monthly compensation under 38 U.S.C. §1114(k), for the loss of a creative organ.

- The BVA voiced an opinion that the appellant cannot do "physically demanding" work, supporting its previous finding that he was capable of performing sedentary employment such as "light manual labor." Although the BVA has voiced an opinion as to whether the appellant is employable, it has not provided reasons or bases in support of its finding that the appellant is employable. The records show the appellant appears periodically in a wheelchair.

- The fact that the appellant has only a sixth or seventh grade education would severely limit the type of manual labor that he could perform.

- The BVA, although it mentioned the non-service-connected disabilities in its discussion, failed to set forth reasons why it was "not persuaded" that the appellant was unemployable based solely on his service-connected injuries.

- The record shows that the appellant has no employment history after leaving the service. Realistically, if he was discharged as being permanently disabled by an ankle injury, the reason for the discharge was that the army had no employment for him, even "light manual labor."

- The BVA further erred by failing to address the different medical opinions expressed as to the appellant's unemployability. In assessing the appellant's unemployability, the BVA may be unable to determine whether the appellant's unemployability is caused by his non-service-connected disabilities or by his service-connected disabilities. If that is the case, then the evidence may be so evenly balanced that the doctrine of the benefit of the doubt found in 38 U.S.C. §5107(b) may apply.

TOWNSEND V. DERWINSKI, I VET. APP. 408 (1991)

In deciding *Townsend*, the court remanded the case to the BVA with instructions to specify the medical authority or medical evidence of record used to conclude that Mr. Townsend's foot condition was not aggravated while in the service. The remand order also directed the BVA to provide reasons or bases to explain why it denied the claim and instructed it to consider the Doctrine of Reasonable Doubt.

Mr. Townsend was discharged from the U.S. Army in 1970, having completed three years of active service including a combat tour in Vietnam. His entrance medical examination was silent as to any physical abnormalities of his feet. However, while in basic training he was treated for pain of the right foot. The examining physician noted in his record that the patient had "flat feet" and a navicular bar in his right foot. The record also mentioned that the patient reported minimal trouble with his right foot before entering the Army. The doctor stated that Mr. Townsend was not qualified for service and should be separated. However, the patient stated he wanted to stay in the service. He was allowed to continue in basic training and upon graduation was given a permanent medical profile that would eliminate any activity that involved crawling, stepping, running, jumping, prolonged standing, or marching. Despite a diagnosis of severe *pes planus* (flat feet) and a limited-duty profile, he was assigned to combat duty in Vietnam. His right foot condition was further aggravated by long periods of standing and heavy lifting duties. He was treated throughout his tour for foot pain. The separation medical examination report noted "pes planus severe—see health record."

A claim was filed by the veteran for his right foot condition in 1983 and was subsequently denied by the local VARO. The letter of denial acknowledged that the entrance examination had not found anything wrong with his right foot and that when discharged he was suffering from severe pes planus. They justified the denial of benefits based on an assumption: "By generally accepted medical principles, pes planus [is] held to have preexisted service and [was] not aggravated thereby." Unfortunately, Mr. Townsend did not appeal this decision within one year of being notified of being denied benefits.

In 1989, the veteran tried to reopen his claim for a right flat foot condition. Again, the VARO denied his action to obtain benefits. This time Mr. Townsend did file an appeal within the one-year time frame. His case was heard in early 1990 by the BVA and denied. The BVA held that "A review of the evidence of record reveals that, there having been no timely appeal, the originating agency's determination of March 1983 became final and in the absence of error, that determination is not subject to revision on the same factual basis." The BVA concluded that "1. A bilateral disorder was not incurred in or aggravated by service. 2. The originating agency's determination of March 1983 was final; the additional evidence received subsequent to that determination does not present a new factual basis so as to warrant the grant of service connection for a bilateral foot disorder."

The case was appealed to the Court of Veterans Appeals and decided on July 25, 1991. The court reversed the BVA decision and remanded it. The court made these points when it sided with the veteran:

- A preexisting injury or disease will be considered to have been aggravated by active service where there is an increase in disability during such service, unless there is a specific finding that the increase in disability is due to the natural progress of the disease. (38 U.S.C. § 1153 (1994).)
- This provision is interpreted by 38 CFR §3.306(b) (1995):

(b) Wartime service; peacetime service after December 31, 1946. Clear and unmistakable evidence (obvious or manifest) is required to rebut the presumption of aggravation where the pre-service disability underwent an increase in severity during service.

- ◆ When read together, these provisions state that once a claimant's disability increases in severity during service there is a presumption of aggravation (i.e., service connection), unless it can be established by clear and unmistakable evidence that the increase was due to the natural progression of the disease.
- ◆ The records show that the appellant's foot disorder increased in severity during service inclusive of the time of discharge.
- ◆ The BVA decision, without a discussion of the presumption of the way it is rebutted, found that there was no error in the VARO rating decision, which had also ignored the presumption and its rebuttal.
- ◆ The court has consistently ruled that the BVA must apply relevant law (even though 38 CFR §3.306(b) was not raised by the appellant).
- ◆ The BVA apparently relied solely on the "generally acceptable medical principles" rationale given by the VARO when it denied the appellant's claim.
- ◆ The failure of the BVA to cite the medical authority or medical evidence in the record to support this conclusionary statement is not in accordance with the law.
- ◆ The BVA decision did not provide the necessary reasons or bases to explain its action.
- ◆ The BVA failed to consider the Doctrine of Reasonable Doubt in resolving the appellant's claim.

Chapter 13 Highlights

The Court of Appeals for Veterans Claims stated that the Doctrine of Reasonable Doubt is meant to be the easiest standard of proof found anywhere in the American system of jurisprudence. The court has told us that the adoption of this standard is in keeping with the high esteem in which our nation holds those who have served in the Armed Services. It is in recognition of our debt to our veterans that society has through legislation taken upon its self the risk of error when, in determining whether a veteran is entitled to benefits, there is an approximate balance of positive and negative evidence. *"By tradition and by statute, the benefit of doubt belongs to the veteran* [emphasis added]."

It has been more than sixteen years since the court first addressed the issue of reasonable doubt in *Gilbert*. Have veterans benefited from this protection? The answer varies among the different levels of bureaucracy. If a case is before the court, the standard of reasonable doubt definitely is scrutinized and applied. If the case is before the BVA, there is a very good chance that the standard will be applied. The BVA is directly under the oversight of the court, and if an appeal is filed with the court and the standard has not been properly applied, the appeal will be remanded to the BVA. However, this is where application of the standard of reasonable doubt practically ceases. Local VAROs have considerable difficulty correctly applying this concept to a claim action. They always say they considered the Doctrine of Reasonable Doubt but the evidence was not in favor of the veteran's claim. Yet the rating is totally silent as to how they arrived at this decision.

If a claim is denied, first request a copy of the complete rating decision and C&P Examination under the provisions of the Freedom of Information Act. Every report has at least two pages. Most ratings run four or five pages, depending on how many issues are being rated. They also include the rating schedule (code and percentage for each disability). Make certain the rating schedule and signature page are included as part of this report. If the local regional office fails to include these pages or any portion of the rating, contact your representative or senator and request his help in obtaining the missing page or pages. A VARO has no authority to withhold any portion of a requested document; it must provide the complete document.

Second, locate the statement concerning the application of reasonable doubt and determine exactly what evidence was used to deny the claim. A rating decision should be analyzed as follows:

- Did the VA obtain all my service medical records and VA medical records? If you did not provide this medical evidence with your claim, then you must request a complete copy of all the evidence used in considering your claim. Did the VA obtain additional evidence that I requested that would support the claim?
- Did the rating discuss all the favorable evidence filed with the claim?
- Did the VA rate all the disabilities I claimed? If not, did it explain why it failed to do so?
- Did the VA provide complete reasons or a basis for its findings? This includes identifying those findings it deems crucial to its decision and accounting for the evidence it finds persuasive or unpersuasive.
- If differences of medical opinions are expressed as to the issue of service connection, did the VA set forth the reasons why it was not persuaded by the evidence favorable to the claim?
- Did the VA cite its medical authority or medical evidence of record to support any conclusionary statement it may have made in the rating?

The third step is to reread the cases cited as part of this unit, especially *Fluharty* and *Townsend*. Remember, the VA cannot deny a benefit unless it can justify its decision. Now that local VAROs are permitted to use single-signature ratings as an everyday practice, the claimant must challenge every denied decision. Rating specialists have neither legal nor medical training to sufficiently qualify them to adjudicate complex medical and legal issues. Do not make the fatal error of assuming that their decision is just or in accord with the evidence or law.

The final step is to file a Notice of Disagreement. When the VA responds with a Statement of the Case, the appeal process is in the works. You have one year from the date of the VA's original notice of denial to submit your formal appeal. A formal appeal is your argument why benefits should have been granted.

Do not be cheated out of what is justly yours by law. Know the rules and do not give up in frustration. Seek a competent advocate to help you through the appeal process.

One last thought: There are some advocates whose expertise ends at filling out forms. Search for an advocate who is knowledgeable of the VA's duty, can apply the concepts of case law to your case, knows where to find evidence to fight your case, and is able to understand the complexities of your medical problems.

APPENDIX A:

GLOSSARY OF ABBREVIATIONS

Numerals

lB *11-56* Physician's Guide For Disability Evaluation
      Examinations

A

AFB   Air Force Base
AMA   American Medical Association
AMIE   Automated Medical Information Exchange
      System
AOJ   Agency of original jurisdiction, where the
      claim was first adjudicated

B

BIRLS   Beneficiary Identification Records Locator
      Subsystem
BVA   Board of Veterans' Appeals

C

C-number claim file number
CFR   Code of Federal Regulations
CHAMPUS Civilian Health and Medical Program
      of the Uniformed Services
CHAMPVA Civilian Health and Medical Program of the
      Veterans Administration
COVERS Control of Veterans Records System
C&P Exam- Compensation & Pension Examination
ination

| CPI | Claims processing improvement model |
| CSS # | indicates a claim number that uses Social Security number |

D
DIC	Dependency and Indemnity Compensation
DRG	Diagnostic Related Groups
DRO	Decision Review Officer
DSWA	Defense Special Weapons Agency
DVA	Department of Veterans Affairs (See VA)

F
| FOIA | Freedom of Information Act |
| FR | Federal Register |

G
| GAO | General Accounting Office |
| GPO | Government Printing Office |

H
| HMO | Health maintenance organization |

K
| KIABNR | Kill in Action Body Not Recovered |

L
| LOD | Line of Duty Investigation |
| LZ | Landing zone |

M
MAP-D	Modern Award Processing Development
MOD	Medical Officer of the Day
MPR	Military Personnel Records

N

N/A	Not applicable
NARA	National Archives and Records Administration
NPRC	National Personnel Records Center
NTPR	Nuclear Test Personnel Review

O

OGC	Office of the General Counsel
OHRE	Office of Human Radiation Experiments
OMB	Office of Management and Budget
OMPF	Official Military Personnel Files

P

PCS	Permanent change of station
POW	Prisoner of war
PTSD	post-traumatic stress disorder

R

RO	Regional Office

S

SOC	Statement of the Case
SSA	Social Security Administration
SSD	Social Security Disability
SSOC	Supplemental Statement of the Case

T

TDIU	Total Disability Due to Individual Unemploy-ablity
TDY	Temporary duty

U

USAF	U.S. Air Force
U.S.C.	United States Code

U.S.C.A.	United States Code Annotated

V

VA	Department of Veterans Affairs
VACOLS	Veterans Appeals Control and Locator System records
VAH	Veterans Health Administration
VAMC	Department of Veterans Affairs Medical Center
VARO	Department of Veterans Affairs Regional Office
VBA	Veterans Benefits Administration
Vet. App.	Veterans Appeals (United States Court of Appeals for Veterans Claims)
VISN	Veterans Integrated Service Network

W

WWI	World War I
WWII	World War II
WWW	World Wide Web

APPENDIX B:

GLOSSARY OF DEFINITIONS

A

Affidavit   A written statement sworn, before a notary public. When the claimant, family, or friends provide such testimony, the VA must accept the statement as evidence and give it proper weight.

Analogous Rating
                 A rating that is based on a similar condition.

Appeal   A request for a review of an AOJ determination on a claim.

Appellant   An individual who appeals an AOJ claim determination.

Armed Forces   U.S. Army, Navy, Marine Corps, Air Force, and Coast Guard.

B

Board of Veterans Appeals (BVA)
                 The VA department that reviews benefit claim appeals and that issues decisions on those appeals.

Board member   A Law Judge, appointed by the secretary of the Department of Veterans Affairs and approved by the president, who decides veterans benefits appeals.

C

Central office   The director of the Compensation and Pension Service, VA central office, shall approve all VARO determinations establishing or denying POW status with the exception of those service depart-

	ments' findings establishing that detention or internment was by an enemy government or its agents.
Chronicity	Of long duration or recurrence (referring to a health problem).
Claim	A request for veterans benefits.
Claim number	A number assigned by the VA that identifies a person who filed a claim; often called a "C-number."
Claim file	The file containing all documents concerning a veteran's claim or appeal.
Compensable	Entitled to compensation benefits.

Continuity of symptomatology

A history of treatment of a health problem.

Court of Appeals for Veterans Claims

An independent United States administrative court that reviews appeals of BVA decisions.

D

Date of receipt	The date on which a claim, information, or evidence was received in the Department of Veterans Affairs, except as to the specific provisions of the Code of Federal Regulations for claims or evidence received in the State Department, the Social Security Administration, or Department of Defense as to initial claims filed at or prior to separation.
Decision	The final product of the BVA's review of an appeal. Possible actions are to grant or deny the benefit or benefits claimed or to remand them to the AOJ for additional action.
Deposition	A statement sworn before a notary.
Determination	A decision on a claim made at the VARO.
DIC	Compensation benefits granted to a surviving

| | spouse, child, or parent resulting from a veteran's service-related death. |
| Discharge | Separation, including retirement, from the active armed forces. |

E

| Evidence | Fair preponderance of evidence. The evidence must be sufficient to prove that the evidence against the veteran's claim outweighs the evidence offered in support of the claim. |

H

| Hearing | A meeting, similar to an interview, between an appellant and an official from the VA who will decide an appellant's case, during which testimony and other evidence supporting the case is presented. There are two types of personal hearings: regional office hearings (also called local office hearings) and BVA hearings. |
| Hostile force | Any entity other than an enemy or foreign government or the agents of either whose actions are taken to further or enhance anti-American military, political, or economic objectives or views or to attempt to embarrass the United States. Pertains to Prisoners of War. |

I

In the line of duty

Referring to an injury or disease incurred or aggravated during a period of active army, naval, or air service, unless such injury or disease was the result of the veteran's own willful misconduct or, for claims filed after October 31, 1990, was a result of his abuse of alcohol or drugs. A service department finding that injury, disease, or death occurred in the line of duty will be binding on the VA unless it is patently inconsistent with the requirements of laws administered by the VA.

Issue   A benefit sought on a claim or an appeal. For example, if an appeal seeks a decision on three different matters, the appeal is said to contain three issues.

L
Lay evidence   Lay evidence provided by a nonexpert.

Lay person   A person who cannot give expert testimony related to the issue being adjudicated.

M
Marriage   A marriage valid under the law of the place where the parties resided at the time of marriage, or the law of the place where the parties resided when the right to benefits accrued.

N
Non-service-connected   With respect to disability or death, means that such disability was not incurred or aggravated, or that the death did not result from a disability incurred or aggravated, in line of duty in the active military, naval, or air service.

Notice   A written notice sent to a claimant or payee at his latest address of record.

Notice of Disagreement

A written statement expressing dissatisfaction or disagreement with a local VA office's determination on a benefit claim; must be filed within one year of the date of the regional office's decision.

P

Preponderance of evidence

> The VA must demonstrate that its evidence is superior to that which was introduced by the veteran before a claim may be denied.

Presumptive period

> The time frame in which an illness must manifest to a degree of 10 percent.

Prisoner of war   A person who, while serving in the active military, naval, or air service, is forcibly detained or interned in the line of duty by an enemy or foreign government, the agents of either, or a hostile force.

Probative   Referring to evidence that tends to prove a particular issue.

Proximate cause   An event that caused an injury or disease and that would not have occurred without such injury or exposure.

R

Reasonable Doubt

> In a VA claim action, the term implies certainty that must be applied before benefits can be denied. If the evidence pro and con is equal to or nearly equal to, the decision must be in favor of the claimant.

Rebut   To contradict or oppose by formal legal argument

Rebuttal of service incurrence

> Evidence which may be considered in rebuttal of a claim of service incurrence for a disease listed in 38 CFR §3.09. This evidence would refute evidence that the condition was service related.

Regional Office

> A local VA office; there are fifty-eight VA regional

offices throughout the United States and its territories.

Regional Office Hearing

A personal hearing conducted by a VARO hearing officer. A regional office hearing may be conducted in addition to a BVA hearing.

Relevant

Refers to evidence that is pertinent, relative, or connected to the point or target.

Remand

A remand occurs when an original decision is vacated by the BVA and the appeal is returned to the regional office or medical facility where the claim originated.

Residuals

A disability left by a disease or operation.

S

Separation

The discharge or retirement of an individual from the service.

Service connection

With respect to disability or death, means that such disability was incurred or aggravated, or that the death resulted from a disability incurred or aggravated, in line of duty in the active military, naval, or air services.

State

One of the fifty states, territories, and possessions of the United States, the District of Columbia, or commonwealth of Puerto Rico.

Statement of the Case

Prepared by the VARO, a summary of the evidence considered, as well as a listing of the laws and regulations used in deciding a benefit claim. It also provides information on the right to appeal a VARO's decision to the BVA.

Supplemental Statement of the Case

A summary, similar to a Statement of the Case,

that the VA prepares if a VA form 9 contains a new issue or presents new evidence and the benefit is still denied. A Supplemental Statement of the Case will be provided when an appeal is returned (remanded) to the VARO by the BVA for new or additional action.

V

Vacate   To reverse an original decision.

Veterans service organization

An organization that represents the interest of veterans. Most veterans service organizations have specific membership criteria, although membership is not usually required to obtain assistance with benefit claims or appeals.

W

Wartime service The following dates are inclusive for formal periods of war in which a veteran will have been considered as serving during a wartime period: World War I—April 6, 1917–November 2, 1918 (veterans who served in Russia from April 6, 1917 to July 7, 1921, are also considered wartime veterans); World War II—September 16, 1940–December 31, 1946; Korean Conflict—June 27, 1950–January 31, 1955; Vietnam Era—August 5, 1964–May 7, 1975 (those who served as advisors in Vietnam any time between February 28, 1961, and August 4, 1964, are also included); Persian Gulf War—August 2, 1990, to a date yet to be determined. Wartime service also means any time in which combat service was performed between January 1, 1947, and a date yet to be determined. Several examples would be the Berlin Air Lift, Lebanon Crisis, Grenada, Iranian Crisis, and Bosnia.

Willful misconduct

An act involving conscious wrongdoing or known prohibited action (*malum in se* or *malum prohibitum*). A service department finding that injury, disease, or death was not due to misconduct will be binding on the Department of Veterans Affairs unless it is patently inconsistent with the facts and the requirement of laws administered by the Department of Veterans Affairs.

APPENDIX C:

SURVIVAL RULES

Action Rule # 1 There is no claim if it isn't well grounded. The burden of proof is on you to provide sufficient evidence that your injury or illness is more likely than not to have been incurred in the service. Otherwise the VA will deny your claim.

Action Rule # 2 Don't file for compensation benefits unless you have all the evidence. This is especially true if you are filing while on active duty. Instead file an Informal Claim for the benefits. This action protects your date of entitlement up to one year and allows you to do the job right. This technique prevents the VA from prematurely denying benefits because you have not submitted sufficient evidence for them to rate the claim.

Action Rule #3 What do you do if your claim is denied? *Appeal it.* Just because the VA said no it doesn't mean they are right. Complex issues such as PTSD, undiagnosed illnesses, and heart disease, for example, often are denied because the individuals responsible for rating the claim have no experience in law, medicine, or occupational limitation imposed by injuries or illnesses. Another reason for so many errors is the adjudication groups are pressured to clear as many claims as possible or it affects their annual performance pay bonus. If the claim is denied, they get credit for completing a claim action.

Action Rule # 4 Know the rules the VA must follow. It's easy to access their statutes, regulations, manuals, legal opinions, and pertinent case law. If they in any way stray from the golden rule then drop the hammer on them.

259

Action Rule # 5 Take your medical records to a non-VA specialist along with the appropriate VA diagnostic code. It is more likely than not that VA medical evaluation will be performed by a physician's assistant, nurse practitioner, or retired general practitioner. The findings of these marginally qualified medical staff members are another reason why many claims are denied. If this happens to you start yelling "flawed examination" by filing a "Notice of Disagreement" (appeal) immediately. Take someone with you when being examined. Later they can offer a sworn statement as to what kind of questions you were asked, how long the exam lasted, what the medical findings were, whether the examiner follow the proper protocol, and whether he or she had your claim file and reviewed it prior to the exam. One last thing: C&P examiners have been known to tell you one thing and file a report that is entirely different. Remember to yell "flawed" and file a NOD.

Action Rule # 6 Are you claiming a disability based on a combat injury or illness? The VA must accept your explanation if your service records show you have a Combat Infantry Badge, Purple Heart, Bronze Star, or Air Medal with V device along with other awards and decorations. This cuts out all the guesswork on their part. They only have to evaluate the degree of disability based on the medical evidence.

Action Rule # 7 Become a Paper P.I.; learn how to track key evidence to support your claim. Here are several examples of places where evidence may be hiding: after action reports, unit's history, sworn statement from those who were with you, and your sworn statement detailing the events and circumstances.

Action Rule # 8 Look for a qualified advocate if you need assistance. You can measure their worth by how well they know VA regulations, manuals, and case law. You do not want to join up with a service officer who can only fill out VA forms. Ask them how many appeals they have filed and how many cases they have won. Look for the service officer who says "Hell yes! I'll go head to head with the VA."

Action Rule # 9 Read every letter from the VA with great care. Immediately after filing a claim (approximately three months later) the VA will send you a notice titled Expedited Action Attachment. Don't let yourself be forced into allowing them to expedite the processing of your claim. You have one year by law from the date they received your claim to submit all the evidence before they can render a final decision. They may even send you a notice after sixty days saying that they are denying your claim for failure to provide compelling evidence. Don't ever believe them! Respond by sending them a "Notice of Disagreement" stating you have one full year by law to submit the necessary evidence to support your claim.

Action Rule # 10 Join and support service organizations. Always remember you are not a "customer." In VA facilities throughout the country there are signs and banners stating, "We support our veteran customers!!!" American Indians expressed it best by saying, "The big Washington chief speaks with forked tongue." Always remember the White House, OMB, and the Department of Veteran Affairs sees you as nothing more than an expense they wish to keep the lid on. You have paid dearly for these benefits. So, to keep what you are entitled to, join with your fellow veterans and dig in. Hold the line when they want to cut benefits. Make them comply with the laws as provided by the Congress. It would be interesting to know how many of the White House staff, including the executives; how many in the Office of Management and Budget; and how many of the political appointees in the Department of Veterans Affairs have had actual combat experience.

APPENDIX D:

TABLE OF AUTHORITY

STATUTES

REGULATIONS

MANUALS

NOTES

Preface

1. The *Veterans Post* is a monthly newspaper for veterans that has been published in the Tampa Bay area for more then 15 years.
2. On June 24, 2005, the Military Officers Association of America made this information available to its membership via its weekly Internet newsletter.

Chapter 1

1. David N. Gosoroski, "Brotherhood of the Damned," the Veterans of Foreign Wars, September 1997.
2. "The Bonus March (May–July 1932)," American Experience, 89, People and Events Release online by Public Broadcasting System. Undated. www.pbs.org (Search "Bonus March 1932").
3. Brian R. Train, "The Bonus Army of 1932," course material for History 151, University of Massachusetts, undated.
4. William Manchester, *The Glory and the Dream: A Narrative History of America 1932—1972*, Publisher Little Brown, 1973), 9–23.
5. *Section: 1 of 1* Federal Bureau of Investigation Subsection S(c) and Conclusion September 12, 1932 Freedom of Information and Privacy Acts Subject: Bonus March
6. Source quoted is Microsoft online Encarta Dictionary. http://encarta.ms.com
7. On July 13, 2005, from the *Time's* Wire Service, this little bomb

was put out to test the waters. "Plan could push veterans out of state nursing homes. A budget proposal that could push thousands of military veterans out of state nursing homes is causing new worries in light of the recent disclosure shortfalls in Veterans Affairs budget. Bush had proposed restricting the VA's long-term care services to those veterans injured or disabled while on active duty, those with severe disabilities, those in need of care after hospital stay and those requiring hospice or respite care."

8. On August 12, 2005, the VBA issued a press release, picked up by the *St. Petersburg Times*, saying that it intended to review 72,000 PTSD claims. This later focused action on those receiving 70 to 100 percent for PTSD. By downsizing the number receiving 100 percent benefits they could shave nearly a billion dollars off the annual compensation costs.

9. This feat was accomplished by denying any claim for which the claimant could not provide supportive evidence within the sixty-day period as prescribed in the first contact letter.

Chapter 2

1. See Chapter 11 for details on what to do when faced with his problem.

2. See Chapters 12 and 13 for steps to take in preparing an appeal

3. See Chapter 10 for detailed information on how to and where to collect evidence.

4. The veteran appealed the first denial of benefits and his claim was certified to the Board of Veterans Appeals, where it was reviewed and returned to the RO on remand. They "fiddled" some time away with a local hearing then gave the vet sixty days to come up with the magic evidence; otherwise the case will be recertified back to the BVA. So far, the veteran has been in a state of flux for four years and it is conceivable it

could take another two to three years to resolve the issue. If the claim goes back to the BVA, another year will be added to the case history. I plan to attack their decision on several fronts in that they ignored case law, the doctrine of reasonable doubt and evidence that was favorable to the veteran, and that they have no proof that what the veteran swore to was not true.

5. *De Novo* is a legal term meaning a review from the very beginning. The VA states that when a claim is appealed the reviewing officer will go through the entire claim file prior to issuing his judgment.

6. In an effort to standardize correspondence, the VA has many generic letters in which the team member has only to fill in certain information or facts. This method of communicating the final decision to the claimant is an attempt to avoid major legal fights over the semantics of words used.

7. *Disabled American Veterans v. Sec. of Veterans Affairs*, 327 F.3d 1339 (Fed. Cir. 2003) The Federal Circuit held that 38 CFR § 19.9(a)(2) was invalid. 38 CFR § 19.9(a) (2) permitted the BVA to obtain evidence and adjudicate an issue not previously considered by the regional office. The Veteran Benefit Administration, to comply with the *DAV* case, created a separate department called the Appellate Management Team. It performs many of the same functions of a regional office, setting up medical examinations and developing other types of evidence.

8. For those interested in knowing the nitty gritty of each of the terms, search the internet using Google and the key words "M21-1MR sub-part I."

Chapter 3

1. Prior to the passage of *The Veterans Claims Assistance Act of 2000*, a claim had to be considered well-grounded before it could advance to the next level of adjudication.

2. This regulation not only spells out what the VA's duties are, but in the event of denial of benefits, it may also provide grounds for a Clear and Unmistakable Error Appeal because the VA failed to follow the regulation exactly as the law prescribed. Secondly, it is a checklist for the claimant as to exactly what he must provide in order to prevail.

Chapter 4

1. Each of these elements will be discussed and illustrated in Chapter 5.

Chapter 5

1. This boundary marker set by law is not chiseled in stone, and there are exceptions in which the VA can and does deny a claim without fulfilling its duty to assist.
2. Mail from members of Congress or the United States Senate receives special handling within all regional offices. If for some reason the entitlement date comes into dispute the VA must acknowledge any communication from members of Congress as your proof they received the notice of intent.
3. The details of VA regulation 38 CFR §3.307 and §3.309 can be found by logging on to the VA website www.va.gov and clicking on "Compensation," then "Directives," then on the link to part 3. Scroll down to the regulation.
4. See Chapter 9 for details on obtaining records.
5. A document sworn before a notary public is evidence in its own right and must be given equal weight with all other evidence when a claim is being rated.

Chapter 7

1. The other four claims that are most difficult are original, re-

opened, and amended claims, and service connection for treatment by VA medical services.

2. If you have Internet access, visit http://www.index.va.gov/boardofveteransappeals. Link down to 1995. Pick a subject and read the BVA decisions. You may come away wondering if the local ROs know what it means to have a "duty to assist."

Chapter 8

1. To reduce the cost of hospitalization of Medicare patients, the government instituted the concept of DRG. It states that for any known condition there is a theoretical point at which the average patient can be released. Medicare pays the hospital for the maximum number of days the DRG determined for the condition being treated. If the patient stays beyond this point, the hospital cannot bill Medicare or the patient for the additional care. The VA adopted this concept in the late 1980s.

2. However, there have been signs that rating members have been showing more consideration to the facts as they pertain to the veteran's claim.

Chapter 9

1. Visit www.vamalpractice.info/newspaper_articles.htm for the news stories behind the headlines.

2. Exceptions: you are rated by the VA as having a service-connected disability of 50 percent or more; you were discharged or separated from the service with a compensable disability and it has been less than a year since your separation; or you are seeking care from the VA for only a service-connected disability.

3. This manual can be reviewed online at www.va.gov.

4. In *Sklar v. Brown*, the court held that if there is a diagnosis by a specialist and the only evidence against the veteran claim is

a contrary opinion by a nonspecialist, then the findings of the nonspecialist should carry little weight.

5. See *Dusek v. Derwinski*, 2 Vet. App. 519 (1992). In this case it was ruled that the VA properly denied the veteran increased benefits because he failed to report for an evaluation examination and failed to provide a good cause for his action. The court noted, "[t]he duty to assist is not always a one-way street."

6. See *Ardison v. Brown*, 6 Vet. App. 405 (1994). The Court ruled that the VA failed in its duty to assist by relying on an examination that was performed when the condition was inactive.

INDEX

38 CFR
  100 percent disabled, 81–102
  Basic Eligibility for TDUI, 85
  Claim's examiner duty to notify, 35
  continuity of symptomatology, 169
  Diseases Associated with Exposure to
    Certain Herbicides, 68
  doctrine of *volenti non fit injuria*
    provision, 129–30
  duty to request records, 226
  entitlement to a total disability rating,
    86
  informal claims, 43–44
  Interpretation of an Examination
    Report, 142–43
  medical evidence, 109–10
  obtaining current copies of, 128
  original elements to be proven, 120–
    21
  Presumption of Service Connection,
    68–69
  Procedural Due Process and Appellate
    Rights, 82
  providing section pertaining to
    disability, 115
  reasonable probability of valid claim,
    140
  reopening claims, 86
  requirements of condition, 122–23
  Revision of Decisions-Errors, 83
  rewriting of, xiii
  Schedule for Rating Disabilities, 49
38 U.S.C.
  1151 claims, 129–30
  doctor qualifications, 136–37
  duty to request records, 226
  limited duty to assist, 225
  Outreach Services, 82
  requirements of condition, 122–23

1151 claims
  adjudication manual sections per-
    tinent to, 120–30
  doctrine of *volenti non fit injuria*
    provision, 121
  elements of, 120–26
  filing for, 127–30
  necessary consequences, 120–21

abbreviations, glossary of, 247–50
action rules, 259–61
Adjudication Division
  grading based on claims cleared, 33
  internal structure of, 19–27
adjudication process, 50–51, 215–16
adversarial contest, 14
Agent Orange, 7–8
Air Force
  contact information, 188
  locator service, 194
Air Medal, 61
AMA. *See* American Medical Association
  (AMA)
amended claim, 47–48
American Legion Magazine, 50
American Medical Association (AMA)
  contact information for, 126
  fee-based general practitioners of, 140
  website, 170
AMIE. *See* Automated Medical Information Exchange (AMIE)
Anacostia River, 5–6
Appeals Management Center, 26
appeals team, 25–26
application, substantially complete, 34–35
archives, military historical, 183–91
archives, military special
  Defense Special Weapons Agency,
    187–89

ABOUT THE AUTHOR

John Roche's involvement as a veteran's advocate began nine years before he retired from the U.S. Air Force. His VA actions on behalf of retired military personnel came to the attention of the St. Petersburg Regional Office's adjudication officer when, as a causality assistance officer, he successfully argued for a widow that her retired air force officer husband's accidental death in the county jail was service-connected.

Immediately after leaving the air force, Roche joined the VA Regional Office adjudication division as a claims specialist. During the three years that he was with the VA, he completed its 1,560-hour formal training program and gained considerable insight into why so many claims were denied. Veterans did not know how to prove their claims; they relied on the VA to do it for them.

His decision to leave the VA was fostered by policies that contradicted the reason he accepted the job. Since leaving the VA, Roche has used his knowledge of the system to help more than forty thousand clients during the past thirteen years as a county service officer. Health reasons caused him to step down as an active veteran's advocate with the county service in 1996.

Roche is a published writer specializing in veteran's issues and has four forthcoming books on the subject. He has written five books focusing on how to get claims approved. His books have introduced him to veterans from all over the United States who have had legitimate claims denied.

Mr. Roche is a lifetime member of the Disabled American Veterans, National Association of Uniform Services, and the Military Officers Association of America. He is also a member of Congressman Michael Bilirakis's advisory board. He lives in Palm Harbor, Florida.